**HOUSE & GARDEN'S
COMPLETE GUIDE
TO
CREATIVE ENTERTAINING**

The generation gap is nonexistent at an all-ages family-friends-and-children party picnic.

HOUSE & GARDEN'S COMPLETE GUIDE
TO

CREATIVE ENTERTAINING

BY THE EDITORS OF HOUSE & GARDEN

McGRAW-HILL BOOK COMPANY
NEW YORK   ST. LOUIS   SAN FRANCISCO   TORONTO

Edited by **HARRIET BURKET**
former Editor-in-Chief of *House & Garden*
Designed by **AUDREY R. FLAMBERG**

CONTENTS

HOSPITALITY AT HOME
AND
AT ITS BEST

Even the simplest party becomes a celebration when it is sparked by the host's own delight. Inevitably this spirit comes across in a genuine warmth of welcome. It is also reflected in a tempo that tacitly gives time for interests to be explored, friendships to develop. And it inspires the exhilaration that comes with a feeling of personal anticipation. This mood of joyous sharing is a natural one, for hospitality is a deep part of our culture and of our finest instincts. But the way we express it changes with the way we live. Entertaining, like a number of other activities today, has broken away from old formulas. People aren't hung up any longer on the idea that you can't give a dinner party without a dining room. Or that a big bash is a bore. Or that you can't entertain with style in the kitchen. There are no more set rules that spell out what a party is to be—or where. The issue is, rather, what makes any party a great one? Whether it's a simple dinner for six, dancing for sixty, or an open house for twice that, your party will be memorable if you give it the best of yourself.

START WITH COMFORT. This nuts-and-bolts part is simply a matter of making things easy for your guests. Remove every hurdle before the party begins so it will get off to a running start. Here is the time for careful planning and organization.

ADD DELIGHT. Color, lights, music, superb food and drink, engaging little decorative flourishes, imaginative ways of arranging flowers; a personal touch that is yours alone. Anything that quickens the senses makes people come alive.

THEN BRING ON A SURPRISE. A little make-believe, a cheerful put-on, a single elegant touch at a small party; one bit of homespun at a lavish "do." Surprise works like a push button to bring people together, to start them talking and make them click.

MAKE YOUR AIM DIVERSION. Which is what a party is all about—a few lovely hours' diversion away from workaday concerns that heighten tensions, dull the wit. A relaxed atmosphere accompanied by good conversation can distill magic.

When people are comfortable, delighted, truly diverted, they are at their best. Then you can depend upon it, they will entertain each other. And they will go home calling your party great.

COCKTAIL BUFFET IN A GARAGE. Transforming a plain, functional space into a glowing party pavilion, *opposite*, is mostly a matter of color and camouflage. Vivid hues on door panels, in abstractions on the walls, in varicolored tablecloths; an indoor-outdoor carpet over the concrete floor; masses of fat paper balls masking the rafters are inspired party panoply. Familiar, festive furnishings: potted palms stationed along the walls, gilded ballroom chairs, small round tables.

CHAPTER 1

THE LIVELIEST PERSONAL ART —CREATIVE TABLE SETTINGS

Like a good painting, a table setting should reflect its maker. And creating charming settings for each meal, for every group of people including your own family, affords day-after-day opportunities to be an artist, to design still-life compositions that are highly personal, endlessly varied, and able to evoke any mood you wish. Your inspiration: a deep-rooted urge to express yourself and to give pleasure. Your tools: color, pattern, shapes, textures, unexpected effects, fresh partnerships, just-right lighting—rather than brushes and paint. Your canvas is the table and the room where you use it. Your only restrictions are those established procedures that are primarily intended for the convenience of hosts and guests when serving and eating. It is a challenging adventure to ring appealing changes on your table, but without resorting to fads or trickiness, which are seldom convincing. Most helpful is always to keep in mind the basic reason for setting a table at all—in order that people may be served or serve themselves, eat and drink, with ease and enjoyment. That they do these things amid a feast for the eyes strengthens the bonds of hospitality.

Every table arrangement begins, of course, with the essentials dictated by the menu—necessary flatware, plates, glasses, whatever. Over a period of time, you can collect various scene-changers: pacesetting linens and serving dishes, a set of captivating salad plates, covered bowls or colored glasses, an endearing tureen, accent pieces that work together and suit your way of entertaining. If you look around your house at the decorative ornaments that give it your particular brand of charm, you may want to experiment with some of them on your table. Try exploring the potential of vegetables, living plants, clusters of fat candles—for focal points. Any composition at a seated meal should be kept low or it will block people's view of one another. Asymmetry is most effective upon occasion; so is a scattering rather than a concentration of attractions. When table space is limited, a pull-up cart to handle the overflow or a buffet arrangement are simple solutions. Here and on the following ten pages—and indeed, throughout this book—is a gathering of imaginative tables to kindle your own creative impulses.

COUNTRY BOUNTY radiates from tables set for an early winter buffet party. Floor-length cloths are cane-patterned in Christmas colors. On the buffet, towering twin centerpieces of fresh vegetables circled with artichoke-shaped candles, a ceramic rabbit tureen that holds the main dish, lettuce-leaf plates, a wicker basket of rolls and a big wooden bowl of delectable salad. Across the room, dessert and coffee placed on another table eliminate crowding and delays.

BEADLE

GRANITSAS

MINGLING OF SHELLS AND FLOWERS. Bunches of fresh violets, *above*, bring instant magic to a long and seemingly casual arrangement of seashells. Round white linen place mats, smaller than the white plates on them, protect the table but allow most of its gleaming surface to show. Such mats make it easy to put settings close together when necessary without too crowded a look.

EXTRAVAGANZA OF SHELLS AND BIBELOTS. A variety of rare objects, *opposite*, turns a dining table into a collector's personal creation. A school of silver fish, silver mugs with horn handles, many nosegays in little containers, precious tiny boxes, provide a feast for the eyes. Dinner plates are shell-shaped; butter plates are real shells and the butter pats are molded in shell forms.

BEADLE

BEADLE

MOOD: SHINING AND SOPHISTICATED. A Lucite table, *above*, seems to float in real and reflected space against a mirrored wall. Set for an after-theater supper, covered lacquer bowls of soup are easily carried on small trays; salad and larger lacquer bowls of fruit are ready for next courses. For panache: tall candelabrum, looking-glass palm.

AMBIANCE: FRESH AS SPRINGTIME. The cool whiteness of a bare table, *opposite*, plays up leaf-green butter plates, napkins, and a flock of fanciful birds. One big bouquet and painted wicker pots of grape hyacinths bring flowerbeds right into the house. Covered amber glass bowls shaped like nesting birds lend lilt to a garden room lunch.

DESIGNER: GILMAN-BROWN   SETTING: MACDONALD FORBES

WHITE, LIGHT—AND FLOWERS. The truly "Good morning" breakfast table, *opposite*, is set in a white-trellised garden room filled with the lush green of topiary trees, ivy, ferns. Light washes across the walls and the organdy tablecloth, laid over a white-on-white skirt. One or two perfect blooms in three narrow-necked vases circle tall contrasting sprays of flowering quince.

DESIGNER: THE GREENERY

PINK, PORCELAINS—AND SERENITY. Tradition and great quality can be teamed with creativity, as shown *below*. For a summer luncheon, rosy Rockingham and glass are underwritten by a cloud-pink organdy cloth floating over damask. Centered on the table, where guests can enjoy every hue and feather, are two pairs of antique Chinese porcelain birds, part of a cherished, rare collection that roosts permanently in the dining room.

MILLER

BEADLE

LYON

GREEN FOR ALL SEASONS. Humble parsley from summer's garden or winter's grocer can freshen any setting. Tightly bunched, *right,* it keeps company with vermeil flatware and owls, yellow and white china and linens, elaborately-cut crystal. Other good green mixers: fresh mint, privet, boxwood, limes, and pears.

BANDANNAS FOR MERRIMENT. The familiar red and white cotton squares that team so well with blue jeans also have tabletop potential. *Left,* they are sewn together for a colorful cloth, used individually for napkins, cut up to cover little shades on a chandelier.

RARITIES FOR RICHNESS. A table for two, *below,* is crammed with delights: painted plates on patterned mats, shells on delicate stands, little brasses, old silverware with ivory handles. Crowd your table with your own favorite possessions for a look of lavish abundance.

MAYA

DESIGNER: ARNOLD SCAASI

PATTERN FOR INSPIRATION. A dramatic motif, *left below,* in the center of a table or cloth can substitute for a centerpiece when space is limited—and spark a dozen ideas. This compass-sun inlaid in a bare stony top is echoed in the garnishing of green leaves on the plates and in the geometry of the salad arrangement.

DESIGNER: HUMBERTO ARELLANO

COLOR FOR QUICK IMPACT. A last minute table setting, *right below,* put together in front of guests after cocktails, relies on boldness for effect. Ingredients: dark, strongly patterned cloth, vivid plates and napkins, a made-ahead pyramid of fresh apples held with toothpicks. White enamel paint on bamboo handles of the flatware makes them look like porcelain.

DESIGNER: COUNTESS MARGARET WILLAUMEZ

GUERRERO

BEADLE

CREATIVE TABLE SETTINGS

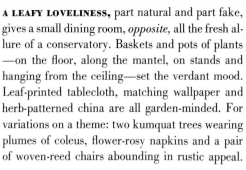

A LEAFY LOVELINESS, part natural and part fake, gives a small dining room, *opposite,* all the fresh allure of a conservatory. Baskets and pots of plants —on the floor, along the mantel, on stands and hanging from the ceiling—set the verdant mood. Leaf-printed tablecloth, matching wallpaper and herb-patterned china are all garden-minded. For variations on a theme: two kumquat trees wearing plumes of coleus, flower-rosy napkins and a pair of woven-reed chairs abounding in rustic appeal.

DESIGNER: MARIO BUATTA

A GEOMETRIC DRAMA is played out on and around a simple dining table, *below.* In colorful contrast to the unadorned white walls and squared-off tile floor, butcher-block wood tabletop is decked out with fringed red mats and napkins, flowers, wine bottles and a baked-clay casserole. Overlooking the scene and abetting it: a wine rack full of bottles within easy reach and underlined by a handwoven length of black and white stripes. Narrower stripes discreetly circle the plates.

ARCHITECT: MYRON GOLDFINGER

MCGRATH

A FRESH APPROACH TO WHAT GOES ON THE TABLE

Entertaining, like a number of other activities these days, has broken away from the old formulas. Most of us now live informally —and we like to give relaxed, casual parties. On the other hand, the woman who has not discovered the fun and satisfaction of setting a formal table on occasion has missed out on a great deal. But even today's formal dinner is different from that of our parents' day. Courses number four at most; place mats often replace the time-honored white damask cloth; china may change pattern with each course. And the overall feeling is exciting and adventurous rather than staid and ceremonial.

Today's parties are so different because the world around us is different. Probably the two factors that have effected the biggest changes in the way we entertain are the lack of household help and the lack of space. Both have brought problems, but they have also worked to our advantage by giving us more honest values and tastes, and improved techniques. Many pretentious and meaningless social forms have disappeared. We have become more sincerely and less formally hospitable. And to help us cope, designers and manufacturers have given us many superbly efficient appliances, handsome and easy-to-clean linens, and china and glass that will go through the dishwasher cycle without chipping or fading.

The new approach to what goes on our party tables depends upon several important factors. Among them: *Where we live.* Planning a sit-down dinner for eight in a rambling house in the country is quite different from giving a dinner for the same number in a three-room city apartment. *How we live*—our interests and activities. *Our budget*—the money we can allocate to party-giving. And *available help*—whether we are still lucky enough to have a housekeeper-cook, can call in a good catering service, or can find someone to serve and clean up.

Within this framework—and with imagination—we can create exciting parties and intriguing tables. We can match, contrast, or mix china; vary linens for different occasions; combine heirlooms with today's plastics; put together delightful centerpieces to share with friends.

THE IMAGINATIVE AND THE UNEXPECTED, *opposite,* delight at a party table laced with surprises. Among the inspirations are alternate place settings: for the women, gold-bordered plates, vermeil flatware, and green mats of a simple weave; for the men, blue-bordered plates, silver flatware, hyacinth mats. Crystal sparkles, wood gleams, bobêches of fake berries circling thimble-shaped candle holders lift colors and spirits high.

HOW TO BUILD A TABLE-SETTING WARDROBE

The intimidating rules that used to be known as the "etiquette of table setting" faded away with the butler and the six-course dinner. Changing patterns of living, eating and entertaining have generated a relaxed, freewheeling approach to what-goes-with-what on the table. We no longer buy china, glass and silver in space-devouring 102-piece sets. Instead we assemble our table-setting components as we assemble our wardrobes—with an eye to use, suitability and variety.

This practical attitude has developed into a whole new party policy, adaptable to any style of entertaining. You can plot your table-setting wardrobe around your own tastes and budget, starting with simplified sets of dishes, glass and flatware; then expanding each category with choice acquisitions that combine with the basics in all kinds of ways for all types of parties. Last, you choose the significant extras—serving pieces and accessories suited to your favorite menus and your favorite ways of serving. The lists at right outline the details. Quantities are not stipulated because these depend so much upon the size of your guest lists, your style of dining and your storage space. You may find that you need two or even three sets of dinner plates, preferably both patterned and plain ones—which you can alternate to suit the occasion and mix for big buffets. Also omitted from this list are linens, which even more are a matter of personal taste. (You'll find ideas for your linen wardrobe on page 26.)

Variety and versatility should be the criteria in selecting your multipurpose accessories. Generally speaking, the only dishes that need to match are those habitually teamed at the table: dinner and luncheon plates, cups and saucers. Dessert plates, butter plates and soup bowls don't have to match your basic china as long as they are complementary in one or more ways—in shape, color, material. Unless you are blessed with a load of storage space, pass up the single-use object. Instead of a well-and-tree platter, for instance, look for a serving platter with a carving-board insert that can double for cheese and bread. Since the essence of the wardrobe plan is to buy only what you need and can use again and again, you can afford to splurge now and then on a fabulous extra that will give your table special cachet. For seated dinners, this investment might be an antique centerpiece or a one-of-a-kind set of fruit knives. For buffets you might venture all on decorative cook-and-serve French earthenware casseroles or on a handsome chafing dish.

CHINA

CHOOSE FIRST

Dinner plates, 10-inch
Cups and saucers
in one or more matched sets, patterned or plain

CHOOSE NEXT

Plates, 6-inch
of any material, for bread, salad, hors d'oeuvre

Plates, 8-inch
decorative enough for dessert and for first-course place plates

Bowls
of any material that blends with your basic china

After-dinner coffee cups
in demitasse size or larger, as you prefer

ADD AS YOU CAN

Conventional soup plates
to match dinner plates (or deep plates, to contrast)

Pots de crème

Ramekins
oven-proof, in shell or leaf shapes

Extralarge coffee cups or mugs
Individual butter crocks

SILVER

CHOOSE FIRST

Teaspoons
in quantity since they have lots of uses

Place spoons, dessert size
in extra quantity if soup figures
large on your menus

Place forks, large

Place forks, luncheon size
to double for salad, dessert
(In patterns that have no luncheon size,
buy salad fork instead)

Place knives, large

CHOOSE NEXT

Carving set

Steak knives

Small ladle
suitable for mayonnaise, gravy, dressing

Large ladle
for soup, punch, stews

Serving spoons and forks

Iced-tea spoons

Butter knives
matched to silver pattern for seated dinners;
in wood, for buffets and casual meals

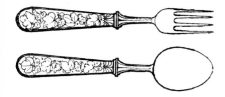

ADD AS YOU CAN

Demitasse spoons

Seafood forks

Fish knives and forks
in a pattern to complement basic silver

Fruit knives and forks
in any material or design

Grape scissors

Nutcracker

Tea strainer

Salt spoons

Cake server

GLASS

CHOOSE FIRST

Stemmed water goblets

Stemmed wine glasses
an all-purpose size,
matched to water goblets

Single old-fashioned glass or
small tumbler
for juice, short drinks

Double old-fashioned
or large tumbler
for iced tea, soft and long drinks

CHOOSE NEXT

Cocktail glasses
in a size and shape that can
double for aperitif wines

Glass plates

Glass bowls
for dessert, cold soup,
or to use as finger bowls

Brandy or liqueur glasses

ADD AS YOU CAN

Champagne glasses
in flute or tulip shapes which are more
adaptable than saucer type

Sherry glasses

Beer mugs

Punch cups

Brandy snifters

Second set of wine or cocktail glasses
in colored glass

Seafood glasses

ACCESSORIES

Teapot

Teakettle, spirit lamp

Coffee pot

Pitchers—tall, medium, small

Cream and sugar set

Ice bucket
large enough to double as wine cooler

Decanters

Cocktail shaker
plus bar equipment: knife, corkscrew,
bottle opener

Large oval platter
in silver, stainless steel or china

Large round platter
in silver or china, for desserts

Small oval platter or au gratin dish
(Platters are best for seated service,
au gratin dishes, for buffets)

Wood board
to fit large oval platter,
for carving, also for cheese

Trays
in assorted sizes for coffee, cocktails,
individual buffet meals

Bowls—large, medium, small
of silver, china or glass

Vegetable dishes

Casseroles and soufflé dish
to double as vegetable dishes at buffet meals

Chafing dish

Warming stand
of electric, alcohol or candle type

Tureen

Set of square dishes (*raviers*)
for hors d'oeuvre service,
also for salads and desserts

Cake stand
of compote type, also good for centerpiece

Wine basket

Bread basket

Pepper mills

Salt cellars

Ashtrays

Menu or place-card holders

Candlesticks
that can be grouped in various ways

Hurricane chimneys

Epergne, compote, sectional *rivière*
for centerpieces

REIGER

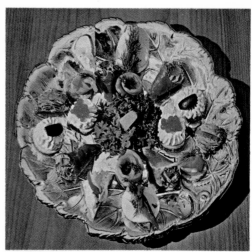

HANDSOME SILVER PLATES, *top left* and *right*, can glorify individual servings of dessert, or can serve hors d'oeuvre regally during the cocktail hour.

CRYSTAL-HANDLED CUTLERY, *left* and *above*, makes a grand appearance for the fish course, then returns in an understated encore for the dessert.

NOBLE TUREEN, *below* and *left*, can reign supreme as a centerpiece or serve the main dish at a buffet.

BEADLE

THE FABULOUS EXTRAS

As the Persian proverb put it, "If thou hast two pennies, spend one for bread, and with the other buy hyacinths for thy soul." Impressed by this logic we suggest a purchase of hyacinths in the form of a superbly beautiful object (or a small set) talented enough to play a repertoire of dramatic roles in your table settings. For instance, an elegant tureen of sterling silver could cradle a bouquet of calla lilies for a centerpiece, or cool splits of champagne in shaved ice, or offer the steaming pièce de résistance at a buffet supper. Antique, heirloom, or brand-new design, wherever and however it is used, a soul-sustaining hyacinth will share its luminous spirit with everything around it, endowing simple designs with unexpected panache.

**CANDIDATES FOR
ONE BIG BEAUTIFUL SPLURGE**

Elegant tureens—silver, ironstone, china
Silver plates
Cachepots—china, silver, fantasy *faux bois*
Epergnes—crystal, tole, silver
Finger bowls in jewel colors—for iced soups,
    desserts, cluster of small bouquets
Tall candlesticks
Individual candlesticks—to group on the table or
    space individually at each place.
Tole urns
Spectacular French earthenware casseroles
Handsome place plates
Crystal hurricane globes
A glorious punch bowl
Collection of pottery vegetables
Chafing dish
Bain-marie
Jumbo brandy glasses
A surtout de table—(sectional flower holder)

FANTASTIC CACHEPOT, *left,* in a *faux bois* finish, offers crudités in a parsley hedge at cocktail time. At a supper party it could hold long breads.

AIRY EPERGNE, *top left,* has four stories of crystal to hold sweets and petits fours at a tea party—or caviar, shrimps and lobster at a champagne gala.

CHOOSING YOUR LINENS

With today's wonderful choice of table linens, you can vary the look of your table settings as freely as you can change accessories to vary your wardrobe. "Table linen" now means any fabric or material that can be used for mats, cloths and napkins, from damask to Indian blankets—whatever looks fresh, lies flat, is easily cleaned. When selecting linens, give a thought to how many people you plan on for sit-down meals. Small round mats can make your table look uncrowded even when it is set for the maximum number. Or a cloth in one lovely color will make the table seem larger. Or a beautiful bare tabletop, polished to a fine sheen and without benefit of cloth or mat, can appear to stretch space. For switches in moods, try see-through laces over wildly patterned cloths. Try mixes: flowered mats on a plaid cloth. Make napkins bright accents—slip vivid ones into contrasting rings or fold them into eye-catching shapes. Tie them into loose bows, Swedish-style, or fold them like a lily, a fan, a bishop's mitre.

FOR YOUR LINEN WARDROBE

TABLECLOTHS: Assorted solid colors, and white. Assorted designs—checks, stripes, florals, whatever—in one-color-and-white, and multicolor combinations. Short cloths, in prints or plain colors, to use over matching or contrasting undercloths and to-the-floor skirts. Sheer short cloths—embroidered, appliquéd, plain— to go over colored undercloths.

TEA CLOTHS: Plain, and embroidered; white and assorted colors; fine weaves, and textured ones.

CLOTHS FOR CARD TABLES: Squares and large rounds for use over folding round tops. And, to mix and match with these, floor-length undercloths in a range of plain colors or prints.

MATS: Varied shapes—oblong, round, free-form, fruit, vegetable. Plain and assorted designs—checkered, striped, flowered.

NAPKINS: Solids in a variety of colors and white, prints and woven designs in several colors— all to mix and match, as accents or complements for your cloths, mats, china.

FUN TO HAVE: As table covers: Indian bedspreads; Spanish cotton rugs; Balinese batiks; Mexican rebozos; American quilts. In place of mats: pairs of long runners to use the length of the table on each side. For trays: mat-and-napkin sets in solids, handsome prints.

26

BRILLIANT PATCHWORK QUILT, *above,* brings on smiles and adds warmth to a winter-holiday luncheon table. Stemmed glasses pick up the lively blue; plain napkins and plates add variety and contrast.

SEE-THROUGH CLOTH, *above,* of appliquéd net, changes character with the cloth you lay under it. For a regal dinner, a tiger-lily glow. For another look, use a cool color—sky blue, shell pink—or even a pattern.

WICKER TRAYS, *below,* deep and sturdy, tote lunch from the kitchen of a beach house to a deckside table and then serve as place mats. Napkins are slipped conveniently through the slotted handles.

MASSEY REPORTAGE PINTO

DESIGNER: MELVIN DWORK

CHECKERED UNDERSKIRT, *above* and *right*, the mainstay of a small candle-lit dinner party and a bright Sunday breakfast. For dinner, the floor-length cover is topped by an elaborately patterned cloth, fringed all around. Raspberry napkins bring out the motifs in the top cloth. Plates add a third helping of pattern, the blue related to both covers. At breakfast, the checks take on a new look with slice-of-egg mats and yellow accents. The same china, milk-glass tumblers and flatware make both scenes.

WHAT GOES ON THE TABLE:
CHOOSING YOUR LINENS

LEE

VIBRANT REBOZOS, *above,* a trio of them in three different colors, crisscross a party table to underline places for six. Napkins repeat the fuchsia of the rebozo. Gleaming white plates act as brilliant relief.

MASSEY

COOL CANVAS MATS, *above,* sturdy and washable, add a green-and-white forest to a luncheon table. Soft touches: napkins neatly tucked under glass plates, and a profusion of flowers straight from paradise.

FLOWERED RUNNERS, *left,* stitched up from varied printed linens, go crosswise on the table, are the basis for a pattern-on-pattern scheme that includes striped napkins, flower-sprigged plates, garden bouquets. Lots of white and greens hold the mixture together.

BEADLE

NATURAL GRAIN, *above*, of the tabletop is beautifully emphasized by wood plates and by the curry-and-orange of the striped napkins.

PASTEL MATS, *below*, plus white and yellow napkins popped into wine glasses bring the freshness of wildflower colors to a round white

BRIGHT SHOCKS, *above*, of yellow tassels around the napkins at the front of each setting contribute gaiety to an informal supper. The plaid cloth is an excellent foil for a potpourri of accessories in wood, pewter and pottery.

OFFBEAT PROPS, *below*, set the scene for an indoor picnic. Guests are seated on cushions and given a terry hand towel (trimmed with festive fringe) for a lapwide napkin. The "table" is yards of pattern laid flat on the floor.

table. The centerpiece bouquet of buttercups is popped into a larger stemmed glass.

BARE TABLETOP, *below*, dark and dramatic, has shocks of white and red. Each napkin torch is made by centering a ring on an open napkin and then pulling the fullness through.

YEE   GRIGSBY

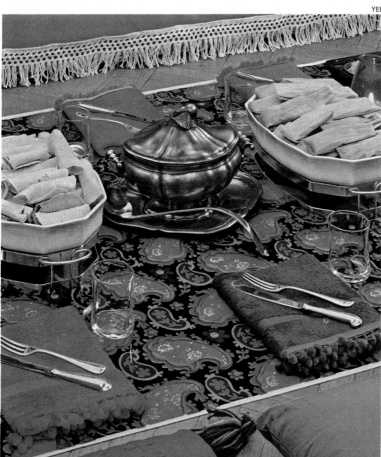

WITH A REPERTOIRE OF NAPKIN FOLDS at your command, you can give your party tables a little added dignity for special occasions and different, amusing touches other times. **THREE USUAL WAYS TO FOLD A NAPKIN,** *right,* assume that the napkin is already folded twice to make a square. *Right:* it is folded again to form a rectangle with the fold to the right and the open corner (whether monogrammed, decorated or plain) at lower left. *Center:* square is turned so open corner faces table edge; right and left corners are then folded under. *Far right:* this way is similar, except that top corner is folded under first, then right and left ones, to form smaller shield. **SIX DECORATIVE SHAPES,** *below* and *opposite,* are easily folded if you spray-starch napkins before pressing.

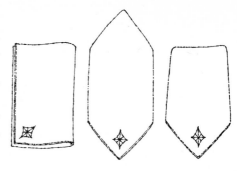

BEADLE

FLOWERBED: Fold napkin in quarters. Take corner that has four free points and fold it to the opposite corner, forming a triangle. Turn napkin over so four free points face downward. Bring two long points of triangle toward each other and tuck one into the other. Turn napkin over. Fold down top point. Tuck fresh flower under fold so that just the blossom peeks out.

BOUQUET: A napkin with a pretty motif in the corner is best for this shape. With right side down, fold the napkin according to easy steps, *far right.* First, fold napkin in quarters (but do not press edges), then turn it over so point A (with design) is at the top. Turn point B up so it is about one-half inch below the bottom of the design. Pleat softly (do not crease or press the folds), and slip the napkin partway into a simple ring. Along with the napkin, tuck in a leafy spray and a flower or two. Place it on table and plump up center fold.

RADKAI

DUTCH CAP: Fold napkin into three equal parts. Turn both ends in to meet at center. Fold top corners down to form a triangle. Turn napkin over, with point of triangle facing down. Tuck one corner pleat into the other to form peaked cap. Put on plates so cap faces as shown, *above.*

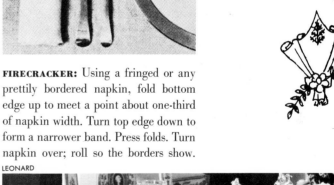

FIRECRACKER: Using a fringed or any prettily bordered napkin, fold bottom edge up to meet a point about one-third of napkin width. Turn top edge down to form a narrower band. Press folds. Turn napkin over; roll so the borders show.

LEONARD

TWIN TRIANGLE: If possible, use a napkin having a decorative edge. Fold napkin in half to form triangle; repeat to form a small triangle. Bring the two long points over to meet at top point. Press folds. Place napkin catercornered on the service plate. Lay a few fresh flowers on the center.

LOTUS: Bring four corners of the napkin to meet at center point. Repeat step (if napkin is large, repeat this step again—it will result in more petals). Turn napkin over. Fold the four corners to center. Hold down at center with fingers or a small glass, reach under and pull out the hidden corners to form petals.

SETTING THE TABLE

A great deal of tradition still underlies our eating and drinking customs, no matter how informal dining today has become. The position of most appointments at each place setting is so established by convention that any personal invention in this area would only result in confusion. It is the security of knowing what is correct in the order of flatware, where to place glasses, butter plates and napkins that leads to relaxed pleasure. Of course, some hidebound rules have given way to a few options: For instance, at informal meals, flatware for dessert may either be included in the place setting or brought in on the dessert plate. Rules for the *overall* arrangement of a table may also be waived when necessity or common sense requires it—as in the arrangement of a buffet or the convenient placing of serving dishes on the dining table. But the more formal the occasion and the more numerous the courses, the wiser it is for everyone's ease to follow classic, traditional table-setting patterns.

KASPER

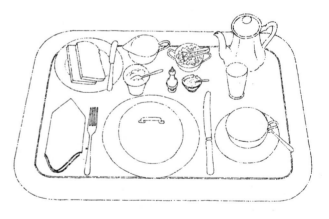

BREAKFAST: As a rule, fruit juice and cold cereal are already on the table, but hot cereal is brought from the kitchen, as are eggs on a hot plate or a soft-boiled egg in an egg cup. Shown above, left to right across the front: napkin, bowl of cold cereal on a plate flanked by a fork and knife for the scrambled eggs and sausages that will follow, cereal spoon, and a spoon for coffee (alternatively, the coffee spoon could be placed on the saucer). Across the back are the butter plate and butter knife for toast or roll, a glass of fruit juice, and the coffee cup and saucer.

BREAKFAST TRAY: The setting includes everything needed for the entire meal (this one has a menu of orange juice, scrambled eggs, bacon, toast, coffee). From left, across the front: napkin, main breakfast plate (with a cover for keeping food warm) flanked by fork and knife, cup and saucer plus teaspoon. Above the knife, glass of juice. In back: on the left, butter plate with buttered toast and a butter knife; on the right, the coffee pot. In between: small cream pitcher, bowl of lump sugar and tongs; jam jar with its spoon; pepper shaker and open salt dish.

FORMAL LUNCHEON: The setting shown is for a three-course meal, and the first course—clams on the half-shell—is already on the table (a *hot* first course would be brought in only after guests are seated). Left to right, in front: napkin, main-course fork, first-course plate, main-course knife and oyster fork (oyster fork is only fork ever placed on right). Across the top: pepper and salt (their location may vary depending on the overall table setting), glass for water and small glass for wine. Butter plate and knife may be placed at top left, but they are often eliminated.

INFORMAL LUNCH: Place setting for a main course and dessert, with coffee served during the meal, is as basic as can be. In front, left to right: napkin, main-course fork, dinner plate, main-course knife, teaspoon, coffee cup and saucer. At top left: butter plate and knife (either this position or straight across the top is correct for a butter knife), dessert fork (often dessert spoon accompanies fork). The one glass is for water. For decorative effect, placement of napkin (and its folded shape) may vary at informal meals from the traditional position just to left of fork.

FORMAL DINNER: For soup, fish and meat courses requiring many appointments, each piece is carefully positioned (dessert fork and spoon are brought in with the dessert service). Left to right, at front: fish and main-course forks; service plate, napkin, place card (optional); main-course and fish knives; soup spoon. Glasses, clockwise from left, are for water, red wine, white wine. Ashtray, cigarettes, matches above service plate are optional. Position of pepper and salt varies, depending on how many people must share them, often are between every two places.

INFORMAL DINNER: The menu is simpler than the one at left (three courses are usual) and calls for fewer pieces at each place. The dinner here: shrimp cocktail (on the table when guests sit down), meat course, dessert. Front, left to right: napkin, main-course fork, salad fork (for salad with main course); service plate with seafood glass and plate; main-course knife, oyster fork. Large glass for water, small one for wine. Top center: dessert spoon with handle at right and, below it, dessert fork with handle at left (if preferred, these may be brought in with dessert).

BREAKFAST TRAYS ALL READY FOR THEIR JOURNEY, *below,* offer a visual pickup with their bright, uncrowded settings. Squares of eye-awakening red, prettily edged, are napkins and mats placed catercorner. Staying nicely warm under each see-through hood: omelets with herbs and bacon. At right is an ample cup for the brew nearby, with spoon on saucer. In back, from left: roll, butter, knife, on butter plate; salt and mill for grinding fresh pepper; juice in a stemmed goblet.

DESIGNER: ANGELO DONGHIA OF BURGE-DONGHIA

BREAKFAST TABLE ALIVE WITH COLOR, *opposite,* launches the day. Set right in the kitchen where cooking aromas spur appetites, the table is festooned with checkered cloth and bandana napkins. Waiting on the patterned plates are fresh strawberries in silvery porringers. The spoon is for fruit; the knife and fork, for mushroom omelets. Coffee spoon rests on saucer. Juice glass is above knife. Centerpiece is a basket of biscuits. The plant at each place setting is to refresh the soul.

DESIGNER: JOHN ROBERT MOORE

BEADLE

34

PARTY LUNCHEON TO HONOR SPECIAL GUESTS, *opposite.* Lavishly embroidered cloth underlays antique Sèvres service plates. Flatware (for consommé, veal scallops, salad and cheeses) includes: meat fork and salad fork on the left; knife for cheeses, meat knife, and soup spoon on the right (the dessert fork and spoon will come with dessert service). Handsome blue and crystal glasses are for water and wine.

CASUAL LUNCHEON TO BRING GOOD FRIENDS TOGETHER, *below,* creates an easygoing mood. Homespun mats are laid with flatware for all courses. From left: main-course fork, salad fork; main-course knife, spoon for sherbet, soup spoon. Nice contrast to the flower-sprigged dinner plates: pewter butter plate, *left,* and milk-glass goblets for water and wine, *right.* The country-fresh scheme of clear blues is dappled with white and flowering plants arrayed on tiles create a lively garden centerpiece.

BEADLE

FOR A FESTIVE BLACK-TIE DINNER, *opposite*, each and every accessory awaits at its time-honored place in a dramatically beautiful setting. Vermeil flatware (for soup, fish, and meat) arranged in order of use, from outside to the plate. Napkin, with place card, centered on service plate. Glasses for water, three wines. Before the champagne glass, a swizzle stick of vermeil. Individual mats, very much of today, let polished wood reflect the serene splendor of gold, white and crystal.

AT A LITTLE DINNER FOR SIX, *below*, appointments are pruned to a minimum on a table arranged to give each lovely piece its due. The absence of nonessentials, such as butter plate and water goblet, is the preference of a hostess who likes an uncluttered look and who favors three delicious courses for a small party. The single glass is for wine. Dessert flatware will come later on dessert plate. Interplay of wood, straw, linen and run of white bougainvillea sets off lacquer plates.

LEONARD

GUERRERO

38

IMAGINATIVE CENTERPIECES

Everything you use to compose a table setting plays a significant part in the overall design—but the element that pinpoints the mood and draws people together is the centerpiece. The mainstay of an enchanting centerpiece could be any one of the great possibilities that are listed below. Whatever you use, keep the composition low—or slim and soaring—so that everyone can see who else is at the table. Much more fun than ho-hum bouquets are surprise centerpieces with the unexpected in their makeup—bibelots, vegetables, flowers used as garniture rather than the whole show. Their unpredictability delights, like the discovery of two pearls in an oyster. Just be sure that anything you choose has a bit of beauty in its own right. And at dinner do include candles. The romantic radiance of candlelight generates a festive spirit nothing can match.

TINY BASKET, *above,* as dainty as a bird's nest, is filled with fresh strawberries, baby's breath, greenery and a single taper, to woo guests to a festive table-for-four at a dinner dance.

THE MAINSTAYS

Cornucopias

Epergnes

Tureens

Tulipières

Small urns

Julep cups

Shapely bottles

Compotes

Candelabra, candle holders

Hurricane chimneys

Plateaux, shallow trays

Baskets, low bowls and vases—all
sizes, shapes, materials

THE COMPLEMENTS

Collections—porcelain figures, shells,
paperweights, whatever

Decorative candles

Potted plants

Fruits, vegetables—fresh, fake

Flowers—garden or meadow, fresh,
dried, fake

Driftwood, rocks, minerals

FOTIADES

LYON

CRAGGY DRIFTWOOD, *above right,* at the crossroad of linen runners on a garden room table, is a fine perch for little bright-eyed owls—made of painted pebbles glued to stay put.

LEAFY HOLDER, *above left,* makes a surprise package of fruits. Heavy green straplike leaves are stapled end to end to make long strands, which are then woven together in a cross.

TULIP CHARMER, *opposite,* a three-tiered *tulipière* from Italy, lets each blossom nod across the way at luncheon guests. With a vase of many spouts, pretty bouquets can be easily created.

FRESHEST CHIVES, *above,* a small forest of them transplanted—soil and all—from herb garden to silver basket are dotted with bachelor's buttons as fresh accents. Cool, too, are light blue napkins, a lime cloth, stemmed glasses.

SAVOY CABBAGE, *above,* metamorphosed. One perfect head veiled by a froth of baby's breath comes to glory on a party table covered in silver lamé. A delectable first course of lobster salad is arranged on—naturally—cabbage leaves.

MUSHROOM MARVEL, *right, top,* sprigged with fern, graces a country dining table. Toothpicks hold the fresh-picked mushrooms to a spongy plastic foundation (such as Oasis, available at the florist) precisely cut to fit the basket.

TURNIP PYRAMID, *right,* turns up on a formal table in a Wedgwood bowl that blends in coloring. How to make the vegetable tower is sketched, *opposite.* Blocks of Oasis are cut in graduated chunks and piled one on the other; allowing space at the rim to skewer the first row of turnips.

BEADLE

SNOW PEAS, *above*, green and delicate, plus a few forget-me-nots, peep out from a Nantucket basket. An inspired switch from the usual bouquet, this mix is all ready to be toted to and centered on a breakfast or luncheon table.

FOTIADES

GREEN PAGODAS, *above*, of peas and beans are today's delights on a luncheon table, tomorrow's feast. To make these centerpieces, string pods of similar length on heavy thread, using a large needle. Tie the peas in separate tiers to woven wicker cones (easy to find at basket shops); then tie and spiral the beans on one string as shown.

MILLER

VEGETABLE TREES, *above*, form an imaginative grove on a terrace buffet. Each tree has a trunk of manzanita root anchored in Styrofoam. Top is an Oasis ball covered with boxwood and different tiny vegetables (pattypan squash, carrots, string beans, cherry tomatoes) all held by tooth-picks. Around the bases: potato "gravel," lettuce "bushes."

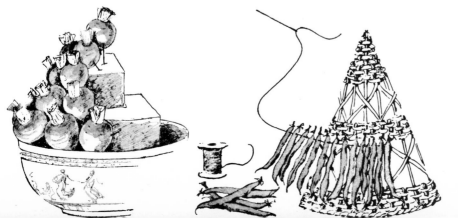

43

MULLER

CENTERPIECES: GLOWING CANDLES

REFLECTIONS, *left,* of plump candles and glass cullets extend the drama on a small table. The glitter and glow of gleaming crystal and lighted candles have a fascination that will last all through the dinner.

SPIKES, *left,* of white candles spark an assemblage of round glass vases that match the candlesticks. In each sphere, a different long-stemmed blossom nods an extra touch of loveliness on a narrow buffet table.

PARADE, *below,* of vigil lights accompanies a pair of Italian angel candelabra down a holiday table festively dressed in Christmas red.

GRANITSAS

FOTIADES

CONSTELLATION, *left,* of squat candles shines among a pretty array for an intimate dinner party served on a marble table. Candles, small accessories, and four tiny vases are composed on two Japanese trays-on-legs. These elevate the arrangement just enough to give it importance.

CENTERPIECES: PERSONAL COLLECTIONS

SEA TREASURES, *right,* from a prized collection of vermeil fish, enhance a dark glass tabletop. In the pond, too, are starfish, shells, coral. More aquatics: silver frog to hold mustard, dinner plates which are rimmed with scalloped scales.

MARBLE EGGS, *below,* assembled in silver holder designed for real ones, add a dash of color to a dinner table. Nearby, pepper and salt shakers are shaped like birds.

YEE

BEADLE
LYON

POTTERY PETS, *right,* most of them antiques from England, come from behind glass doors of a collector's cabinet to graze on a low tray at a dinner party. The mossy bed is pied with fern and red and yellow zinnias, and forested with two primrose trees.

THE DELIGHTS OF COLOR

Clear fresh colors—in china, linens, glasses and in cook-and-serve ware—can be as stimulating to your table settings as armloads of freshly picked flowers. And, like flowers, such colors can be put together in wildly contrasting combinations, in mixtures of subtle pastels or in lovely monotone combinations. You can stage a color buildup by assembling linens in layers of different colors. Or you can revel in a big splash of one color in the background, then add accent colors in dishes and accessories. These accents might bring out a minor motif in the china pattern or be a completely unexpected hue (almost every scheme benefits from a surprise). Or you can keep to a black-and-white scheme, then pour a concentration of a wild hue into one small area where it will delight throughout the meal.

With color as the magic, you can mix linens and accessories to give a basic china wardrobe many different looks: a flowered pattern can suggest at least as many table settings as the colors it contains; a geometric border can be theme or accent—all according to the color company it keeps.

DESIGNER: BRETT WINSTON AND HELEN WALLACE

MASSEY

DRUMBEAT SCHEME, *above,* of red, white and blue quickens the simplest of settings—a kitchen's dining corner. The white table gets its initial punch of color from mats and napkins. Bouillon cups and saucers reinforce the red. Blue takes on the accent role in plates, flowers, goblet linings.

FLOWERBED COLORS, *left,* mixed as they grow in the garden, bring outdoor joys to a simple luncheon table for two. Yellow, like sunshine, touches almost everything, uniting the table and its surroundings. For an unexpected springtime accent, plates introduce a delicate robin's-egg blue.
DESIGNER: MICHAEL LA ROCCA

ANEMONE HUES, *opposite,* play unexpectedly against tangy orange on a table arranged for a fondue party. Mats and napkins in purples and raspberry start the composition fairly quietly. The bread baskets in more purple plus pink build up the scheme. Then tangerine pots and deep blue plates bring to a fine climax stronger related colors.

BEADLE

BEADLE

CHANGE OF SCENERY, *this page,* for plain china, is quick and easy with a switch of linens. The three settings vary greatly in coloring and mood, yet have the same white earthenware dishes and the same flatware, too. Diverse backgrounds, plus a switch in glasses and centerpieces, make all the difference. *Above:* For dinner-party elegance, a muted tweedy cloth and crystal, sparked by orange accents. *Above right:* For a swinging luncheon, an op-art fling. White dishes get bold support from matching napkins, a colony of antique bottles bearing carnations. *Right:* For supper on the patio, a cloth of Japanese silk. Napkins and glasses repeat the blues (they could have echoed the orange or yellow instead).

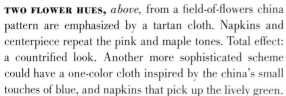

TWO FLOWER HUES, *above,* from a field-of-flowers china pattern are emphasized by a tartan cloth. Napkins and centerpiece repeat the pink and maple tones. Total effect: a countrified look. Another more sophisticated scheme could have a one-color cloth inspired by the china's small touches of blue, and napkins that pick up the lively green.

THREE STRONG SOLIDS, *top right,* and not an ounce of multicolor pattern, bring enormous verve to a circular luncheon table. Blue mats and rich purple napkins make the yellow china stand out against muted beige surface.

DOUBLE DAZZLE, *right center,* comes from two glowing colors in a surprise combination. The china's vibrant pink sings out again in the handblown crystal and in the linen napkins—all set forth on a bright yellow tablecloth.

PALEST NEUTRALS, *right,* let off-white take the lead in a refreshingly subtle scheme. Diagonal stripes of the cloth, golden flatware and a ring of yellow flowers are enough to strengthen the gold border design of the china. Pots of succulents provide a shot of strong living color.

THE SNAP OF BLACK AND WHITE

KEEN TEAM, *this page,* of graphic black and icy white, played any number of ways, always make a table look fresh and pretty. A wonderful way to bring off black and white is to combine the boldness of a stripe or plaid with the softness of a curvy pattern. And always spike the setting with a good swack of lilting color, like a splash of tiger lilies or tulips. *Top right:* Potent plaid and solid napkins set off a dainty china pattern. *Top, far right:* Smooth white table with black and white iris on china, real ones in a blue vase. *Center right:* A mix of patterns, all small in scale, get zip from checkered napkin. Tulips shed sunshine. *Center, far right:* Solid cloth, dark as charcoal, sets off chrysanthemums, real and otherwise, and makes the most of vermeil flatware. *Bottom right:* A husky plaid and sturdy shapes create a country look. *Bottom, far right:* Gleaming black goblet accents two geometrics—a lattice design in the cloth, and the classic motif of the china.

CARNIVAL COLORS, *opposite,* a whole carrousel of them, have a romp on a holiday party table. Layers of contrasting linens—a good way to create color excitement—include striped mats and plain napkins in two shades of blue on a round cloth (its solid coloring steadies the pace somewhat). Mats, copies of Indian fans, are cut from cardboard, then decorated. Centerpiece bowls of flowers are modeled in terra cotta—then gaily painted.
DESIGNER: JACK BAKER
ECKERT

BEADLE

GOOD PARTIES START WITH A PLAN

CHAPTER 3

HOW TO PLOT A SMOOTH PARTY COURSE

Every good party begins with a careful plan. If you tend to shy away from setting a course on the theory that it muffles spontaneity, give the matter a second thought. All great artists—actors, writers, painters, musicians—seem to perform naturally, effortlessly. But if you look behind the scenes you find that the appearance of easy outpouring, so magical to the audience, is based on much practice and experience. Party-giving also is an art, though fortunately a simple one to learn, and the party that seems to give itself without any effort is a personal masterpiece on which the hostess has lavished a great deal of planning, inspiration and love.

In general, party plots involve three themes: the people, the food and drink, and the setting. They also involve time—generous measures of it, not only on the big day itself but the day before, the week before, or more. Your plan should be beautifully detailed, which means it will be too much of a chore to carry all of the many steps in your head. Don't try. Write everything down; complete notes have long-range advantages. Having worked out one party from A to Z, writing down every single thing, you'll discover later that a great deal of the procedure will be the same for almost every other party you give. Others can easily be varied, giving you a whole spate of entertaining maneuvers for little more effort than it takes to create just one perfect party.

Nobody gives a party every day and many of the essential steps will be forgotten in a surprisingly short time. So a written outline, to be truly helpful, should be supplemented by a party record—notes on what worked, what went wrong, what food and drink were served, what arrangements should be improved upon. These two—the plan and the record—can add up to a party "log" which will become your most valuable ally every time you are a hostess. At the end of this chapter you will find samples for a buffet supper and for a little dinner. The pages between will take you through every step that is worth considering when planning any kind of successful party.

WHAT KIND OF A PARTY TO GIVE

To settle this one, the most important person to consult is yourself. Real hospitality is not merely a matter of sharing *something*, but of sharing the very best you can create. So the type of party to give should depend on what you do best. It may not be the kind you think is expected of you. It may not be anything like the festivities most of your friends dream up. It may, on first thought, seem too simple. No matter. People always enjoy and appreciate a superlative one-dish meal like oyster stew far more than an indifferent four-course dinner with all the trimmings.

Ask yourself a number of straightforward questions and be honest with your answers. What dish do you cook most successfully? Ratatouille, perhaps? Even if it is not a usual main dish, consider it as the starting point for a menu, maybe a buffet dinner: beef Burgundy, ratatouille and buttered green noodles, plus a compote of fruit. If you have a cook or plan to hire one, what is *her* special forte? It would be smart to plan your menu around that.

How about your house—does it lend itself more happily to indoor or outdoor comfort and gaiety? Your dining table may seat twelve but can you serve them as gracefully at the table as you could from a buffet set up in the living room? Do you have space in your living room or foyer where you can put extra tables for four or six? What day of the week and what time of day will give you the most possible time for preparations? How much help can you count on—or would you be happier coping entirely on your own?

After juggling all these considerations, you're pretty sure to come up with a formula that involves a minimum of problems and complications—*the* party that you handle especially well. Stick to it. Since you're not apt to invite all your friends to the same "do," why not repeat it a month or so later for a second group, even once again for a third. But don't try to elaborate on your most successful pattern until you have followed it often enough to smooth out all the kinks and learn the procedure by heart. At that point, begin to create variations and your proven triumph will blossom into a repertoire. Your buffet dinner might be turned into a seated one by adding a first course that is served in the living room—prosciutto and melon, perhaps—and substituting beef à la mode for the beef Burgundy. And for a hearty Saturday lunch you could team the ratatouille with baked Italian sweet sausages and substitute crusty buttered bread and a tossed greens salad for the noodles.

You may also discover that your talents and facilities under certain circumstances can well be adapted to a second master plan. For instance, you might work out one kind of party for indoor entertaining—perhaps a Sunday night supper of soup and make-it-yourself sandwiches in the kitchen—and still another inviting scheme for balmy days when you can stage a meal outdoors. How about a make-your-own-salad Sunday lunch on the terrace, with bowls of mixed greens, shrimp, turkey and ham slivers, raw vegetables, and a lineup of dressings? Or you might give a seated dinner

with a small guest list—or a cocktail-buffet for a crowd. The options are all yours. You will find that with few exceptions (perhaps the celebrations before a wedding) your best party, whatever it is, can be shaped to suit almost any hospitable occasion. The only limitation is one of common sense: base your timing on the way your friends live. It would be stupid, for example, to pick an hour when most of them like to be on the golf course, in church, or asleep because they must rise early in the morning to commute.

WHAT KIND OF HELP WILL YOU NEED?

The best kind of help to have for a party is someone to do the things you dislike doing or cannot do well. So the choice should be as personal as deciding what kind of party to give. Help can also free you to spend more time with your guests, but that problem can usually be met in other ways such as advance preparation and well-thought-out serving arrangements. Here is a checklist of possibilities:

A DISH-AND-GLASS WASHER. Any hostess, even the most ardent do-it-yourselfer, usually appreciates having someone to clean up after the party. It need not be a professional—any reasonably competent female, from the high school girl down the road to your cleaning woman, can be a big help. She needn't arrive until the party is well under way and she needn't set foot outside the kitchen until she departs.

A COOK. If you don't enjoy cooking, hiring a cook would be the natural choice. In the case of a buffet party, you could probably swing everything else by yourself. In fact, the cook needn't necessarily be on the premises during the party. He or she could come in the morning or afternoon and prepare all the main dishes, leaving them for you to warm up.

GENERAL HELPER WHO CAN SERVE. If you do enjoy cooking and look upon it as your creative contribution to a party, a general helper would be your best bet. Her duties would be to cope with some last-minute chores, watch over any final cooking such as green vegetables, toss the salad and serve at a seated dinner for eight or fewer. (You might have to help her by serving one dish from your place at the table, and the host could pour the wine.) At a buffet party she could serve the main dish as the guests bring up their plates, remove empty plates and perhaps pass the dessert. In any case, she would be responsible for clearing the living room of empty glasses and used ashtrays at some point before dinner is over.

A BARMAN. Someone to mix drinks is obviously essential at a large party. Better figure on a bar helper for every twenty guests. But a barman is also important at smaller parties, even during the cocktail hour preceding a dinner party. Everything is sure to run more smoothly if the host as well as the hostess is free to be with the guests, and allowing the guests to make their own drinks is bound to create confusion. If a professional barman seems a bit too grandiose for your ménage, you might look into the possibilities of getting a student. Recently, bartending has become a popular way for college and graduate students to make extra money. Inquire at the student employment office of a nearby university. A bright-looking young man in a white mess jacket may well fit into your party scene better than an imposing professional.

A WAITRESS. If you are planning a seated dinner or luncheon at which all or most of the food is to be served at the table, be sure you do not give one waitress a bigger job than she can handle. The rule of thumb is one waitress for every six to eight diners, depending on the complexity of the menu and how much you can speed things up by arranging two or three dishes on one platter, passing sauces around the table, etc. Don't forget that even at a black-tie dinner, your guests would rather serve themselves from a buffet than sit and watch their food get cold because one nervous waitress can't serve everyone fast enough. If you are lucky enough to have a full-time cook-waitress, an extra person to help her at a seated dinner party can be a good investment.

For a buffet party of any type, a waitress would be a useless extravagance unless she also helps with the preparation and cleanup. For a cocktail party, one or more waitresses may be helpful depending on the size of the party. But if you can set up your bar and your hors d'oeuvre in spots where everyone can reach them without running into traffic bottlenecks, you won't need a waitress. Even for a cocktail party, one all-around helper in the kitchen is apt to be worth three waitresses passing trays in the living room.

A CATERER. You can, of course, eliminate 90 per cent of the work involved in giving any kind of party, simply by hiring a caterer. But while this kind of help might be the wisest course for certain large parties—a dance, for instance—a catered party is apt to lack a personal touch, unless you make a determined effort to inject variations of your own. Here's where you can bring into play a principle that can be applied to any table setting: use color to enhance all of the little look-alike tables—perhaps cloths in a rainbow variety. Today, most caterers have a choice of colors to offer. Many times the standard little gilt chairs can also be obtained in color. And plan a menu that is different!

CONSULTATION AND INSTRUCTION

Some hostesses are convinced that the time to hire party help is the moment it occurs to them to give a party. Not a bad idea—except that you could end up with a firm commitment from the best party help in town only to discover that most of your friends were taking off that week for Canada or the Caribbean. A better system might be to negotiate a date. Consult the help first as to what days or evenings they have open. Then you can confer with the guest of honor (or the one couple you want to be sure can come) and safely suggest two or three alternatives. Once the date is set, confirm it immediately with the help. Early action is all the more important when you are planning to have a particular helper who has worked for you before. Others may be available, but it will take you twice as long to explain everything to someone who doesn't know your house or your kitchen.

If you are not going to have a "regular" who has seen you through many parties, a conference *before* the day of the party is highly desirable; in fact, mandatory in the case of a cook. Even if you only talk together on the telephone, be sure you are in agreement about the work to be performed, how much food preparation will be involved, what kind of uniform will be worn and who will provide it, exactly what time the helper will arrive, how late she may be expected to stay, and how she will get home (you may have to provide transportation). And of course you will want to know how much she will charge or, if you have obtained her from an agency, whether she will expect a tip. In the case of a cook, you will not only want to go over the menu but also want to be sure what ingredients will be needed, in what quantity, and whether you or she will do the marketing.

In addition to the advance conference, any kind of helper except an experienced cook should be given a sheet of written instructions including the menu, a list of which dishes will be used for what, and a timetable (more about that later in the chapter). It will take time for her to read and absorb this and ask you questions about it. She will also need time to change her clothes and, if she is new to your house, to become generally oriented. So be sure to set the time of her arrival at least an hour before you want her to start working. And in planning your own schedule, leave yourself free during that hour to give her as much attention as she may need.

PLANNING YOUR GUEST LIST

People make a party. An indifferent meal may be quite overlooked if the company is congenial and stimulating. Even a disaster like running out of Scotch will be quickly forgotten by a guest who has spent the evening talking to fascinating new acquaintances. So apart from obvious first decisions such as date, time, type of party and help, a good party plan really starts with a carefully planned guest list.

The smaller the party, the more important the guest list becomes. Naturally, if you are inviting only two couples for dinner, you have already concluded they will enjoy meeting each other. But once you decide to add a third, your list demands special thought. When it grows to over twenty, of course, there is more of a chance that each guest will find at least a few others he will like, if only because all are your friends. But don't count on this. Putting together a group of people who will sparkle in each other's company is truly an art. Some hostesses do it intuitively. Others learn by experience. To have one person or one couple to build the list around gives it a focus. So even if you have no reason to cite someone as guest of honor, it is a good idea to start with one couple that you definitely want to include and proceed as if the party were actually being given for them. Of all the rest of your friends, whom would they most enjoy meeting? With whom would they have similar interests?

If you do have guests of honor, especially if they are from out of town, it is nice to ask them if there are any people they would particularly like to see. If there are, be sure to invite them, even if you don't know them personally. But find out all you can about them to serve as cues to the rest of your list.

ACHIEVING GOOD BALANCE

A small party of eight to eighteen should strike a neat balance between similarities and contrasts, familiarity and novelty. Some people should know each other (makes for warmth and ease) but not more than one or two should know *everybody* (more stimulating to meet new people than to see the same old faces). To be avoided at all costs: a group where everyone knows everyone else except for one couple whom none of the others know.

If possible, try not to have any two guests in exactly the same business or profession. This won't matter so much if the two are a man and a woman—less likelihood of their becoming engulfed in shop talk. Two mothers with children in the same local school may find it hard to resist "mother talk." But two people who work with quite different aspects of a broad field like art, or health, or finance, are likely to have enough in common to serve as a conversational starter, yet not so much as to freeze out other guests. Extracurricular interests are important, too—an avid enthusiasm for a particular foreign country, or for gardening or collecting antiques.

Variation in age also adds liveliness to a guest list. Even if the people you want most to invite are all about your own age, make a point of adding at least one couple considerably older or considerably younger. You won't have to worry about a generation gap if you give due thought to how well their individual interests relate to those of the other guests. And one thing you can count on: older men always enjoy a chance to talk to attractive young women.

A perfectly composed guest list will give each guest both a sense of reassurance and a tingle of surprise. One of the greatest compliments a hostess can overhear is the comment: "You never can tell who you're going to meet at her parties."

THE INVITATIONS

Sending out the invitations is perhaps the nicest part of party planning. It calls for so little effort and puts you in the pleasant position of broadcasting good news, since everyone loves to receive an invitation even if he can't accept.

When should you send them? The general rule is: long enough in advance of the party so that most of those on your list are likely to be free, but not so far ahead that acceptance seems mandatory. This usually works out to about three weeks, but the timing will vary according to the season of the year and the nature of the party. If you were planning a large cocktail-buffet for the Thanksgiving-to-New-Year season or the busiest month at a summer resort, you might want to give people longer notice. Yet ten days might be ample for a small dinner in the city in August, or in the country in early spring or late winter.

TELEPHONE INVITATIONS

The type of invitation you send will also vary somewhat according to the party. But there is one form that is always acceptable today: invitation by telephone. Granted, it is somewhat more time-consuming. You may have to make three or four calls to reach a few busy people—as opposed to writing a few lines on a card and addressing an envelope. But when you do talk to them you will learn immediately, or at most by the next day, whether or not they can come. If someone cannot, you can invite an alternate right away, rather than having to wait a week or so for the mail to bring regrets, then scurry around at very nearly the last minute to line up appropriate replacements. (This is a sure way to ruin a beautifully conceived guest list.)

One disadvantage of telephoning is that you run the risk of a misunderstanding over details like time and date. But you can take care of this by following up each acceptance with a reminder card. They come partially engraved, ready for you to fill in:

> **Just a reminder that**
> Mr. and Mrs. Gordon Watkins
> **expect you**
> on Tuesday, January 19
> for Dinner
> at 7:30 o'clock
>
> Black tie   17 Locust Drive

The same information could be written out more informally on the lower half of the inside sheet of a folded informal—or on a visiting card:

> Dinner
> Tuesday, January 19
> 7:30 o'clock
> Mr. and Mrs. Gordon Watkins
>
> 17 Locust Drive

Telephoning is essential in the case of guests of honor since you must be sure they can come before using their names in inviting your other guests. If you opt for written invitations, be sure to send one to the guest of honor, even though he has already accepted. Write "just a reminder" in the lower lefthand corner. For a party of more than twenty, of course, telephone invitations are impractical, both because of the time they would take and because of the inevitable lapse of time between your first call and your last. If someone receives an invitation several days after he has heard about your party from another guest, he is bound to wonder why it took you so long to get around to him. So if you do telephone invitations, be sure to go through your whole list as quickly as possible, leaving messages, if you can, for those whom you can't reach. Written invitations, no matter how large the party, should all go out in the same mail—they should never be sent in batches.

The most formal type of written invitation is fully engraved or engraved except for the guest's name which is written in by hand. Today these are rarely used for private parties except for "once-in-a-life-time" events such as weddings and debutante dances—and occasionally a formal reception. A private dance is always called "a small dance"—never a ball. If it is to be given at a club, the name and location of the club appears in the body of the invitation instead of the house address, which is transferred to the lower left, directly after R.s.v.p.

ENGRAVED CARDS TO FILL IN

Much more popular today is the partially engraved invitation you can fill in according to the occasion.

> To meet Senator and Mrs. Kevin P. West
>
> Mr. and Mrs. Gordon Watkins
>
> **request the pleasure of**
>
> Mr. and Mrs. Linderman's
>
> company   at Dinner
>
> on   Thursday, August 12
>
> at   7:30   o'clock
>
> Black tie
> R.S.V.P   17 Locust Drive

A supply of these partially engraved cards can be a good long-term investment since they can be used for almost any kind of party apart from something as informal as a brunch or a barbecue.

VISITING CARDS AND INFORMALS

More informal is the invitation written on a visiting card (postal regulations require that the envelope measure at least 3 by 4½ inches). An invitation from a couple should always be on a "Mr. and Mrs." visiting card unless the party is a luncheon or tea to which no men are invited. In that case the hostess uses her own personal card. The essential facts are written above and below the engraved name and the address is added in the lower right-hand corner if it is not already engraved there.

> Buffet supper, Saturday, May 9
> 7 o'clock
>
> **Mr. and Mrs. Gordon Watkins**
>
> R.S.V.P   **17 Locust Drive**

> To meet Mrs. Gordon Watkins, junior
>
> **Mrs. Gordon Watkins**
>
> Tea, Tuesday, June 1
> 3 o'clock
>
>   17 Locust Drive

If there is to be a guest of honor, the name, preceded by "to meet" or "for" ("in honor of" is too formal), should be written across the top of the card and the rest below the hosts' names. It is not always necessary to specify the type of party if the hour makes it obvious. In the U.S. "six to eight" could mean nothing but cocktails, while "seven o'clock" or "eight o'clock" are bound to mean dinner.

> **Mr. and Mrs. Gordon Watkins**
> Friday, February 26
> 6 to 8
>
> R.S.V.P   17 Locust Drive

> For Mr. and Mrs. Ben Cain
>
> **Mr. and Mrs. Gordon Watkins**
> Thursday, September 23
> 8 o'clock – black tie
>
> R.S.V.P   **17 Locust Drive**

An alternative to the visiting card is the folded informal with the pertinent information written on the lower half of the inside, leaving the outside clear except for the engraved name.

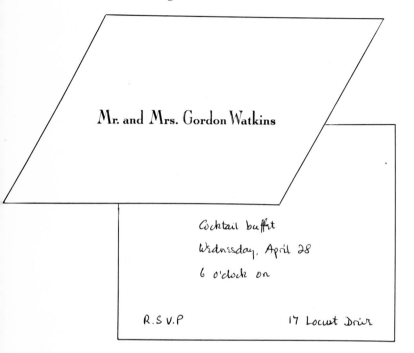

Mr. and Mrs. Gordon Watkins

Cocktail buffet
Wednesday, April 28
6 o'clock on

R.S.V.P   17 Locust Drive

Although on fully engraved invitations almost every word must be spelled out, you are free to use abbreviations and numerals on visiting cards or informals, as long as they are perfectly clear. When should you use R.s.v.p.? Always for a luncheon or dinner or any party where food will be served. Some people feel a reply is not necessary for a large cocktail party, but it is perfectly correct and many times desirable to ask for one. Knowing approximately how many are coming can be a great help, not only in planning drinks and hors d'oeuvre but in arranging your house. Unless you specifically state "black tie," it is to be assumed that dress will be informal, so there is no need to add that. Anyone who is uncertain as to *how* informal will telephone to ask. When that happens, be as specific as possible without seeming to dictate—"You might wear a long informal skirt, but the men are not dressing," or "Pants would be fine, or a short dress, maybe sleeveless." Nothing is more frustrating to an uncertain guest than to be told "Wear anything you like. You always look lovely."

Except for the most formal black-tie, seated, full-service dinners and dances, handwritten individually composed notes are perfectly acceptable as invitations. But they seem unnecessarily time-consuming, especially if you are asking more than two or three couples. Of course a note is always very personal, but then so is a telephone call.

For a very special party, such as one to celebrate raising the rooftree of a new house, you might want to make your own invitations, perhaps on colored paper. If you or someone else in the family has the talent, you might decorate it with a pertinent sketch. But the wording should be the same as on a standard invitation and written by hand as on a visiting card or an informal. Strictly to be avoided are commercial invitations with "cute" or purportedly humorous artwork and wording that starts with "you are invited. . ." or characterizes your party as "a big bash."

ACCEPTANCES AND REGRETS

When it comes to acceptances or regrets, guests today have considerable leeway. But there are two musts: Any invitation should be answered as promptly as possible. And both acceptances and regrets should repeat the vital facts—date, day of the week, hour, and type of party—so that the hostess can correct any misunderstanding. To arrive for a party on the wrong day is probably the height of embarrassment. But it can also be embarrassing to discover when you get to a party that you are expected for dinner—not merely for cocktails, as you understood—and you have to leave because of another engagement. As a rule, a regret should also give a definite reason—"because we will be in Boston that week" or "John's mother will be visiting us and we have tickets for the symphony that evening." But in regretting a formal invitation, it is unnecessary to say more than "because of a previous engagement."

Any formal invitation worded in the third person requires a handwritten reply also worded in the third person with each line centered nicely across the page. For any other kind of invitation a telephone call is adequate although, if you fail to reach the hostess herself, it would be more friendly to follow up a message of regret with a personal note stating why. An invitation by telephone, of course, requires an on-the-spot "yes" or "no" once you have consulted your engagement book. But if for some reason you must clear the date with another member of the family who is not home at the moment, a return call should be made no later than the next day.

A personal note is always a polite way to accept or regret an invitation—or, in the case of a good friend, a more informal message written on your visiting card: "Delighted to come for dinner at 7:30 on Friday, March 9," or "So sorry we can't make it for cocktails on the 24th. Bob's boss is coming for dinner." There is no need to sign such messages but if you do, draw a line through the engraved name.

PLANNING THE MENU AND DRINKS

As we mentioned at the beginning of the chapter, the best starting point for a party menu is your own culinary specialty. It doesn't have to be esoteric. Even baked beans when superbly cooked can be the nucleus of a party menu (although they would certainly give the signal for a hearty informal buffet). You can balance their homeyness with more sophisticated choices for the salad or dessert. What is more apt to seem boring to your guests is a combination that has become a cliché. Chicken, for instance, doesn't have to be accompanied by peas. How about serving tiny whole okra or artichoke hearts with it?

Assuming you have more than one culinary specialty, there are other considerations to be taken into account. If, for instance, your special forte happens to be a rich, rather substantial dessert, you had better save it for coffee-and-dessert parties, since today almost no one seems to care for an elaborate dessert at the end of a party meal, unless it is an exceptionally light luncheon. Fruit, cold soufflés or not-too-rich ices and mousses are more in order.

In deciding on your main dish, an important consideration is whether it can be prepared a day or at least several hours in advance, warmed up at the final hour and, if necessary, kept waiting. Even if you have a cook in the kitchen, she will have enough to do without having to prepare and watch the main dish at the last moment. Skillful party planning will assure that the food *can* be served promptly, but no hostess should be burdened by the thought that if for some unforeseeable reason it is not served promptly, everything will be ruined. That rules out certain serve-immediately dishes such as steaks, soufflés, even certain roasts if you want them done rare. Save these for intimate dinners-for-six at which you can explain the situation ahead of time and prepare your guests to be ready to eat on signal.

BUFFET MENUS

Also to consider in planning your menu is how you will serve the food. For a buffet meal, where guests may take some time to serve themselves, it is especially important to choose dishes that will not suffer from standing on candle warmers or warming trays. It is also important to remember that a guest who is literally serving himself has a plate in one hand and cannot maneuver more than one serving spoon in the other. (For salad, which almost always requires both a spoon and a fork, space should be left on the table where he can park his plate while using two hands.) "Fork food" that never requires the use of a knife is the general rule for buffet parties, but may be relaxed for seated buffets where each guest is given a place at a sturdy table set with a full complement of silver. It is a must, however, for more informal parties at which everyone is free to eat wherever he pleases. Even when he is provided with a small table he will not be in a comfortable position to cut meat. And any dish that tends to be messy should be avoided because of the danger of spills. Spaghetti, for instance, or corn on the cob can be a trial to eat if you are not seated at a standard dining-height table. One advantage of a buffet meal, on the other hand, is that you have room on the main buffet or an auxiliary to set out a choice of sauces and garnishes. An Indian curry with its many accompanying condiments is eminently adapted to buffet service.

MENUS FOR SEATED DINNERS

For a seated dinner where the food is to be served at the table, you have quite different things to think about. If you are relying on one waitress, the main consideration is speed so that the food will not get cold. You can help achieve this by selecting at least two dishes that can be served on one platter. The meat can be arranged around a mound of rice or pasta, or individual servings of vegetables can be ringed like a garnish around the meat. A sauce or gravy, or perhaps the rolls, may be passed around the table from guest to guest. But don't plan to do this with more than one accompaniment—two or three are apt to cause confusion. And if your table is laid with its maximum number of place settings, you may have precious little room to spare for bread-and-butter plates and other extras. Better eliminate the need for them when you plan your menu. Some rolls, for instance, can be served already buttered.

FIRST COURSES

Should you have a first course? At a buffet meal it is unnecessary. In fact it tends to defeat the whole purpose of the informal buffet, which is simplicity. And if you serve at least one hot hors d'oeuvre or a platter of shrimp with the cocktails, you really don't need it. But at a seated dinner it is somewhat nicer to include a first course than to launch immediately into the main course as soon as your guests sit down. Often it is fun and makes the whole meal go more smoothly if you serve the first course in the living room—a quiet signal of the end of the cocktail hour and a pleasant transition between that and the move to the dining room. In either room the dish may be served in individual portions to dispense with the complications of passing a tureen or platters and in the dining room it may already be on the table when the guests are seated unless it is a hot dish that is apt to cool off too quickly. Among the numerous choices for first courses are a single vegetable such as fresh asparagus or artichokes; prosciutto with melon or fresh figs; seafood Newburg or *en coquille* (if the main course is going to be meat). Soup is an excellent beginning to any meal, but before you decide on a hot thin soup for a party, think twice. It must be hot so it can't stand waiting, and it is easily spillable, which makes it a challenge to an inexperienced waitress. Better choose a cold or jellied soup, which is now acceptable the year around, or, in the case of a luncheon or late supper or stay-on-after-cocktails party where the only other food will be sandwiches or salad, a hearty soup that can be served in deep cups or mugs.

PLANNING THE DRINKS

When it comes to planning the drinks you will have to shift gears and think primarily of your guests' tastes rather than your own resources. No one expects you to have a bar as fully equipped as that of a restaurant. A good supply of the standard favorites will be sufficient. But "standard" varies from community to community around the country. In the northeast it would include Scotch, bourbon, gin and vodka. But you may be aware that one of your guests is partial to Canadian whisky or to rye. (A truly perfect hostess would keep a list of her best friends' preferences, even if she couldn't foresee those of new acquaintances.) If so, it would be hospitable to add that liquor to the "standards." And be sure to include dry vermouth so that you can offer martinis (even at a large party it is not necessary to offer an alternate type of cocktail). Are your friends, or at least the particular group of guests for this party, adventurous in their drinking? Unless you are quite certain that almost all of them are, do not limit the drinks to one esoteric choice such as may wine or even champagne. Although most people love champagne, one guest might vastly prefer a simple Scotch and soda. If you must be ready for him and for other possible wine and champagne shunners, there is little point in serving the offbeat drink in the first place. If you want to make one the feature of a special party, announce that fact in the invitation so everyone will know what they may expect.

Aperitifs or fortified wines such as Dubonnet or sherry may not be among the standards, but some people prefer to start out with wine if they suspect that wine will be served with dinner. One choice is usually enough since most people who like one, like them all. It might be the dry vermouth you will have on hand anyway for martinis. But be sure you have enough —a large bottle can disappear very quickly when two or more guests are drinking it on the rocks. If you serve sherry, be sure it is dry—nothing is as disheartening to a sherry lover as to be offered a sweet or "cream" sherry before a meal. Above all, do not make the mistake of classifying the aperitif drinkers with the nondrinkers, giving them skimpy drinks or omitting to ask them if they would like seconds. For the true nondrinkers, you should be prepared with soft drinks— tomato juice, ginger ale, cola, tonic, or perhaps simply Perrier water.

When it comes to selecting wines for a luncheon or

dinner, gourmets are much more flexible than they used to be. You can be, too, at a small intimate luncheon for four to eight people, offering whatever wine suits your personal taste as an accompaniment to the food you are serving. But for a larger group it is simpler and perhaps more discreet to stick to the traditional conventions: red wine, at room temperature or slightly cooler, to go with red meat or chicken cooked with red wine; white wine to go with chicken cooked otherwise or with fish. Not more than one wine is necessary, especially at a buffet meal. And that one wine may be champagne, served throughout the meal regardless of what the food is.

Coffee is taken for granted at the end of a party meal, but it is unnecessary to offer another beverage unless you think that some of the guests would prefer a decaffinated coffee. To serve tea properly is too complicated except at teatime. Brandy and liqueurs add a gala touch to the finale, but they are not necessary. Many of your guests might very well prefer to wait awhile, then have a long drink before going home. You may serve brandy without liqueurs but a choice of liqueurs without brandy is not apt to be very popular since almost all liqueurs are sweet.

REMEMBER YOUR BUDGET

When you are planning your menu, by all means consider your budget. If you put it out of mind, you may come to a rude awakening after the party is over and realize you have spent so much that you won't be able to give another party, even a small one, for a long time. It is not that difficult to cut costs if you go about it the right way. Two ways *never* to cut are to fudge on the quality of the food or drink or to skimp on the quantity. Extra liquor will always keep— that much less to buy for your next party. Extra food, with the exception of a few things like salad, can be frozen to be used later for family meals. But the cost of each dish on your menu should be studied carefully. You may get some surprises. For instance, a casserole that does not seem expensive when you prepare it on a family scale may become very costly when multiplied to party proportions because of its many ingredients. A good quality roast might be cheaper. In any case, veal almost always costs less than beef of comparable quality, and chicken less than veal.

Vegetables vary tremendously in price even when equally delicious. You can dispense with certain side dishes entirely and they never will be missed. And no one will be disappointed if you fail to produce caviar or wild rice. On the other hand, one small splurge, perhaps on the first course, can add distinction to a meal that is based, for the most part, on low-cost ingredients. Prosciutto, for instance, is not cheap, but the limited amount that you would need for a prosciutto and melon first course would balance a main course using ground beef. For a large party particularly, a substantial amount of expense can be saved just by selecting a main dish that calls for relatively inexpensive materials. The fact that they are the best of their kind and beautifully cooked is all that will concern your guests.

PLANNING YOUR TABLE SETTINGS

The third big item on your party-planning agenda is the setting, which begins, of course, with your table. Even more than the food, the things you select to go on your table give you the greatest scope for creativity and for making your party personal.

A party table should be a picture, a joy to look at, whether it is laid with heirloom silver and china for a seated dinner in the dining room, or with colorful pottery and rough linen for a soup and sandwich lunch in the kitchen. But it must also work, which means it must be designed so that the food can be served easily and gracefully and eaten in comfort. That in turn will depend on what you are going to serve and how you plan to serve it. There is one rule that applies to every type of table setting from buffet to seated dinner: *Don't crowd it.* If one table doesn't give you room enough for everything you need, use an auxiliary serving table nearby or an easy-to-maneuver cart on wheels.

For a seated-and-served dinner, "don't crowd it" means not only plenty of room on the dining table but enough space back of the chairs around it so that the waitress can move easily in serving each guest from the left. (In a pinch she may have to double back and start again on the other side, or she might have to serve one person, preferably a member of the family, from the right.) If your dining table seats eight comfortably don't try to squeeze in two more. Either limit your guests to eight or invite an additional couple and set up a small table for four nearby or in an adjoining room. (Often in giving a party you will discover that the best solution to the problem of having two guests too many is to invite two more.) The extra table need not match the setting of the main table, but it should be equally attractive, and the hostess should preside there at the start of the meal. Later, perhaps at the end of the main course, she might change places with the host so that each will have a chance to visit with all their guests. But the meal always starts with the host at the main table.

DRESS REHEARSALS

An excellent idea—in fact an essential aid to your planning—is a dress rehearsal. Whether your party is to be large or small, seated or self-service, set your table exactly and completely as your guests will see it. Include flower holders and serving utensils as well as all the dishes, glasses, silver and napkins—everything except the flowers themselves and the food. If your powers of visualization are not all they might be, here is your chance to see the flaws and correct them. Two colors or two patterns may not look as dreamy together as you imagined, or the centerpiece you had planned on may be too big for the available space. Don't wait until the flowers arrive to find out!

Candles should never be on a table set for a meal to be served before dark. After dark, their romantic glimmer is enchanting, not only on the party table but in the rest of the dining room, the living room or the entrance hall. If candles would tend to crowd your table, however, you can dispense with them as long as the table can be safely lighted in some other way— perhaps by an overhead chandelier. At a seated dinner, the candles should be the opposite of the flowers—i.e., tall, above the eye-level of the guests.

Napkins can play an important role in the composition of the table setting—either by forming a lively contrast in color or pattern to the cloth or plates, or by being folded in a specially decorative manner (see page 31). For a seated meal, the size of the napkins is not so important as long as they are at least 12 inches square. But at any type of buffet meal where guests may be sitting on sofas or perched on terrace walls,

the napkins cannot be too large. If you don't have or can't find any large enough in the colors you want, try linen or cotton place mats. They can be folded to look like napkins and your guests will bless you for your thoughtfulness.

How about ashtrays? If you are a nonsmoker, you are very apt to forget them in planning the table setting for a seated meal. If you strenuously disapprove of smoking you may be tempted to omit them deliberately. But a party is no place to reform your friends, or embarrass them. If you are absolutely sure who smokes and who doesn't, you can provide ashtrays only for the smokers. Otherwise it is safer to place one— a tiny one perhaps, plus a small holder containing two or three cigarettes—in front of each place or between every two places.

Salts and peppers also may go at the top of each place setting, if they are very small. Larger ones usually look better between every two places.

HOW TO SEAT YOUR GUESTS

At a seated dinner for six, ten, fourteen or eighteen (if anyone has a table that long), the hostess sits at one end of the table with the host, facing her, at the other end. Traditionally, the hostess always sat at the end where she could face the door to the kitchen, but today she might elect to sit at the end nearest the kitchen so that the waitress can set unobtrusively before her any dish she is to serve from her place.

In either case, the man guest of honor sits at the hostess' right, and the lady guest of honor at the host's right. But this arrangement won't work if the party comes to eight or any larger multiple of four. No matter how you try it you will be left with two men sitting next to each other and two women sitting side by side—both situations to be avoided if at all possible. And this is possible, at an evenly balanced party, if the hostess simply moves one seat to the right, yielding her place at the end of the table to the man guest of honor. Here is how the two plans work:

Arrangement for six (or ten, fourteen or eighteen)

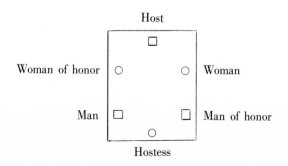

Arrangement for eight (or twelve or sixteen)

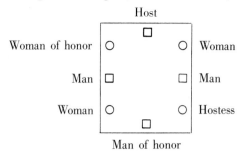

The host always sits at the head of the table. If there is no official hostess, a woman sits facing him at the other end, but does not act as hostess. The man guest of honor, in this case, sits to the left of the woman on the host's left. If a woman is entertaining alone at a party for eight or twelve, she may keep her place at the end of the table but there will be a woman facing her at the other end.

Husbands and wives should never be placed side by side, but engaged couples always sit together.

Even if you haven't specifically designated one couple as guests of honor, give some thought to which guests merit the two honored places. As a rule, precedence should be given to a guest invited to a meal for the first time; a stranger brought by a guest; a much older person; someone whose position deserves special recognition such as a clergyman. In the case of two guests in the same category, as a simple courtesy a visitor from abroad would take precedence over an American. (Low men on the totem pole, incidently, are house guests and children of the family.)

Wives have the same precedence as their husbands, but if the man guest of honor is unmarried, the place at the right of the host goes to the wife of the man who is next in order of precedence. The reverse applies when the woman guest of honor is unmarried.

Except in official circles in Washington, few hostesses today concern themselves with precedence once the guests of honor are placed. Much more fun, and much more conducive to a lively party, is to seat together people you feel will especially enjoy each other. This might mean two people who don't know each other but whom you have been wanting to bring together because they have so much in common. Or you might put a woman who was about to take off for a foreign country next to a man who had once lived there. Unless the party is very small, close friends are best left apart. But you might seat together two old friends who haven't seen each other for a long time.

The same considerations apply in seating guests at a large party where there are several small tables. The man guest of honor always sits at the hostess' table, the woman guest of honor at the host's.

Will you need place cards? Definitely "yes" if you have two or more tables. If you have only one table for six or eight, you can probably direct all the guests to their seats without fumbling. For any larger number, place cards, although not obligatory, can save you mental strain and save guests the embarrassment of having to stand there until you get around to them. Most people rather enjoy the hunt for their names and it often serves as a conversation starter between people who have not had a chance to talk to each other before dinner. Even when you do have place cards you can help speed the seating by directing the guests of honor and anyone who seems to be having a hard time finding his place. A little chart under your own place plate can give you the cues in case you forget your plan.

TIMETABLES AND CHECKLISTS

Getting ready for a party is a little like getting ready for Christmas. Some people do everything in one great whirlwind that leaves them exhausted and glassy-eyed. Others spread out their preparations, gradually building up their spirits to a festive peak.

If you were to sit down and make a list of every single thing, large or small, that ought to be done in preparation for a large party, you'd probably be surprised at how many of them could just as well be done anywhere from two days to two weeks in advance. For instance: ordering liquor; polishing silver; marketing for everything except meat, fresh fruits and vegetables; ordering flowers or plants, extra ice, or anything that has to be rented; rehearsing your table setting. The last item might well be the first on your schedule for it is then that you will note whether you will need extra dishes or glasses; what should be washed, polished or pressed; whether you will want to buy something new. Make out a two-week schedule for yourself and try to take care of a few important things every day. On the next page are some checklists to remind you of what will need looking into:

China

Glasses

Silver

Linens

Serving dishes

Trivets, hot trays, candle warmers

Flowers and containers

Candles

Liquor

Ice cubes

Mixers and soft drinks

Cigarettes and matches

Little tables

Coat closet and hangers

Guest towels and soap

Cash to pay extra help

EQUIPMENT TO BE RENTED FOR LARGE PARTIES

Coat racks and hangers

Extra chairs

Folding tables or round tops for bridge tables

Large platters

Large coffee urn

The smart hostess is the one who gets everything possible done *before the day of the party*. Many things can be done *one* day before. If the house or party rooms are to be cleaned, don't leave that until party day. Marketing for meat and most vegetables can be done the day before, as well as a good part of the cooking. Certain meat dishes are actually improved by twenty-four hours of "aging."

Some things, of course, *must* be left until the day of the party—fixing flowers, setting tables, etc. But most of these can be done any time from early morning on. A hostess who does not have a job and whose husband and children take off for office and school early in the day can even set her table in the morning. Also on the big-day schedule will be lots of little tasks such as putting out fresh candles and arranging crackers on trays. They take only five or ten minutes each and almost no effort, but a string of them can kill two hours very easily. Don't leave them until late afternoon. (You can cover the crackers with plastic wrap.) For an evening party to start at 7:00, everything except truly last-minute jobs like filling ice buckets should be finished by 3:00. After that your time should be about equally divided between resting, dressing, going over the evening's plan with your helper, and taking care of the just-before-guests-arrive musts. Depending on the type of party and type of help, you might want to be dressed when he, she or they arrive at 5:00 so you will have one free hour to answer their questions and another to tend to final business. Or you might wait until 6:00 to dress, leaving your helper with the last-minute list. One word about timing: If your helper for a dinner party tends to be slow, or is new to your kitchen and uncertain, do not flinch from deceiving her about when the guests are expected to arrive and what time you plan to serve dinner. Setting her timetable ahead by half an hour, or even longer, may be your best insurance against a long drawn-out cocktail hour.

HOW TO KEEP A PARTY LOG

A compendium of party case histories, your party log will soon become your most valuable possession as a hostess. It will keep you from embarrassing repeats, show you when you *can* repeat with impunity, save you from making the same mistake twice. In your log you record the guest list for each party, the menu, the decorations. If you have a Polaroid camera, on certain occasions you might take photographs of your table setting and paste them in the log as visual reminders. Record any awkward goofs, too. Note how much food and drink you ordered and whether it was enough or far too much. And if you are exceedingly businesslike, you might include a tally of the cost.

Your party log should be a loose-leaf book small enough to fit on the cookbook shelf. Use some of its pages for jotting down festive ideas and others for keeping records on each party you give.

The story of each party should be told in two parts —the Party Plan and the Party Record—as you will see on the next two pages. The Party Plan is a working schedule to be tacked up in the kitchen for constant reference during party preparations, then saved in your log and used in drawing up other plans. The Party Record is a kind of postmortem that will alert you to the need of revisions and things to remember for your next party. Particularly successful plans—including your "best" party—might be implemented by several Party Records with different guest lists.

You can amplify the log, of course, by adding any checklists, timetables or other details that would be useful to you. Perhaps a daily schedule of the preparations you want to get out of the way during the two weeks before the party. Or a list (to go with each Party Plan) of the serving dishes to be used for each kind of food, which is something one-time helpers always ask about. In the back you could list names and telephone numbers of helpers and agencies, party-supply firms, florists and other relevant services.

VISUAL REMINDERS

You might reserve several pages of the log for rough sketches or cut-out pictures of attractive serving or centerpiece ideas that you pick up when dining out.

TABLE DECORATIONS

Brilliant multicolor Paisley bandannas thrown over red and white checked cloths.

A Severa, Lisbon

Flat fern-edged nosegays with flowers arranged in a mosaic of blues, violets, reds. Lyons, France. Note: Try a row of these down the center of a long table.

HORS D'OEUVRE

Rosette of smoked salmon with a center of cut limes. Salmon sliced thin, then folded in triangles.

Hawaiian Village

Playing-card sandwiches--pate with truffles, cheese with pimiento garnish.

Hawaiian Village

Canapés passed on Japanese lacquer fans. Particularly pretty: cucumber sandwiches on dark green: cheese puffs on blue.

Tokyo Hilton

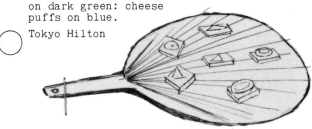

FIRST COURSES

Cold curry soup in a coconut; chicken salad in a scooped-out orange—fresh switch on fruit containers, first course instead of dessert.

Caneel Bay

Butterfly shrimps with delicious shrimp sauce (could not figure out ingredients) served in a scallop shell.

Charles à la Pomme Soufflée
New York

Cold scooped-out artichoke filled with sauce mousseline. Could also be done with vinaigrette sauce.

Caravelle
New York

MAIN COURSES

Shiny mirror rounds in place of platters—quick glitter for a buffet. London Hilton. A grand substitute for that big round platter I've never been able to replace.

Cool decoration for a cold platter: ice frozen in a fancy mold on a thick lawn of parsley. Trout in aspic arranged on parsley. La Reserve de Beaulieu. Lots of possibilities: cold chicken, variety of cold cuts, etc.

Crab and lobster butterfly: medallions of lobster arranged on lobster shell, crab shells filled with Russian and seafood salads. Ritz, Madrid Note: Could be individual plate or whole platter—depending on the size of lobster, shells.

FOTIADES

SALADS

Big luscious heads of
Boston lettuce opened out
(hearts removed) to hold
cold vegetables and fish
salads on the buffet.
Grand Vefour, Paris.
Also try with Bibb or
heads of Boston for small
individual servings.

DESSERTS

Dessert baskets of
crisp chocolate, very
edible. Wonderful for
orange or coffee
mousse. Dolder, Zurich
Note: Baskets would be
even prettier formed
on a brioche mold.

Prettiest platter imaginable:
icy cold tiny whole beets,
carrots, potatoes, green
beans, zucchini in precise
piles. Sharp cream dressing
served on the side.
Hotel de la Ville, Rome.
Note: Arranged on a huge
round platter would be
spectacular for a summer
Sunday buffet.

Flat basket of tiny bunches of
red, green and black grapes, each
on a grape leaf. Relais du Cheval
Blanc, Beaune, France.
Note: A similar arrangement on
a tiered compote would make a
handsome centerpiece.

Another attractive do-it-yourself
salad: flat basket of greens and
garnishes to choose from and dress
on the spot with oil and vinegar.

Harry's Bar, Venice

Baked Alaska in a
scooped-out pine-
apple—ice cream and
pineapple chunks, but
no cake!

El Convento, San Juan

PARTY PLAN—PARTY RECORD

The Party Plan and Party Record, *below* and *opposite page*, illustrate the kinds of information you will want to keep in your party log. The plan *below* was worked out for the party on page 70—a small buffet dinner to be given by a hostess who has only a general helper by the evening—not a cook, but one who can be depended upon to follow instructions. The black line separates the hostess' tasks from those of the helper.

PARTY PLAN #1
for Buffet Dinner, page 70

MENU	WINES
Shrimp Newburg	White Bordeaux
Rice with chives and peppers	
Asparagus	
Green salad	
Rolls	
Fresh strawberries with kirsch	

TIMETABLE

Week before: Check bar, order liquor, wines. Don't forget sherry, kirsch.

Day before: Boil shrimp, shell & devein. Wash greens, wash & peel asparagus. Wash & hull strawberries. (Cover each with plastic wrap and refrigerate.)

Day of party: Arrange flowers, set buffet, coffee, and bar tables. Make salad dressing. Chop chives and green pepper. Prepare Shrimp Newburg up to addition of cream & eggs.

5:00 Helper arrives, go over timetable with her.

6:00 Fill ice bucket, water pitcher. Put strawberries in serving dish, add kirsch.

7:00 (guests due to arrive.) Put asparagus on to cook. Put on water for rice, when boiling add rice.

7:15 Finish Shrimp Newburg.

7:30 Drain asparagus, drain rice, add green seasonings & butter, keep hot.

7:35 Put rolls in oven to warm. Add dressing to salad and toss.

7:45 Transfer food to serving dishes, bring to table. Place warmed plates on buffet, announce dinner.

While guests are eating: Empty ashtrays, clear glasses from living room. Make coffee, set bar for liqueurs.

While guests serve themselves salad: Clear main course plates. Set strawberries on coffee table.

Half hour after coffee is served: Remove coffee cups.

PARTY RECORD

DATE Wednesday, April 7, 1971

OCCASION
Welcome home party for the Petersons

GUEST LIST
Alan and Jane Peterson
Carl and Ruth Hutchinson--regrets (Wednesday school board meeting)
John and Suzanne Simmons
Ann Bouvard
Jean-Pierre Dupré

MENU	DRINKS
See Party Plan #1	Usual bar

WINE
Pavillon Blanc du Château Margaux

TABLE SETTING AND DECORATIONS
On buffet table (table behind sofa), black and white chintz to match slipcovers, topped by plain black cloth.
Yellow napkins rolled up in mirror-paved napkin rings.
Blue-bordered Lenox dinner plates and dessert plates, dark crystal compotes for strawberries.
Bar set up on white Parsons table; dessert, on glass-topped coffee table.
Flowers: at one corner of buffet table, big bouquet of white tulips and lilacs; on bar table, pots of red tulips; on coffee table semicircle of hyacinths, ivy, pick-a-back.

NOTES
Three guests did not drink coffee-- must remember to have a pot of decaffinated.
Completely forgot we did not need knives on the buffet table!

The plan for the seated dinner, *below,* was worked out for the party for six on page 82. This hostess likes to cook, prepares as much as possible the day before and plans menus with dishes that can be easily finished or reheated by a waitress who also serves the dinner.

PARTY PLAN #2
for Seated Dinner, page 82

MENU   **WINES**
Prosciutto and fresh figs   Meursault–
  (serve in living room)   Perrières
Chicken baked in sherry and cream
Artichoke hearts
Wheat pilaf
Spring salad (separate course)
Poached pears, spice cookies

TIMETABLE
Week before: Check bar, order liquor,
    flowers (to be sure they
    have the right kind).
Two days before: Poach pears.
Day before: Cook artichokes, remove
    hearts, refrigerate. Make wheat
    pilaf, make cookies.
    Wash greens and refrigerate.
Day of party: Press tablecloth, napkins.
    Arrange flowers. Set dining table,
    arrange sideboard and bar.
    Make salad dressing. Mix cream,
    sherry & seasonings for chicken,
    refrigerate.
5:30 Waitress arrives, go over
        timetable with her.
- -
6:30 Fill ice bucket, water pitcher.
        Arrange cheese & crackers on tray.
7:15 Put chicken under broiler to
        brown slightly.
7:30 Guests due to arrive.
7:35 Pour cream & sherry over chicken,
        transfer to oven.
7:45 Heat up pilaf.
7:55 Baste chicken.
        Heat up artichoke hearts in double
        boiler.
8:00 Arrange prosciutto on figs.
8:15 Serve first course.
        Transfer all food for main course
        to serving dishes.
        After guests are seated in dining
        room serve chicken and pilaf
        (on one platter), artichoke
        hearts, sauce for chicken.
While guests are eating:
        Clear first-course plates and
        glasses from living room, empty
        ashtrays.
        Make coffee.
8:50 (about) Serve second helpings.
9:00 (about) Clear table, set salad
        plates and salad at my place.
9:15 (about) Clear table, serve
        dessert.
        Take coffee into living room.

PARTY RECORD
DATE Monday,
May 10, 1971

OCCASION
  To honor Gordon's counterpart in London,
  John Brooks . . . and wife.

GUEST LIST
  Mr. and Mrs. John Brooks
  Bill and Alice Cummings
  Bill and Evelyn Stair––regrets
  (leaving May 9 for Italy)

MENU   **DRINKS**
  See Party Plan #2   Usual bar

                    WINE

                       Meursault–
                       Perrières

TABLE SETTING AND DECORATIONS
  Flower-embroidered organdy cloth and
    napkins with flowered Limoges china.
  Lettuce-shaped faience plates for salad.
  Hand-painted Limoges dessert plates plus
    cut-crystal compotes.
  Flowers: In the niches, big bouquets of
    carnations, mimosa,
    chrysanthemums and lilies,
    with a few pieces of fruit on
    shelves. On the table,
    carnations, chrysanthemums,
    apple blossoms laid out right
    on cloth and circled with a
    few kumquats with leaves.
  No candles because they would interfere
    with flowers. Using chandelier above
    table worked out very well.

NOTES
  Everyone was happy with demitasse so
    there was no need of keeping large
    cups in reserve on dining room
    sideboard.

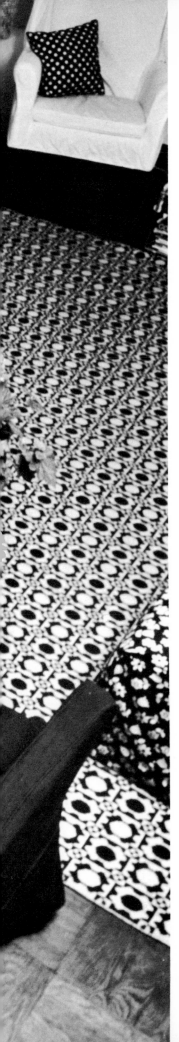

TODAY'S MOST POPULAR PARTIES CHAPTER 4

Every successful hostess has her favorite way of entertaining, usually based upon the kind of party she can best handle. We can't say it too often—recognize what you do well with the help and space available—and do no more. You can find interesting ways, within your scope, to entertain anyone from a visiting diplomat to a young country cousin without trying to do what is "expected." Indeed, it is in doing the unexpected that you make your parties individually your own. Today's most popular parties fall into seven patterns—within these patterns there are, of course, many variations:

BUFFETS OF ALL KINDS, at all times of day, as large or as small as you wish, as informal as a luncheon of cold meats and salad after a hard-fought tennis match or as formal as a black-tie evening by candlelight, with all the trimmings.

THE CLASSIC SEATED DINNER, by all odds the party pattern most conducive to the full enjoyment of superb food and good conversation. Six or eight guests are the perfect number—small enough for strangers to get acquainted, large enough for a stimulating play of viewpoints and personalities. But when the space is limited and there is no one to help with the serving, the party might be as small as a congenial foursome.

LUNCHEON GET-TOGETHERS, special way to entertain special women guests during the week (a favorite way to honor out-of-town guests) and on weekends a great way to gather couples together informally. The weekend luncheon is usually a lively, personal party and one that many hostesses specialize in—particularly in the country.

THE BREAKFAST OR BRUNCH—really a luncheon but with a slightly earlier hour and a menu based on delicious breakfast dishes. Usually a relaxed weekend event that includes guests of both sexes. Also a good way to handle a morning committee meeting.

THE TEA PARTY, most feminine of all, and a fitting way to bring together friends of varied ages and interests: your own contemporaries, mothers and grandmothers, the clergyman's wife, a neighbor moving in or a neighbor departing. A mother might honor her new daughter-in-law by introducing her to her friends at teatime.

THE "COFFEE" at any hour of day, becoming more and more popular, especially among young people. The morning coffee may top off a committee meeting; the afternoon coffee takes the place of the traditional tea. Evening coffee parties start sometime after dinner—anywhere from 8:30 on. Coffee at its best and most glamorous is served, accompanied by a festive dessert and liqueurs—and, later in the evening, highballs.

THE VERSATILE COCKTAIL PARTY with as few as six or eight guests or as many as forty or more. Newcomer to the cocktail scene is the cocktail buffet, less elaborate than the traditional buffet supper, more festive than the big cocktail "do" and now outshining it in popularity—a wonderful way to get friends together informally.

ALL-AROUND-THE-ROOM BUFFET, *left,* lets guests mix and mingle happily. Along one wall, a table for drinks to start the party. Then to a delectable main-course buffet, with seating on nearby sofas and chairs. Dessert gets people on the move again: it's set on the coffee table in the middle of everything—which is conducive to lingering after-dinner talk with friends. (Step-by-step details for planning this party are on page 68.)

BEADLE   DESIGNER: LUCAS KING

A DIVISIBLE FEAST, *this page,* superbly organized on several large buffets, handles a 200-guest supper with aplomb. In one area dedicated to cocktails and hors d'oeuvre, a seafood bar is on a traffic-wise circular island, *below left.* At one end

of the main buffet, *top,* guests pick up a napkin-flatware log and a plate, then select from dazzling foods, *top left.* Surprises range from whole figs in baskets to hot dishes in bains-marie. Guests eat in an adjoining area at any table they choose, return for dessert of berries, grapes and peaches, *above,* or pastries at another buffet.

THE BOUNTIFUL BUFFET

Small wonder that the buffet party is America's favorite, for nothing so well expresses a spirit of openhanded hospitality. Today, in a nearly servantless era, entertaining at buffet meals solves a problem which would otherwise keep a lot of us from asking our friends to the house as often as we would like. The buffet party is definitely one which can be handled without benefit of help—even for a large group, if necessary.

Buffet parties can be large or small, they can take place at any time of day—from late afternoon through late supper—indoors or outdoors, all through the house. They can be completely informal and a sort of perpetual-motion affair with guests serving themselves, then taking their plates to wherever they prefer to perch. (At a "perch" buffet of any size, be sure to provide plenty of little folding tables and chairs so everyone has a place to sit and prop his plate.) Or they can be quite formal, with guests seated at little tables set for anywhere from four to twelve, often with place cards. A black-tie buffet dinner is one of the most auspicious ways of staging a really partyish party.

But regardless of size, time of day or degree of casualness, all buffet parties follow one basic pattern: the food and drink are arranged on a buffet table or sideboard, and guests serve themselves to at least one course. You can take it from there and ring all sorts of changes. For a small seated buffet dinner without help, the first course could be served in the living room, the table fully set in the dining room, food on a nearby buffet. Guests move in when invited, serve themselves and take their plates to the table. They might then return to the living room for dessert, followed by coffee.

For really large parties, consider setting up a series of special buffet tables for the different courses—a long one for hot casseroles, cold meats and salads; mini-buffets for wine, dessert, coffee. Also, for large get-togethers, buffet tables can be stationed in different rooms to expedite traffic. For these occasions, even though you may do all of the cooking yourself, you will find it desirable to have at least one helper in the kitchen and several waiters to clear tables and take care of empty glasses and keep things generally neat and tidy.

For menus for buffet parties, turn to page 247.

BUFFET FOR STROLLERS, *right*, at a house-wide housewarming, offers hearty fare to guests who began the evening with cocktails in nearby family room. All delectables can be picked up in the fingers so everyone can continue to browse. Party progresses into living room for dessert and coffee, and onto a deck for liqueurs.

GRIGSBY

OPEN-KITCHEN BUFFET, *above*, makes a country weekend luncheon pleasant and easy to manage for a small group. The food is informally arrayed on a work table and counter. The host does the carving, and guests help themselves, then sit by the hearth or move to a dining table in the living room.

SPANISH-STYLE SMORGASBORD, *opposite*, within the dining room, invites luncheon guests to circle about and choose from an exciting variety of *tapas*—tasty dishes native to Spain—and to return for more as often as they please. On the dining table, a pitcher of sangria to accompany the meal.

BEADLE

BLACK-TIE BUFFET, *below,* is a come-back-to-our-house-for-breakfast party to cap a country-club dance. Rented tables and chairs are set up in the dining room (stripped of its customary furniture) and red by the yard adds gaiety. Inexpensive cotton, plain and plaid, makes cloths and napkins. Poppies everywhere are of felt. For the buffet, champagne plus fare akin to an English breakfast.

BEADLE

AN ANTIPASTO PARTY, *below,* begins at a terrace kitchen. The buffet table—spiked with the garnet red of the cloth, napkins and flowers—groans gently with cheese, sausages, breads, wine and more. After making their choices, luncheon guests proceed to the grill to help themselves to a casserole of veal and mushrooms. Coffee and fruit for dessert are nearby. Guests eat in comfort at completely set tables.

ARCHITECT: JAIME PARLADE; TABLE SETTING: JOAN ARNOLD

THE GALA DINNER PARTY

The most flattering and hospitable of all invitations you can give or receive is the one to a little dinner at home. Good conversation, delicious food and a lively intimacy for the guests make the small dinner party a star occasion. Most people agree that the ideal size is no fewer than six and no more than twelve. But the size and degree of formality may well depend upon available help. If you have none at all, or if someone to serve and clean is the only possibility, then your party will of course be informal. You can arrange your table in the living room, the dining room (if you have one) or in a comfortable family room or living-kitchen. Your menu will consist of no more than two or three courses; usually only one wine is served. Even with a helper in the kitchen, the hosts assist with the service or handle it entirely themselves. On such occasions consider serving the first course in the living room. During cocktails consommé can be kept simmering in a samovar and at an appointed time you invite guests to help themselves. Or the hors d'oeuvre you serve with cocktails can take the place of a first course—shrimps with a sharp sauce, antipasto, tiny cheese tarts piping hot from the kitchen.

When the occasion warrants a formal dinner, you will need a good cook and a trained butler or one or more waitresses. Never attempt a formal party without adequate assistance. Your table, carefully set in the dining room, wears a distinct aura of elegance. (See table setting for a formal dinner on page 33.) Place cards may be used. This is the occasion for your most handsome table appointments, your most spectacular recipes, your most cosseted wine. And after dinner, something unexpected in the way of entertainment—some music, perhaps, or the viewing of a new film.

For menus for gala dinners, turn to page 244.

JOYOUS WELCOME, *opposite,* to a dinner for ten comes from a happy scheme of yellow and white with lots of sparkle and from personal touches that convey the fun of planning a special "do": armfuls of flowers and favorite animal figurines for the centerpiece; butter molded in pretty shapes; home-brandied peaches in the champagne.

PARTY SPIRIT, *right,* for a small dinner comes from the imaginative use of fresh oranges to spike dainty flowers in the centerpiece and at each place. The other colors are soft, so the table is completely at home with the room's pale yellows, greens and wood tones.

BEADLE   DESIGNER: JACK HARTRICK

MAYA

GREAT SPLASHES OF GREEN, *above,* with white and silver make a dining table look cool as a bower—and especially refreshing for a summertime dinner party. The centerpiece, purposely emphasizing greenery rather than blossoms, is echoed by more greenery banked behind the table. White damask etched with silvery pewter gray sets off the solid-color plates, the gleaming silver bowls lined in brilliant green enamel, the green napkins. Easily served by one maid, or by the hostess alone, this dinner for six includes an iced soup first course that can be on the table when the guests sit down.

FOTIADES

FLOWER-AND-LIGHT CENTERPIECE, *above*, and a profusion of designs inspired by the riches of India create a warm mood for a dinner on a winter's night. The fancifully shaped clay lamps (or you could use vigil lights) burn for hours, so the table stays pretty for lingering after-dinner talk. Patterning a felt cloth are temporary motifs of colored powder. These versions of an Indian folk art are made by shaking artist's pigment (confectioner's sugar or talcum will also do) onto the cloth through stencil boxes having pinhole designs. Outsize napkins are cut from different bold Indian cotton prints.

81

DESIGNER: RICHARD NEAS

A DINING ROOM IN FULL BLOSSOM, *opposite*, welcomes guests to the table after they've had the first course in the living room. Two gigantic bouquets encircled by fruit are arranged like eighteenth-century paintings in the niches. In airy contrast, single flowers—apple blossoms, carnations, chrysanthemums and one splash lily—are laid on an organdy cloth embroidered with delicate sprays. And here and there are fresh kumquats winged with tiny leaves. To make serving easier for the hostess, she skips bread-and-butter plates, and places the dessert silver above each setting. (For full details on how this dinner party was planned, and its menu, please turn to page 69.)

SNUG ALCOVE, *right*, in a small apartment can be a flattering dining spot for a chosen few, especially if you conjure up a guest's favorite dish and set the table with very special pieces. On this table for three, the cherished tureen, service plates and octagonal soup bowls are from the beginnings of a pewter collection. Interesting contrast to the heirloom pewter: bright trays of plastic-laminated fiber glass.

A CONGENIAL KITCHEN, *below*, open to the dining room is the friendliest of settings for a gourmet dinner. The hostess-cook can always be at the party, not a part-time recluse by the stove. The dining area is as international as the menu is apt to be: French table set with mugs and a mix of pottery in blue and green; American chairs; old English hutch; Mexican tile floor; Portuguese tile walls.

YEE

BEADLE   DESIGNER: AUDRE FIBER OF FIBER-JEHU, INC.

BEAUTIFUL BREAKFASTS

For a change, it's fun to plan a party to start the day instead of ending it. Twelve noon on a Saturday or Sunday might be your shining hour. But although breakfast parties are especially fun on weekends, there are also occasions on weekdays when they are a good entertaining solution—for a morning committee meeting made up of men and women, or women alone; for an all-ages group before or after sports; for wives of husbands attending a convention or other business meeting; as an informal reception for a recently married young couple.

The breakfast or brunch party is in many ways a luncheon but with food eaten at breakfast—waffles, scrambled eggs, sausages, codfish cakes and the like. It can be served buffet-style, and you can use your best silver serving dishes without having everything look too formal. Or it can be a seated party for anywhere from four to twelve people, sometimes with the host or hostess cooking at the table—maybe in a chafing dish on a handy serving cart, or on a waffle iron stationed close by. Drinks served before breakfast are of quite a different nature from those that precede lunch or dinner. There has to be a particular alchemy to top-of-the-morning drinks, compounded of one part clean flavor and one part hidden stimulus, such as can be found in a Bloody Mary, a screwdriver or a salty dog. And of course there's nothing more delightful than champagne.

For breakfast and brunch menus, turn to page 243.

BEADLE

NO-HUNT HUNT BREAKFAST, *left,* takes its cue from the English countryside but skips the fox part. The cynosure now is a group of hot dishes (among them, kidneys sauté, tiny sausage cakes in wine, clam fritters) on a living room's traditional hunt table. A buffet-style Sunday breakfast is fun to revive as a nonstuffy reception for a newly married couple or for friends just back from vacation haunts.

A WAFFLE GALA, *opposite,* with a raft of different fruit syrups to make it festive, could take place on a porch, in the kitchen, or wherever. On a Sunday morning, this is a peaceful way to be with close friends or to entertain a neighbor's weekend guests. To ease service, the waffle iron is on a convenient serving cart and the baking is done to order right at the tableside.

CHAFING-DISH BRUNCH, *opposite,* for friends planning to watch the tennis matches, starts at a time comfortable for late risers yet sufficiently early to get to the first game without a rush. A cart near the hostess' chair simplifies serving. Tiers hold fruits, brioches, coffee. And hot from the chafing dish on top comes creamed chicken. To make this an occasion, there's wine, too. But first a round of Bloody Marys or a choice of fruit juices.
BEADLE

EARLY BIRDS' REPAST, *below,* for weekend houseguests gives Saturday a bright beginning. Especially if the eye-opener takes place where morning sun streams in—for instance, a porch turned into an informal dining area. A garden bouquet, flowered china and a roomy banquette create an easy mood. Over a simple meal of juice, country-fresh eggs, sausages and a home-baked loaf to be cut at the table, everyone can decide on the activities ahead.
HORST

LUNCHEON PARTIES

Lunching together during the week is one of the most popular ways of entertaining among women. To honor a houseguest or the houseguest of a close friend might be the occasion for a luncheon on the formal side; for an informal luncheon, simply to get together several good friends whom you know will enjoy each other. Anywhere from four to twelve make a pleasant luncheon group, and it is possible to handle an informal party of this size without help. A formal luncheon, like a formal dinner, must be fully served. Place cards are frequently used, especially if the gathering numbers twelve or more. Guests are invited for one o'clock. The party may begin with a light aperitif, sherry or a cocktail; wine or champagne may be served during the meal. The menu should be light and delicious. For the informal luncheon two courses are plenty; for the formal, three are adequate. For both, set your table with your prettiest china and linens. Fresh flowers make a lovely centerpiece or you might bring out a treasure from another part of the house—a pair of antique cockatoos or a choice tureen. The weekend or holiday lunch is something else again, since men may be present. Your menu is then heartier. For menus for luncheon parties, turn to page 243.

WEEKDAY RESPITE, *opposite,* is a refreshing luncheon get-together to meet a new neighbor. Adding delight are lots of garden flowers and an easy mix of flowered patterns against the glowing mahogany table. A tiny cow (from the antique dresser) and green leaf plates on which to park hot buttered rolls, make amusing complements to the cheerful blue Staffordshire china.
DESIGNER: AUDREY KOEHLER

SATURDAY INTERLUDE, *right,* built around a light lunch is a marvelous way for two couples to catch up on each other's news. For a cozy dining spot, a small table in the entrance hall has its tartan skirt topped by crisp linen, tiny straw baskets of nosegays.
STOLLER

BEADLE

YEE

SIMPLE PLEASURES, *opposite*—good food, good talk, some favorite things—enhance a luncheon for four close friends. Flowered china and linens on the wood table echo the room's relaxing scheme. So that the hostess can manage easily without help, coffee pot and cups are placed at one end of the table, wine at the other, the makings for a light lunch on a nearby sideboard.

GRACIOUS ACCOLADE, *above,* for an out-of-town visitor, is a small luncheon meticulously planned, carefully served. The table is a gentle composition of pale and rich hues sparked by a variety of shells from the hostess' collection. Used as soup bowls, bread-and-butter dishes, and as a handsome flower-filled centerpiece, the shells make a cool, creamy contrast to gold-banded china.

A WELCOME TO SPRING, *below,* makes a charming cause célèbre for a city luncheon. A seasonal fling with flowers offers a change from urban bustle: blossoms are tucked in napkins, woven into a nest for the centerpiece. Served in the living room where guests can relax in armchairs, the meal starts with the first course on the table and the wine close by for second pourings.

BEADLE

TEA AND COFFEE ANYTIME

Tea and coffee parties have much in common. They can be as formal or as informal as you wish. They can take place at any time of day—from midmorning until midevening—and they are a relatively inexpensive way to entertain. At a late-morning or late-afternoon reception, both tea and coffee may be served; see *right*.

One normally thinks of a tea party taking place in the afternoon, but also consider spiced tea as a midmorning refresher; after-dinner tea as an alternative to the demitasse; Russian tea as a conversation piece for late-evening gatherings. The perfect tea occasion is, of course, five-o'clock tea. Whether the party is large or small, this is the time to make everything lovely-to-see with flowers, pretty linens, delicate china, dainty food—perhaps a decanter of sherry. The correct service for afternoon tea is based on one major premise: the hostess pours the tea herself. At a large reception, however, it is clearly impossible for her to welcome many people and pour as well; therefore she asks a friend or relative to take her place at the tea table.

The coffee party, morning, afternoon or evening, is one of today's most popular ways of entertaining, especially among the young. The morning "coffee" usually comes about because of good works; there's a meeting or a group gets together to address envelopes—coffee is the obvious refreshment, accompanied by sweet rolls. The afternoon coffee

GUERRERO

party is often a social occasion for housewives who are frequently tied down through luncheon. It begins with coffee and dessert, leaves plenty of time for good conversation, bridge, or Mah-Jongg. The evening party has the same components—coffee and dessert—but is a party for both sexes. Brandy and liqueurs are often served, or champagne with a festive dessert. Set out demitasses and regular coffee cups, dessert plates, forks and napkins, and plan to use all your small tables. Have *lots* of good hot coffee. Irish coffee, espresso or flaming café diable can make the gathering a real occasion, and for wakeful friends, be sure to provide a decaffeinated brew. For menus for tea and coffee parties, please turn to pages 245 and 246.

AFTERNOON PAUSE, *left*, over teacups in the garden brings a few friends together in a little slice of time. The table is covered with batiste laid over a white cloth to emphasize the delicate tracery design. The white pineapple-embossed tea set is combined with plates and cups and saucers of pastel blue stoneware.

TWILIGHT RECEPTION, *opposite*, offers tea in the classic way and coffee with a non-traditional twist—whipped up with milk and melted chocolate for a frothy drink. Another surprise: striped cotton cloth as background for wedding-present silver.

YEE

GRAND-SCALE GALA, *opposite, right,* for a large number of people, calls for an array of the prettiest desserts imaginable. For convenient one-stop service, coffee *et al.,* are set out on a single long table.

TINIEST GARDEN PARTY, *opposite, far right,* just for four, informally mixes casual china with an elegant tea service on a rattan table.

HIGH-TEA DELIGHTS, *opposite, bottom,* roll into the living room on a commodious cart. Each accoutrement is so lovely, no embellishments are needed. A teapot masquerading as a tulip adds fun.

DESSERT PARTY, *left,* early in the evening, is festive yet nonfuss. Dessert and more are carried to the living room in two tray-loads. The first conveys cups, bowls, and a berry dish with cherries, grapes, sour cream and sugar. On the second, coffee and a light liqueur.

AGENDA HIGHLIGHT, *below,* for a midmorning club meeting is steaming coffee and, with it, coffee cake and doughboys. For the buffet, a checkered cloth covers card tables.

YEE

DESIGNER: MELVIN DWORK

BEADLE

THE VERSATILE COCKTAIL PARTY

Probably the easiest and most flexible way to entertain a number of people is to give a cocktail party. The hour may be anywhere from five o'clock on (although on Sundays and holidays, especially in the country, people are often invited for cocktails before lunch), and the group may be large or small. The most successful cocktail parties are those that are large enough for the guests to have an agreeable choice of companions, but not so huge that there is no room to maneuver about comfortably.

Small cocktail parties can be delightful. Relatively little work—a choice of drinks and simple food may be set up in the living room—they leave the hosts free to talk and enjoy their guests. To consider: a wine, or sherry or champagne party as an occasional alternative to a small cocktail get-together. Less expensive, wine parties are growing in popularity with young people, can be festive and fun—provided the guests all enjoy wine, which is important to know.

Large cocktail parties *should* be a friendly gesture to a wide group of acquaintances whom you would like to see and have know each other; they should never be allowed to degenerate into a pay-off-obligations gathering of people who may have nothing in common. In planning a large cocktail "do," be sure to give your most thoughtful attention to the flow of traffic, convenient service of drinks and imaginative food. A nice touch of hospitality would be soup (served in cups) or strong coffee, or both, passed towards departure time.

Today there is a growing and pleasant custom of prolonging the party into a cocktail supper. Drinks and hors d'oeuvre are served first, followed by a buffet that might be quite simple or very elaborate. Or the buffet may be set up during the entire party. Guests serve themselves, frequently are seated at little tables. The cocktail buffet differs from the usual buffet supper in that the menu is simpler, the party may end considerably earlier and it is a drop-in affair.

A GENIAL COCKTAIL-SUPPER, *opposite,* practically runs itself—and does it beautifully even in a small room. The buffet, planned for open-all-night service, includes foods (some hot) that can be kept delicious for hours, and appointments that add continuous glitter. The bar, *below left,* and coffee spa, *right,* are set up in other parts of the room to ease traffic.

CONVERSATION FARE, *above right,* is served with a bit of showmanship. This spectacular offering has fresh oysters topped with horse-radish sauce and served individually in tiny sake cups—fun, tasty and quick to down.

IMPROMPTU RENDEZVOUS, *right,* for a small cocktail party is a big oval table transformed in a minute to an elegant self-help bar. Located in the entrance hall, sparked by crystal and silver, it provides a fast, festive start to the party.

YEE

FESTIVE TRAY TRICK, *opposite,* set up before the party starts, offers a complete, self-contained feast (drink, food and flowers, too) for each guest. Hors d'oeuvre on each tray are intentionally varied to encourage trades—and talk—between strangers.

PORTABLE POTABLES, *below,* plus snacks and supplies can be tucked into wicker trays, ready to go whenever you feel like serving. In one basket, a loaf of wedge-shaped sandwiches made from a round bread which has been sliced horizontally.

BEADLE

ADULT-STYLE OASIS, *left,* for a large-scale house-warming, has all the mixers and trimmings for fix-it-yourself cocktails. Dominating one end of the table is a bowl of cold gazpacho nestled in ice.

IRRESISTIBLE MAGNET, *below,* of lobster and a tart sauce, is arranged on a terrace table for on-the-spot nibbling. To cheer guests, a house-wide party might have such lures in many strategic places.

GUERRERO

FOTIADES

LARGE
COCKTAIL PARTY,
SMALL SPACE

Fitting a king-size cocktail party into a limited area—and doing it so that everyone has a chance to talk comfortably with friends—is a matter of realistic planning. With astute logistics, you can see to it that everything needed is readily at hand, that the party moves easily, and that no mob scene ever builds up.

Thanks to a series of great ploys, no crush whatever develops when forty come for cocktails in the one-room apartment, *right*. To turn it into a party place, a drastic rearrangement of furniture is called for. Chairs, tables and a sofa bed which normally form one big conversation area are moved to clear more floor space for action, open up wide traffic lanes and, at the same time, make several small seating groups. The effect of the furniture realignment, *below right*, may be dismaying when the room is empty, but it will be quite different when the place is full of people.

Since the apartment has no bedroom and none of the existing closets can house forty extra coats, a hiding place for them is provided in the foyer. A rented coatrack is stashed behind a curtain made of dime-store ribbons, stapled around a tension pole, which is then mounted near the ceiling.

One way to induce guests to move about is to deploy food and drink in rather widespread areas, and provide speedy service at the bar. The bar here is set up in the foyer. Selection of drinks includes Scotch, bourbon, gin and, as all parties should, a nonalcoholic beverage (one of the best: a good mineral water). Cocktails, which take time (and some elbowroom) to concoct are premixed and ready in flasks. Since something less than a dinner but more than a mere nibble is a cocktail-party necessity, a variety of hors d'oeuvre is cached at strategic spots—on bookshelves, a table, a low cabinet. Really sustaining food, a hearty hot dish, waits in the kitchen, ready to be brought in toward the end of the party as a pleasant concluding note.

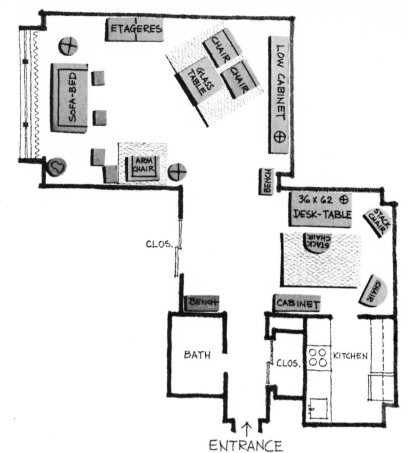

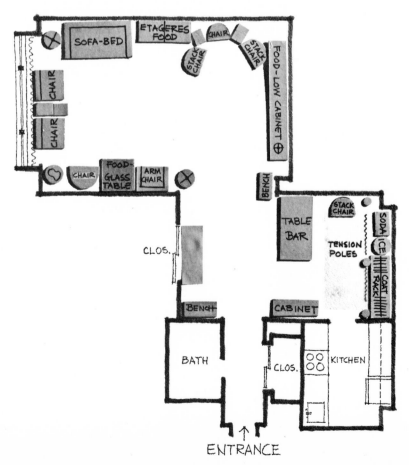

FOTIADES

MAYA

PARTY SPA, *top left,* is the foyer desk, protected by cork over a plastic liner. Behind the ribbons, extra ice, more soda, a coatrack. *Top right:* Between books on the étagères, canapés on Japanese trays. *Above:* Toward the party's end, a curry dish is brought from the kitchen on a hot-tray cart. *Left:* A fabulous extra—a caviar seascape on a brass tray. Shells hold accompaniments at base of the immense block of ice; knives jut from the coral.

101

HOW
TO
MAKE
SPACE

Making the most of space has always been an American forte, and nowhere does this talent show more tellingly than on the party scene. Dining is no longer defined in terms of a single room and, as a result, new forms of entertaining are evolving every day to suit our freer, more fluid pattern of living. Space-making and space-stretching are the "in" things for, paradoxically, it is often those without a proper dining room who give the most parties. The idea of dining all over the house has taken hold, and many rooms are now planned with this extra purpose in view. Living-room tables are meant to hold not only lamps and ashtrays but also tray suppers. Family rooms have tables that double for dining as well as games. Halls are often furnished with drop-leaf tables and side chairs for small supper parties. Savvy hostesses are aware that folding chairs, extension tables, tray tables, card tables with big, round latch-on tops, tea carts, cocktail tables that rise to dining height are the invaluable supplementals that make it as simple to give a party for sixteen as for six.

Today we are definitely more concerned with the personal touch in entertaining than with perfection. After all, who ever dictated that the proper manner of dining was to sit up straight and make polite chitchat with the guests on either side of you? Certainly not the great eighteenth-century hostesses and wits who valued good food and sparkling conversation over the refinements of protocol. More friendships were launched at intimate little suppers in the private chambers of Versailles than in the intimidating splendors of the banqueting halls. The art of entertaining is, above all, to keep your guests happy and relaxed and the conversation flowing, an achievement devoutly to be wished and much more likely to happen in the personal atmosphere of a living room, a library, a family room or even a kitchen than in the conventional confines of the dining room.

ART GALLERY harbors guests for after-dinner coffee and conversation. Carpeted floor and big squashy cushions prompt low-level lounging in a latter-day simulation of the Turkish corner. Carpeted shelf, by day a stretch-out spot, becomes buffet counter holding coffee service, plate of petits fours.

NAAS   DESIGNER: WARD BENNETT

DINING ALL OVER THE HOUSE

Who but out-and-out traditionalists still insist that the only proper venue for dining is the dining room? Certainly not today's liberated hostesses, who recognize that the place to entertain is wherever it happens to be most pleasant at the moment, sometimes in the dining room, many times in other parts of the house. In spring, a garden room green with plants or a sunny nook by the library window. In summer, by the sea-sprayed window of a beach-house living room or on the breeze-swept coolness of a porch. In winter, undoubtedly in the warm heart of the kitchen or before a blazing fire in the family room. The hour, too, dictates the setting. Intimate little suppers after the theatre might be hatched against the luxurious background of a guest room or the final stage of a dinner party might move to a cushioned corner where guests can stretch out at ease. Many hostesses prefer to assess their space and facilities sensibly and find the place that best fits the size and mood of the planned party. Even when the family is alone, it lifts the spirits to change the place where you dine.

YEE

SUMMER LIVING ROOM, as invitingly crisp, cool and fresh as a garden salad, is sufficient to stimulate flagging appetites on a hot day. Sustaining the mood, the sleek lacquer table is bare except for bright ovals of place mats set for a one-course luncheon—moves that cut the work of entertaining to a minimum.

COUNTRY KITCHEN, *right,* enticingly wrapped in the appetizing smells of cooking, is a warm and welcoming setting in which to entertain weekend guests. With its beguiling mixture of family mementos, primitive paintings, gay wallpaper and antique furniture, the room has a very personal ambience.

GRIGSBY

GUEST ROOM, *above,* as elegantly ornate as the Brighton Pavilion, lends an atmosphere of intimate luxury to a dinner for six. Folding chairs and adjustable backrests that enthrone guests on the bed supplement armchairs. When temporary dining furniture is whisked away, the room returns to its normal state, *right.*

DESIGNER: WILLIAM PAHLMANN

STUDY as fresh as a garden, *right*, with rose-painted screen, cheerful butterfly chintz on chairs, becomes an impromptu breakfast room where the day can start out in a sunny mood.

DECK IN THE TREETOPS, *below*, with all-weather wood benches and chairs, turns into a dining porch at the first hint of a warm day.

STOLLER   ARCHITECT: HENRI JOVA

BEADLE   DESIGNER: JAMES TILLIS OF MALLORY-TILLIS, INC.

LIVING-ROOM CORNER team of banquettes and square coffee table with the places set on adjoining sides, *above*, serves four people comfortably, without any sense of improvisation.

GARDEN ROOM, *right*, combines the indoor pleasure of well-padded chairs with the outdoor delights of sun-lit luncheon in a garden ambience, the cool sparkle of a glass-topped table.

DESIGNER: JOHN BRASWELL

107

SPACE: DINING ALL OVER THE HOUSE

TWO-WAY DINING KITCHEN with a cooking counter as the bridge, *below*, enjoys the best of both worlds. For a spring luncheon, omelets and salad can be made on the kitchen side, served over-the-counter to guests sitting at the table.

FAMILY ROOM, *bottom*, with a game table big enough to seat eight in front of the fireplace, is the natural choice for a family-and-friends Sunday supper and get-together with perhaps a huge pot of cassoulet (the perfect one-dish meal), wine, French bread and a bowl of fruit as the centerpiece.

BEADLE

KORAB
BAER

ARCHITECT: WILLIAM W. WURSTER

DINING AREA of the kitchen can be quickly set up for a ready-when-you-are breakfast for weekend houseguests. Kitchen counter draped with matching tablecloth becomes a sideboard bearing orange juice, fresh coffee, chafing dish of hot food and bowl of eggs to be cooked to order.

HALLWAY freshened with plants and a fantasy-forest wallpaper makes an enchanting, intimate corner for Sunday breakfast when the dining room seems too large, the kitchen too mundane. Riot of spring flowers on the floor-length tablecloth and napkins matches the bouquet centerpiece.

HORST

DINNERS MINUS A DINING ROOM

The impulse to give a seated dinner party need never be frustrated by a lack of conventional dining space or conventional dining furniture. Almost any room will stretch to party proportions if you assess it imaginatively, even a crowded living room or one-room apartment. Almost any table you happen to have will serve, if you are inventive about arranging the place settings. If you are prepared to go to the new lows and give a party on the floor, Moroccan, Indian and Oriental fashion, you don't even need chairs. If you aren't (and this should depend on the age and limberness of your guests), there's no reason to give up. Nowadays, chairs are rarely expected to match tables on any count: design, period, wood or finish. It is, in fact, considerably more innovative to use a mixed bag of dining chairs, open arm chairs, pull-up chairs, director's chairs, even garden chairs, and should the guest list expand beyond your seating capacity, there's always the caterer to call on. Dining in the living room gives you a chance to break away from the rigid traditional seating patterns, too. If your guest list includes more women than men, as it is very apt to these days, you can gracefully obscure the imbalance of the sexes by arranging the place settings checkerboard fashion on a long, narrow table—this also helps to disguise an uneven number of diners—or by using tables that seat three or five instead of the usual two-by-two pairing.

SEATED DINNER without a dining room is no problem if you are prepared to give up the amenities of the living room for a few hours. All it takes is a call to a caterer to rent extra tables and chairs that will augment your regular dining furniture, and you can seat as many as twenty guests. (Additional flatware, linens and china can be rented, too.) For serving, it is advisable to set up a buffet and let guests help themselves, or each man serve his dinner partner. After dinner, the living room can be returned to its original state in minutes, while the guests move to another room for coffee and after-dinner drinks.
FONSSAGRIVES

LYON

PLANNED PARTY in a living room that doubles for dining is a small miracle of organization and timing. Hours before, the table is set and the centerpiece of tiny white flowers and variegated green leaves arranged in a crystal *rivière, above.* First course of melon is brought from the refrigerator and put on the table just before the guests sit down. Meanwhile, in the kitchen, *above right,* the main dish, dessert and salad greens, all prepared ahead, have been taken out of the refrigerator, the main course reheated and the salad mixed. When the guests sit down, the food is brought into the living room on trays and arranged within arm's reach of the hostess, *right,* who can serve every course easily without having to jump up from the table.

MAYA

DESIGNER: SARA LITTLE TURNBULL

A TRIO OF DINNERS in a space-shy, one-room apartment revolves around a wheel-about table with extension top that can be set up anywhere depending on the menu and number of guests. *Top left:* instead of place mats, dinner is served on trays that speed table clearing. When guests sit down, soup is already on trays in covered bowls, main dish waits in casserole, dessert on a desk-turned-server. *Above:* For another foursome dinner, soup is poured from an insulated pitcher into bowls on gold lacquer trays. End-of-the-table centerpiece is a handful of zinnias plunged into a lush basket of ferns. *Left:* At a dinner for six, the table is pushed in front of the sofa to stretch the seating space. The plates for fish and meat courses are stacked on place trays, in the Scandinavian fashion; sturdy mugs set in a row hold condiments.

DINNER ON THE FLOOR, *right*, Japanese-style, needs only floor cushions, low tables and an Oriental chest pushed together to provide dining space for six. The main dish of sukiyaki is cooked in an electric skillet on the hearth, with ingredients all lined up nearby.

LEONARD

**CHECKLIST
OF FURNITURE
THAT MAKES
ENTERTAINING EASY**

Card tables with folding
    round tops
Tray tables
Nesting or stacking tables
Small tables that can be
    grouped together to
    make a large one
Cocktail table that rises to
    dining height
Long folding table for buffets
Small coffee or end tables, to
    hold trays for buffet meals
Bar cart, with glass storage
Tea cart, with warming shelf
Folding or stacking chairs
Pull-up chairs
Mushroom stools
Foam-wedge ottomans
Cubes, to use as tables, stools,
    for storage
Inflatable furniture for indoor
    or outdoor parties
"Knockdown" furniture that
    can be reassembled
    as needed
Floor cushions

PARTY CLOSET, *left,* holds a
mighty haul. On recessed upper
shelves: eight folding tray tables,
two round 45-inch folding-table
tops, ceramic centerpiece, punch
and salad bowls, drop-front box
for coasters, ashtrays, bins for
candles, paper napkins. Glassware trays (plastic planters from
dime store) on back of door fit
into recess above shelf. Below
shelf: eight folding chairs, two
card tables on diagonal, space-
conserving tracks, silver serving
pieces, as well as projectors for
color slides and home movies.

YEE

SPACE-SAVING IDEAS FOR PARTY GEAR

Party-givers are inveterate collectors. In no time at all every available inch of space is chockablock with the paraphernalia of entertaining. There are ways, though, to amass everything you could possibly need for any type of party without exhausting your existing space. Mostly this is a matter of good sense and good management both in buying and in storing what you buy. When you add a piece of furniture, let it have a double purpose: a cube end table with storage room inside, a coffee table with a folding base and tray top, an étagère that can turn party-server, holding dishes and food on each tier. Large serving pieces such as tureens and punch bowls should be decorative enough to stay out in full view, holding a mass of leaves or a pile of fruit. When glasses are a storage problem, it's worth investing in a set of the stacking type. Hunt for unused space, such as the back of a kitchen or closet door where you can have racks for linens, trays, place mats. Closets work better if they are divided into compartments with space for bulky furniture, adjustable shelves for tall centerpieces, narrow slits for trays, drawers where untidy objects like ashtrays and coasters can be filed. And don't overlook the possibilities of prosaic dime-store objects for organizing storage, such as clear plastic stackable boxes to hold linens, flatware, candles.

MAYA

HELMS

MIEHLMANN

TINY TABLE, *above,* is a tiered Chinese wedding basket that splits into five trays to provide guests with individual holders for drink, and hors d'oeuvre plate.

SILVER STORAGE behind china-closet door, *left,* consists of a nontarnish cloth lining that is faced with loops to keep flatware in place, easily visible and shiny.

BAR CABINET, *far left,* painted like a poster, is compact and roomy. The center well holds bottles while a refrigerator and sliding shelves for glasses are fitted neatly into the four sides.

PARTY GEAR, gets stowed away in shipshape fashion in closet compartmented to take card and tray tables, also vases.

OTTOMANS of featherweight foam keep the seating pattern of a party fluid; they can be stacked or grouped in small space until the moment comes for them to split apart.

SUPER SIDEBOARD, *above,* covered with anodized aluminu[m] veneer, is masterfully designed to give the maximum stora[ge] space for linens, flatware, china, trays and serving piece[s]. When closed, it is a handsome and striking asset to any roo[m].

BEADLE

SLIM WALL RACK fits a week's supply of wines in any tight corner. Bottles rest on their sides in open cradles so the labels may be quickly identified.

TABLE LINENS hung on slender towel racks in normally wasted space behind a kitchen door, *below,* stay uncreased, are as colorfully composed as a pop art painting.

TINY TRIANGULAR TABLES, *bottom of page,* brilliantly lacquered, can join forces to make two small square tables, a large rectangle or the triangle, as shown here.

MAYA

MULL[ER]

TRAY TABLES, *above,* as boldly striped as a zebra, com[e] out of hiding to be set up as individual place settings in a[ny] corner that the hostess' fancy dictates. Here they are warm[ly] entrenched before a roaring fire for a cozy winter suppe[r].

SPACE-SAVING IDEAS FOR PARTY GEA[R]

CLUSTER OF TABLES, *above,* at different heights from cocktail to dining, take up less room than one huge table for a family party of grown-ups and children ranging in age from tot to teenager.

LINEUP OF LOW TABLES and floor cushions on a straw-covered loggia floor adopts a space-saving, air-cooled fashion from the Middle East. After guests have dined, the pillows stack up, tables space out.

ICE HAMPER nearly two feet high, with metal lining, glass lid, leather cover, holds all the ice needed for a huge indoor or outdoor party, yet takes up minimum of room behind bar.

TEA CART with built-in hot-tray shelf to keep food warm, handy second tier for plates, napkins and silver, rolls the first course into the living room for smooth switch from cocktails to dinner.

CONVERTED CABINET of the Victorian era fitted with curved shelves of plastic laminate, is lacquered white, lined with palm-printed fabric and has interior capacious enough for the fittings of a full-fledged bar.

TURTLE CANDLE, *above,* couched on a bed of polished pebbles in a Japanese lacquer tray serves a dual purpose as both decoration and illumination for a party table on a terrace.

COLORFUL COMPACT CUBES, *left,* are a boon to small apartments as end tables, extra seats or plopped before a sofa where they become sturdy serving tables for cocktails, after-dinner coffee, or for buffet meals.

NEW
PARTY
PATTERNS

Ringing changes on a familiar theme is the special forte of every hostess with a true talent for entertaining. For practicality's sake she may adopt a general format that copes smoothly with the idiosyncrasies of her house, her kitchen and her friends' schedules. But she is always adding new twists to that basic pattern. Every party she gives means another opportunity for her to improvise and experiment. If colors and patterns and bibelots are her passion, she dreams up a new centerpiece or concocts a new table setting. If she loves to cook, or simply delights in imaginative food, she surprises her guests with an unexpected menu or one very special dish. She may come up with a lively new form of entertainment or decide to start—or end—the party at an unconventional hour. The setting may be a small apartment, a poolside, a wine cellar or a stable. But always there is a clear and evident concern for people. You can see this in the care and trouble that is taken in making out the guest list, in arranging the seating, and in dozens of other little attentions for the comfort and pleasure of her guests. For she knows that a good party is neither a ritual to be performed for its own sake, nor a display of virtuosity. A party is a gift to friends—from beginning to end solely a matter of giving them a good time. Today's new party patterns couple an uninhibited delight in the unexpected with the knowledge that anything goes, as long as it goes smoothly and is fun.

ZODIAC PARTY, *opposite,* is the most fabulous of birthday parties—it celebrates every guest's birth date at once, as well as your own. A lively astrology theme spikes the room decorations, the table arrangements and the evening's activities.. Here, the living room is cleared and almost every strong color under the stars brought into play; so are lots of designs as highly individual as horoscopes. A gypsy mix of gaily painted cardboard chairs line up to form banquettes. Overlaying the white felt cloths are black and white zodiacs cut from printed fabric and varicolored paper plates showing each guest's sign. Napkin colors and place cards match plates. For mood lighting, crystalball lamps flash on and off. After a buffet supper (heavenly food, of course) comes dancing in the middle of the floor to the music of a live combo, and tête-à-têtes in some private corner with a guest astrologer.

BEADLE

MENU

Avocado and lobster mousse
with cold green sauce
Vegetable pie
Russian salad
Champagne

IRRESISTIBLE FARE is arranged so each food is a star. *Above:* In a brimming bowl set on a coffee table, an anchovy dip is garlanded with mixed crudités. *Left:* Seafood glistens around a decorative mold of ice set on a metal tray (where it lasts for hours). To make the mold, water is frozen in a large bowl, and shells and coral imbedded during the chilling. The shell on top contains the sauce. *Below:* A lavish dessert buffet is the climax to the demi-dinner. Among the tantalizing assortment are crepes, with a choice of fillings, cooked on the spot.

GRANITSAS

DEMI-DINNER

Newcomer to the party scene is the demi-dinner, a new kind of party with a new menu, a new hour, new flexibility. Its menu: two courses only—hors d'oeuvre and dessert—but each bountiful, delicious, surprising. Its timing: a starting hour around six-thirty, a festive finale around ten (so guests with a long drive home or an early rising can leave before midnight). Its flexibility: no set tables, no main course. That means guests can drop in any time, circulate or settle down, even leave for a previous engagement and return later. Some people come in street clothes, some in black tie, others dressed for a dance later in the evening. There are always new people to talk to, other viewpoints to be shared.

The food is as variegated as the constantly moving parade of guests. Diverse cold hors d'oeuvre are at help-yourself stations in several different areas. Hot hors d'oeuvre are passed on one big tray after another, each with its special treat. The many choices add up to a hearty, delightfully unexpected replacement for the first two courses of a routine dinner. Then at the stroke of ten, the gala climax is revealed—a lavish buffet of cakes, mousses and other desserts, irresistible even to weight-watchers. The array draws all guests, who happily rationalize they haven't had dinner so they can revel for once in dessert. And they do, returning to the buffet again and again. Coffee is served in the living room, and guests linger or leave as they like.

MENU

Hors d'oeuvre:

Caviar; Crudités, anchovy dip; Fruits de mer; Sliced fillet of beef on French bread, savory sauce; Shrimp Tempura; Chicken porcupines, hot marmalade dip.

Desserts:

Lemon mousse; Chocolate mousse; Chocolate cake; Orange cake; Pineapple brownies; Crepes with choice of apricot puree, strawberries, sour cream.

HEARTY HORS D'OEUVRE, *above,* of the hot variety are all finger foods attractively arranged and passed on large silver trays. *Right:* Caviar station offers the delicacy iced in the tin, with lemon wedges, bowls of chopped onion, sieved egg and sour cream alongside.

RAVE BUFFET, *top left,* of favorite dishes spreads wall to wall. Guests help themselves, then sit at a close-by table, *above,* simply set with cross-wise runners. Contrasting poultry dishes, *left,* a galantine of chicken and a gold-touched turkey, wait to be carved. The formidable menu, *top,* written over a hand-painted sprig of herbs, becomes a souvenir for guests to take home. Below the bill of fare, the meal's triumphant conclusion, a croquembouche.

GREAT RECAP DINNER

TROMPE L'OEIL PARTY

To discover a very favorite dish on a party menu gives a person that loved and pampered feeling—as if the dinner were planned just for him. To make each and everyone at your party feel that way is the happy idea behind a second-time-around party. It's made up solely of dishes your guests have commented on, never forgotten, and can't wait to sample again. If you are planning such a red-letter event, keep in mind that a buffet is virtually a must—otherwise dishes might number too many or not lend themselves to a well-planned dinner menu. Then, too, a buffet with all the dishes, from first course to last, set forth in splendor, lets everyone know what delights are in the offing. (Only in the case of something like a hot soufflé is a dish brought in at the last moment.)

Star among stars of the encore meal, *opposite*, is a Golden Bird. For this Midas-touched recipe from India, a turkey is roasted in the usual way, then decoratively covered with thin gold leaf, which adheres easily with butter. Sharing main-course honors with the hot turkey and a cool complement to it is a galantine of chicken. The dessert, a tower of tiny puffs filled with rum-flavored butter cream and glazed with caramel, terminates the buffet like a marvelous piece of sculpture.

A trompe l'oeil dinner is an exercise in fool-the-eye mischief that's fun at any time of year—and a marvelous escapade for April Fool's Day. An all-out trompe l'oeil party is a masquerade with one big difference—the foods come in disguise, not the guests.

For the fanciful dinner here, the eye-foolers start with the table. At each place, one knife or fork or spoon is a full-size cut-out photograph. Place mats are pretend antipasto platters—paper plates decorated with pictures of sausages *et al.* cut from magazines (shadows are painted on for realism).

Every course comes to the table incognito. In each soup bowl, crisp noodles form a nest around a raw egg (this is doused by hot consommé). Chopped salad hides in hollowed-out tomatoes. What appears to be an apple is actually made of grated cheddar and butter, shaped, then painted red with vegetable coloring. For the grand finale: a cake baked in a lamb mold, iced, fleeced with coconut, set out in a bed of ice-cream flowers.

FANTASY FILLS A CENTERPIECE, *right*, to overflowing. In, around and above a vast brandy snifter are pomander balls, ribbons, paperweights, fruits, eggs, a dove. *Top:* A paper-plate mat holds a pseudo-antipasto course: a savoy cabbage, stuffed with ground meat is tied up to look like a fresh whole cabbage; red wine sits in a wire carrier, white wine in an ice-filled china washbasin.

MENU
Trout glazed with aspic
Eggs Surprise
Stuffed tomatoes
Galantine of chicken
Golden Bird
Cheese pastry
Croquembouche
Champagne

MENU
Egg-in-a-nest consommé
Fillet-of-flounder fans
White Bordeaux
Capons encircled by deep-fried potato eggs
Stuffed cabbage, Majolica
Red Bordeaux
Tomato Surprise salad
Garden-of-Eden cheese
Springtime cake   Ice-cream flowers

JAPANESE FEAST

International parties, with their unusual fare and delightful decorations, are rising high on the list of today's favorites. One foreign theme that lends itself particularly well to our love of outdoor entertaining comes straight from Japan. A Japanese dinner can offer double delights—an exotic feast plus the fun of watching food being cooked on the spot.

The party on these pages started well before sundown on a terrace where everyone gathered for cocktails and watched tempura, the first course, being deep-fried over a hibachi. (Cooking is swift but the dish is a masterpiece of preparation. The major chore—paring and slicing vegetables—is done ahead and the ingredients arranged on a tray as attractively as if they were hors d'oeuvre.) While an expert chef, abetted by the more adventurous guests, did the cooking, others helped themselves to completed morsels, using chopsticks or fingers. For the next course, which was cooked in the kitchen, everyone trooped in to fill their plates from the stove and enjoy the rest of the feast indoors.

To help you plan such a party, many adult schools now offer short courses in Japanese cuisine and sources for foreign foods are springing up in many cities across the country.

MENU

Sashimi (thinly sliced raw tuna)
Tempura
Shoyu sauce with ginger and horseradish
(for dipping Sashimi and Tempura)
Sukiyaki   Rice
Watermelon   Choice of beer or white wine

YEE

STEPS TO THE FEAST, *above,* are lighted by candles in sand-filled paper bags. *Opposite:* On the terrace, where the Japanese meal starts with a tempura cookout, ingredients are prettily arranged on a ceramic table. Boat-shaped dishes of very thin wood, the Japanese version of paper plates, will soon be heaped with the first course. Close by, waiting for the cooking to begin, are the hibachi and saucepan of batter. *Below:* Guests help themselves to tempura directly from a napkin-lined pot used for draining just-cooked pieces. After the first course, the party moves indoors for sukiyaki and dessert. *Below left:* On the pass-through panel between the kitchen and the living room, bottles of wine, pottery goblets and watermelon are arranged like a still life.

DESIGNER: JACK LENOR LARSEN

HORST

DESIGNER: MAC II

DINNER AND GAMES

When everyone at your party is comfortable and re-laxed, good things happen naturally. That's the thinking behind this about-face party—an easygoing, "don't-dress" dinner followed by an evening of games, that adds up to a complete change of pace for many party-goers.

To clear the way for spontaneity: Keep dinner arrange-ments on the informal side. Offer a wide choice of games —some new, some old, some for two players, others for four or more. And encourage a play-wherever-you're-comfortable policy by providing a mix of chairs, plus a haven of pillows for those who may prefer the floor.

For this kind of party, plan to serve dinner on several small tables and, wherever possible, make them part of existing furniture groups in the living and dining rooms. The advantage: tables will be on stage, not in the wings, so you'll have very little moving of furniture for games later in the evening. Choose a simple menu that allows the first course to be on the dining tables. For the main course, attractively arranged platters could be set out on a sideboard or other small table for buffet service. Or dinner plates could be served from the buffet and passed to seated guests by the hosts or a waitress.

After dinner, guests choose their favorites from the games you've assembled, and turn the room into a playground. The party may end early or late, whenever players finish a round or two and decide to continue or call it a night.

AN ENGAGING MEDLEY, *opposite,* of vivid colors, patterns, flowers, foods and games, give a party the spontaneity of a happening. *Top:* A mix of chairs is pulled up to a dining table set before the sofa. *Far left:* A potpourri of pillows is handy to comfort floor-sitting backgammon players. *Center:* A hamper on the floor brings flowers down to where game participants can enjoy them. *Center right:* Two round tables let guests dine in small relaxing groups. *Bottom left:* Ticktacktoe game on coffee table is fun for early arrivals. *Bottom right:* Instead of flowers, the party centerpiece is the first course—a basket of crudités. Each guest cuts off as much as he wants, and adds French dressing. *This page:* Dinner is set out, ready to be served.

MENU
Crudités, French dressing
Baked steak
Creamed spinach ring and fresh carrots
Stuffed baked potatoes
Beaujolais
Endive and watercress salad
Toasted French bread
Port-du-Salut
Meringue soufflé, marmalade topping
Coffee

BRILLIANT BUFFET, *left,* signal
its location with an airborn
centerpiece of balloons that ar
slipcovered with black and whit
fabrics. Below them, milk-glas
goblets sport eyelet napkins
Above: A pot of rillettes of goos
inlaid with black olives. *Top:* A
cubist study made of bread. *Be
low:* White platter of cotechin
(dark sausage); and an aromati
dunk of olives and anchovies fo
cauliflower and other raw vege
tables that are white as can be

OP-ART BUFFET

Op art, gayest of the lively arts, makes a great motif for a party—particularly one to celebrate New Year's Eve. For an unusual revel, *opposite*, op art comes to the party via a black and white scheme for everything, food included. The party's bright innovation: a new, decidedly untraditional hour for a New Year's event—six to eight-thirty, which considerately gives guests the choice of going on to later parties well fortified by substantial food and champagne, or spending the rest of the evening peacefully at home without feeling deprived of a year-end celebration.

On the buffet for this party: a dazzling black and white print cloth, lots of milk glass and white china, black pottery and plastics. Plus food as close to black and white as possible.

A black-and-white menu is challenging to devise. Your plans could include breads, white-as-can-be cheeses, seafoods, and cream sauces, to name a few basics, with black olives and caviar for accents. And you can always stretch the scheme with anchovies, pâtés or with roast meats that are crusty dark on the outside and juicy within.

MENU

Chicken liver pâté
Rillettes of goose
Roast beef   Burgundian mustard
Cotechino (any dark Italian sausage)
Crudités and tapenade
Breads and butter
Champagne

VIENNA BRUNCH

A Sunday brunch can be a beautiful way to entertain—especially when you give it a spectacular theme. For most people, late on a weekend morning is a fresh and lively time for a party, and guests are apt to arrive in an expectant mood. For a brunch full of surprises, you might decide on Vienna, city of dreams, as your inspiration. As befits a city famed for its creamy concoctions and outstanding composers, the foods should be rich, and music always in the air (provided by a pianist you hire). Instead of cocktails, the brunch, *right*, starts with a fruit course served buffet style in the living room. Afterwards, everybody sits at one table to enjoy, among other things, wedges of an astonishing pancake dish. This is built of thin crepes spread alternately with creamed chicken, creamed ham and mushrooms, layered in a spring-form pan (with the side removed, they look like a cake), then covered with a rich Mornay sauce, slathered with Parmesan cheese, and set in the oven until glazed. During the meal, passages from Haydn, Mozart, Johann Strauss and others serenade the party.

MENU

Mélange of fresh fruits
Viennese layer pancakes
Salade Mimosa
Lemon caraway casserole bread
Gold dessert
Champagne   Coffee

MAYA

GAY AS OLD VIENNA, the brunch table, *above*, is bedecked with a bit of springtime madness: Hurricane shades filled with eggs alternate with bowls of blue forget-me-nots on a blue cloth. Assorted coffee cups are varicolored, whacking big. *Top:* Each white linen napkin has the menu printed within a blue fruit-and-flower wreath. *Below:* A mélange of luscious fresh fruit arrayed on a small buffet table for the first course is the only one guests serve themselves.

RENOIR PICNIC ON A BARGE

Before your friends scatter for the summer, why not think up a marvelous farewell party for one and all. A meandering picnic along a little inland waterway is a lovely way for everyone to bid each other bon voyage. This isn't too difficult to arrange since a surprising number of towns and cities have canopied barges for hire, some mule-drawn, some horse-drawn. Once you hire the boat, preparations are less than you might think. You bring the food, of course, but you have no tables to set and no need for professional help on board. All you need for a bar and buffet are extra tables.

To make a barge party truly memorable, you might conjure up an enchanting nineteenth-century aura by basing the invitations, dress and provisions on a Renoir theme. For the Renoir picnic, *opposite*, on a Pennsylvania canal, invitations were sent in individual hampers with instructions for guests to bring their own china, silver and wine glass to the scene. At the same time, everyone was asked to look as Impressionist as possible in a costume evocative of the master's paintings—a command that brought forth a flurry of parasols and peg-top pants, down from the attics. Guests embarked at one o'clock, settled down to enjoy cocktails, a masterful Gallic repast and scenery, while old dobbins pulled them gently downstream until the end of the party at sundown.

PICNIC WARES, *above,* are toted in a hamper sent to each guest along with the invitation. *Below:* Cold French fare starts with a truffled pâté de foie. *Bottom:* On a buffet table laid with a polka-dot cloth, what looks like a Flemish still life is really a lobster salad hidden under the shell which is bedecked with artichoke hearts, garlands of lobster-meat medallions and truffle-topped hard-cooked eggs. Also on board to enjoy: a noble assembly of cheeses, a distinguished wine. *Left:* Printed menu (mime of ones from Maxim's famous restaurant) is destined for scrapbooks where it will help party-goers keep pleasant memories green.

MENU

Truffled pâté de foie
Pinot Chardonnay
Lobster salad Parisienne
Mixed vegetable salad in mayonnaise
Fruits and Cheese

MAYA

DINNER-DANCE IN A STABLE

MENU

Marinated cold cauliflower
Crabmeat salad
Curried egg salad
Baked glazed ham
Chicken and artichoke casserole
Puligny-Montrachet
French bread, fresh sweet butter
Strawberry Bavarian cream

The best time for an outsize dinner-and-dance party: summer, when you can use both outdoor and indoor areas. The best way to bring them together: a lively overall theme. The best place for the party: an original setting on your own grounds. You could turn a garage and driveway into a bistro with café tables. Or, if there is an unused structure on your property, why not convert it to a party place, as was done with the carriage house, *this page* and *opposite.*

The occasion: a dinner-dance with a theme inspired by a family collection of animal figures. These served as centerpieces on each table, also as clues to the seating arrangements. On a terrace where guests met for cocktails, a paper model of the dining tables was set up, complete with place cards and a tiny toy animal keyed to each centerpiece. After checking these clues, guests crossed the lawn to the stable house and easily found their places. Later came hours of dancing to nonstop music by two alternating combos.

ELEGANT STABLE DINING is at banquettes in the stalls, *right,* and at round tables in the carriage room, *opposite.* In keeping with the party's animal theme, jungle motifs and colors unite the two areas. A curtain-fabric print covers some tables, a related solid on others. The meal is largely buffet, with waiters on hand to pass platters for second helpings, serve dessert.

LEONARD

LYON

DESIGNER: ALICE SPAULDING BOWEN

ENCHANTING SETTINGS, *opposite,* for outdoor and indoor tables are only a few yards apart, and dining room doors are kept wide open so all guests feel they are part of one big party. Terrace table is protected by a canopy worthy of a maharaja and lighted by hanging lanterns of silk and pewter. *Left:* The initial gathering place for all is the long terrace, leafy setting for cocktails. Cushions on the wall make pleasant perches for guests. *Bottom left:* On each of several trays placed within reach of small groups, there are drinks for four and a complete selection of hot and cold hors d'oeuvre. The pair of containers holds enough iced martinis to supply refills, so no one has to spoil good conversation by the interruptions entailed in going to the bar or signaling a waiter. *Below:* A harpist in an idyllic setting plays relaxing music during dinner.

MENU

Chicken consommé with
julienne mushrooms and chopped dill
Saddle of lamb   Snow peas
Red Bordeaux
Endive and beet salad   Parsley dressing
Chocolate soufflé   Custard sauce

AN INDOOR-OUTDOOR PARTY

A refreshing table-setting gambit makes it possible to invite many more guests for a seated dinner than an indoor dining area holds. The trick is to set equally lovely tables in two quite different, but adjoining sites, indoors and out. This is relatively easy to accomplish by switching furniture about and making imaginative use of things from all over the house. You might, for example, take a pair of wing chairs outdoors for regal-looking host and hostess chairs. By making the outdoor setting resemble a full-fledged dining room, you intertwine the comforts of a seated dinner with the airiness of a fête champêtre. (Add a little light music and you imbue the scene with the magic of a musicale, too.)

Tables for the indoor-outdoor party, *this page*, are equally beautiful, equally desirable, so every guest feels well treated. Settings are not identical but they do have visual links. For instance, linens and dishes differ, but their colors and delicacy are related. And similar hurricane candles and masses of flowers are combined in both centerpieces.

WINE-CELLAR FEAST

For the adventurous, wine tastings have become a favorite at-home entertainment. After the tenth or twelfth go-round, however, the novelty of a straight tasting of a large group of wines tends to pall. A kindlier extension of stand-up wine tastings is a lunch or dinner party with wines and foods that enhance each other. This new party pattern gives you a latitude extending from the classic dinner with its progression of great dishes and wines to a simple, but original, buffet. For the epicurean menu, *right*, planning of the foods came first, then wines selected to complement them. The charming setting for this dinner was the label-patterned tasting room, *opposite*, adjoining the wine cellar of a connoisseur.

Beluga caviar White toast
Dom Ruinart Blanc de Blancs
Icelandic shrimp in potato baskets
Green horseradish sauce
Montrachet Marquis de la Guiche
Crown roast of lamb
Madagascar rice and wild mushrooms
Fiddlehead ferns
Château Cheval Blanc
Cheese soufflés
Musigny Cuvée Vielles Vignes
Comte Georges de Vogüé
Peaches poached with champagne
Raspberry sauce
Schloss Vollrads
Trockenbeerenauslese
Coffee
Cognac Grande Champagne

QUICK WINE PARTY

BEADLE

A new, carefree pattern in wine parties has a fresh young beat. A far cry from sophisticated tastings, the fledgling wine party is basically a small buffet of several red wines and a half-dozen cheeses. A few chilled white wines could be added, along with a mild cheese, bread and sweet butter. A sampling of this kind is quick to put together, easy to manage for a few or a crowd. And it can get by in very little space. For one such party, *left*, a coffee table holds the basics. Each cheese has a flag with its name to guide guests. To turn a tasting like this into a supper takes only a few additions (see menu, *right*), which can be ready on a nearby table.

Bresse Bleu
Taleggio
Tomme de Savoie
Double Gloucester
Appenzeller
Bel Paese
French bread
Sweet butter
Blanched almonds
Neuchâtel
Chianti Ruffino
Dézaley
Beaujolais Brouilly
Cold beef salad
Fresh fruits

CHILDREN'S PARTIES

Behind every party worth its ice cream and cake stands a resourceful mother with her pleasant smile, nerves of tempered steel and a plan she follows to the letter. The plan begins with a guest list, its length limited according to the size of the party area. One good guide is to invite as many guests as the host's age—five for a fifth birthday, six for a sixth, and so on. Plan a theme to get everyone in the party mood and carry it through with invitations, decorations, activities, and sometimes even clothing. Next, decide on a time limit (from an hour and a half for preschoolers to three hours for ten- and eleven-year-olds), write it on the invitations, and stick to it. Jam-pack the allotted time with things to do, exuberant alternating with quiet; keeping a list of extras in case the main event fizzles. By and large, the under-four set likes play-alone games: blocks, balls, crayons and pull-toys—lots of them help avoid squabbles (some might double as favors). Older guests are more competitive and the more exciting the treasure hunt or relay race, the better they like it. Above all, have plenty of prizes and favors; the surefire way to have the party rated tops is lots of loot to cart home. The party table is the pièce de résistance. Here and on the following pages, a grab bag of party ideas, all intended to elicit gleeful squeals from small participants and keep mother's smile genuine to the end.

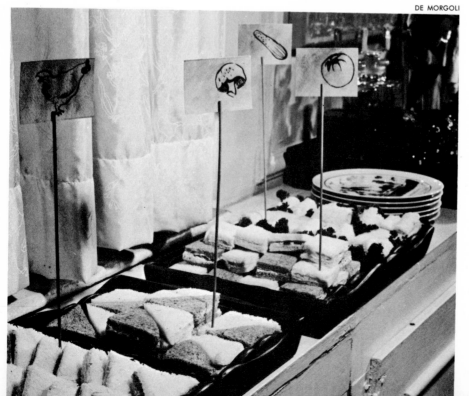

DE MORGOLI

JAPANESE PARTY, *opposite page,* lets girls of ten or eleven sit on floor cushions, sample exotic oriental flavors, giggle over fortune-cookie forecasts. On a table crisscrossed with sailcloth obis are lacquer fans in a hibachi, *kokeshi*-doll favors, and, swaying above, a paper parasol. Food is simple but special: pineapple on bamboo skewers, chow mein with rice and crispy noodles, cookies and tea from Japanese kettle. For each guest, chopsticks *and* a fork.

PARTY SANDWICH BOARD, *left,* with paper and bamboo signposts that help nibblers choose exactly what they like. You can buy French parchment signs very much like these, handpaint or letter your own, or cut and paste saucy pictures from magazines.

BLOSSOM-TIME TABLE, set in a garden for romantic little girls, has wicker place plates and a centerpiece of apple blossoms in a wicker garden basket. At each place is a little clay flowerpot filled with fruit sherbet and sprouting a candied apple-on-a-stick.

POSTER PARTY for pre-teen girls, where blowups of last year's festivity are matted on the wall; poster cutouts under acetate form attractive place mats. The centerpiece, a poster-yellow birthday cake polka-dotted with fat, white after-dinner peppermints.

CARNIVAL PARTY for unpredictable kindergartners, stars drumsticks-in-a-basket lunch served up on its own shiny plastic tray. Table is spread with wipeable, field-flowered oilcloth; centerpiece is a bouquet of paper napkins; bright-colored favors, looking like fat candles, are kaleidoscopes.

CHUCK-WAGON PARTY TABLES for pint-sized cowpokes are bales of hay loaded up with frankfurters to grill, fresh rolls, baked beans, apples, doughnuts. To catch spills: striped lap-cloths the size of saddle blankets. Flatware is wood, plates unbreakable plastic. To take home: stack of ten-gallon hats.

GRIGSBY

DESIGNER: NORMAN LALIBERTÉ

NAPKIN TREE, *above,* a painted branch in a base of florist's clay, has blossoms of calico clipped on with plastic clothespins—useful later on for securing the napkins to the wriggling young guests.

FANCIFUL FLYING UNICORN, *above right,* has cotton tails for pinning, a mask for blindfolding small contestants. To make, glue on or appliqué fabric cutouts, decorate with embroidery and trimmings.

CHINTZ CHAIR BACKS, *right,* at a party for tots, are really smocks to protect party clothes. Felt rounds on plates keep bowls from skidding; matching bows dress up the cups. In the basket, birthday cupcakes, each with a lighted candle for wishing.

TEDDY BEARS in gay apparel, *below,* sit in place at the gaily canopied party table while little girls romp and play in the garden. After the ice cream and some merry-go-round cake, each bear will leave for home in the arms of his favorite small guest.

MULLER

DESIGNER: DAVID EUGENE BELL OF BLOOMINGDALE'S

A BACKYARD HOBO PARTY is a natural for grade-school boys, who love to outdo one another with patchy jeans and outrageous hobo hats. Begin with the invitations, perhaps cutouts of battered stovepipe hats with flip-up paper daisies. Along with party details inside, be sure to announce the costume of the day. Let the garden gate greet the guests with a railroad lantern and a rustic road sign that points the way to the hobos' campfire (formerly the family barbecue pit). As soon as the last tramp arrives, break the ice with a treasure hunt, handing each guest a bindle—a dime-store cotton handkerchief on a stick—to fill with his treasure and keep afterward. For refreshments, hamburgers grilled before their eyes, served up with french fries and carrot sticks on tin plates painted and personalized (more take-homes) with nontoxic paint. For dessert, ice cream, chocolate cigars, and a birthday cake that has been cleverly concealed under the overcoat of a backyard scarecrow. To make scarecrow, set an angel food birthday cake on a thick styrofoam base that is a few inches wider than the cake, and skewer both cake and base on a broomstick stuck solidly in the ground. Attach a coat hanger at scarecrow shoulder height and drape a coat around the styrofoam, not touching the cake. Top the pole with an innocent-faced straw head and floppy felt hat, and stuff a little straw at cuffs and hem.

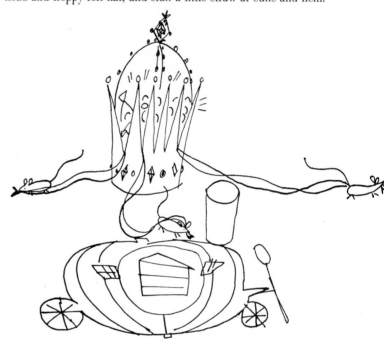

A PARTY FOR PRINCESSES can turn even tomboys into ladylike Cinderellas for an afternoon. Invitations might be parchment scrolls, tied with velvet ribbons and mailed in tubes. On party day, decorate the door with a life-size blowup of a magazine princess, or make her yourself of cut and folded paper. The party-starter could be a game of pin the crown on the princess, followed by a session of quiet crown-making with foil, lengths of chiffon and assorted sparkly trimmings. Luncheon might be grown-up creamed chicken in patty shells or individual brioches, served on oilcloth pumpkin-coach place mats. And, as the pièce de résistance, the birthday cake, discovered at party's end under a golden crown centerpiece heaped with bags of gold-wrapped chocolate coins and beribboned with gay streamers tied to tiny white take-home candy mice.

CIRCUS PARTIES, indoors or out, thrill both boys and girls of almost any age if you begin with a bang and keep all three rings going full speed. Invitations to the greatest party on earth might be cards that look like circus wagons, with detachable animal namepins to wear to the party. Marking the door or gate might be a baggy-trousered paper clown, with circus pennants and balloons lining the path through which the guests march to recorded calliope music. For the opening act, hand each guest a paper bag filled with scissors, crayons, bits of yarn, marking pens and shiny paper, and set them to work making paper-bag animal masks. Give prizes for the best. Children keep masks on for a game of petrified animals, in which they move and make noises like circus beasts while music plays: They must freeze in position the moment it stops. Anyone who moves is "out." For lunch under the big top, have mock pizzas (tomato sauce and melted mozzarella on English muffins), candy apples, popcorn, punch, and for dessert, ice cream served in bowl-topped beer glasses decorated with stick-on clown faces and ice-cream-cone clown hats. The birthday cake hides beneath an inverted hatbox decorated to look like a circus arena, with paper pennants, glued-on paper animals and, around the edge, a parade of wooden circus ponies for guests to take home.

PORTER

PARTY GAMES: ACTIVE

POP-THE-BAG-RELAY: Divide guests into two teams on facing rows of chairs and give everyone a paper bag. At the signal, each in turn dashes around his row of chairs and back to his place, blows up the bag and pops it. The first team that finishes wins the game.

KING-OF-THE-RING: Everyone puts one foot inside a circle chalked on floor or grass, then grasps ankle with hand. At signal, players try to shoulder and shove each other from ring. Anyone who lets go of his ankle or who puts other foot in ring is "out."

BACKWARDS TUG-OF-WAR for two: Competitors stand back-to-back at room center, bend down and grasp right hands between their legs. Winner is the one who pulls the other across the room.

PARTY GAMES: QUIET

WHERE IS THE RING? With one blindfolded player in the center, other guests sit in a tight circle passing a ring around a long string and chanting, "Ring-a-ling, who has the ring?" At the last word, center player unmasks and tries to guess. When he does, the child with ring is "it" for next round.

TOSS THE PENNY: Put a half-dollar in a pail of water. Line up the players. Whoever drops a penny squarely on the coin wins it.

ARCHITECT: Pass out paper and pencils. Blindfold everyone and have them draw a house, garage, car, tree. Remove masks for comparing mixed-up arrangements.

PARTY
CANDLES

BEADLE

CIRCUS ANIMAL CANDLES in big-top colors, *above*, parade around a candle clown whose hat burns all the birthdays from 1 to 10.

CHOIR OF ANGELS scarcely one inch tall, *above right*, are dressed in pastel robes and hold miniature candles on their heads, while they "sing" happy birthday at the tops of their soundless wooden lungs.

CANDLE FLOWERS, *right,* of blue, red, magenta and pink, can bloom on icing stems and leaves. Just one inch across, their centers change color as they slowly burn.

WOODEN LOCOMOTIVES, *above,* pull shiny bright-colored one-inch railroad cars with birthday-candle cargoes along frosting tracks.

PAINTED ANIMALS with candles on their backs, *right,* march in twos around center ring of candy-striped candles three inches tall.

GRIGSBY

FLOCKS OF BALLOONS, *opposite page,* turn a garden into a birthday wonderland for ten little girls at a summertime party. Rows of balloons on strings pegged into the ground line the front path and back garden, where balloon clusters swing like never-never grapes from the trees. The centerpiece is an Around-the-World balloon, its basket (weighted with a paper-wrapped brick) piled with birthday gifts. After all the presents are opened, strings are snipped, letting clouds of balloons float skyward. Then young guests with balloon favors skip up and down the street, finally pile into the fabulous "balloonmobile" bound for home.

BIG DOTS, LITTLE DOTS, *left* and *below,* mostly on paper throwaways, make a festive party that you clean up by making a quick tour with the trash barrel. Glass-topped table, its base wrapped in a dotty paper cloth, holds paper plates, cups and napkins, plastic forks and a centerpiece of tangerine flowers on an orange base. More oranges (nature's own polka dots), pierced with straws, wait on plates to sip as first course of a hot-dogs-and-beans lunch. The franks are served on corkscrew-tailed German wooden sausage-servers destined to accompany guests home. The biggest dots of all cover paper chairs sturdy enough to support a grown man (or a bouncy party-goer). Afterward, the chairs can be stacked for storage or unfolded and then stashed away flat.

YEE

HOW TO TURN A BIG PARTY ON

T he wonderful air of spontaneity, the glowing aura of warmth and friendliness that makes a big party a great one is not a matter of happenstance or talented ad-libbing. Both of these can turn the trick at an intimate get-together, but the true vitality and success of an outsize gala depend on how well you lay your plans and work out your logistics. To make it marvelous and memorable, you must put your stamp in large letters on the party's several facets *in advance*, because in many ways your personal stamp is your stand-in; at a big party you can't be everywhere at once.

Anticipate the party's progress step by step, from your guest's viewpoint as well as your own. Concoct a festive marker for the driveway or dress up your everyday one so people won't wonder if they've found the right address. Be sure you have adequate parking space, even if you must borrow a neighbor's field and hire a minibus to shuttle guests from car to house. (That breaks the ice between strangers fast!) Enlist a few close friends to come early and help with introductions.

If you are planning a buffet dinner, think up ways to make the help-yourself part go as smoothly as possible. Figure out how to simplify the serving of wine and other drinks. Take the time to plan the seating—then there will be no timid souls looking for a place. This doesn't necessarily mean place cards. How about a balloon tied to the back of each chair, the name written with a felt-tipped pen—or a flower given to arriving guests to direct them to the tables with flowers in corresponding colors. Or you might revive a Victorian custom and hand each man as he enters a card with the name of the lady he is to take in to dinner. Make your decorations larger than life. To be seen and create an impression in a room filled with people, decorations must be stunning in concept, color, scale. In your house they will add a surprise to rooms furnished on an intimate scale; in a hotel ballroom they will conquer architecture designed on a scale too grand for easy friendliness.

Think up an enchanting menu. People do not go to a party primarily to eat, but an excellent meal always helps to make a party memorable. Concentrate on in-season food or regional specialties—or dishes that help to carry out the theme of the party.

BRILLIANT PARTY DRESS, *opposite,* for the buffet at a house-wide gala quickly tells a crowd where the food is—out here on the terrace. High and handsome signals: wildly colorful banners of felt with glued-on designs. Spirited too, a papier-mâché horse with fanciful trappings and the table's covering of hot-pink felt striped with a magenta rebozo. Unique foods, part of what makes a great party a new experience for everyone, are presented with a flourish. Carved wood bowls from Ethiopia contain the main course, an East African curry, rice and condiments. For the centerpiece, a tiered, wood compote holding red vigil lights, whole and halved pineapples, slices of melon. On a small table, lacquer bowls filled with additional condiments. For more about this party, turn the page.
ECKERT

It takes bold colors and strong effects to kindle a crowd of guests and stand up to real live competition. To quote the host of this high-flying bash, "You've got to go big and you've got to go high and you've got to hit hard, if they are going to be seen over the milling crowd." *They* are a galaxy of mood-lifting devices that you can copy or adapt or use for inspiration—and they come up strong through several rooms here.

The flamboyant "do" on these pages is a farewell party given for lots of friends before a glittering trip around the world. The theme: unabashed splash interpreted a dozen ways. The man behind it: an artist with boundless imagination, no inhibitions, and students who make enthusiastic helpers. So you're not an artist and teacher and you can't call on a classroom to aid and abet you. But perhaps you are deft on your own and have talented children who can lend a hand. Begin with a wide-open mind and eye. Dare to make changes in the house that can ignite sparks or increase comfort. Rearranging furniture, camouflaging walls and tables, painting small areas if you want to go all out, using posters, flowers, pennants, tassels, a palette of screaming colors— these are some of the means for staging a spectacular. With felt and glue you can make banners to hang on high. With fabric and pins or a staple gun you can cover tables, walls, whatever. By juggling familiar things you can create a brand-new merriment. Give your inventiveness free rein—and a boost from the fun ideas shown here.

PARTY PANOPLY ALL THROUGH THE HOUSE

HOT BLAZING COLORS, *right,* splashed on one wall key a normally lively living room to party pitch. Shelves, repainted from lavender to red just for the occasion, show off sprightly folk art from the host's collection. For instant impact: awning-striped canvas across a window, magenta felt cloth on a round table. Massed flowers, real and fake, echo painted ones. *Below right:* Ethiopian bread baskets on papered pedestals look like an exotic miniature village, actually offer a wide assortment of cocktail tidbits. *Center,* and *below, far right:* Two of the small dining tables, each zingy enough to sustain a party by itself, present competing lures to guests. Vibrating color schemes—one magenta and chrome yellow spiked with black and white, the other purple and hot red, pink, orange, cooled with blue—and zesty centerpieces make a mockery of repetition. Even the dessert, tangerine ice garnished with lemon blossoms, is served two ways: in covered lacquer bowls on yellow plates and in double glasses (usually used for seafood cocktails) on Mexican tin plates. *Left:* Wicker group at one end of terrace provides cocktail-time seating for wandering guests, with hors d'oeuvre at hand and a pot garden in view.

PARTY DESIGNER: JACK BAKER

ECKERT

ASHLEY

PARTY DESIGNER: CHARLES KOFLER

OPEN HOUSE BY CANDLELIGHT is larger-than-life-size hospitality—generous, romantic, a wonderful way to say "Merry Christmas" or to welcome all your friends after you settle into a new house. And if that house has a bit of history behind it, play it up—to give your party a special grace. On this page, a big gala re-creates the old-time bounty and gaiety of a nineteenth-century house, beginning with an engraving of it, *above right*, on the invitations. Christmas wreaths and massed flowers hold their own in the high-ceilinged front hall, parlors and dining room, even when the party is in full swing. Firelight and candle flame evoke the ambience of the carriage age. Food is served on Canton plates and platters that hark back to clipper ship days. *Top left:* A variety of crudités, as eye-catching as a nearby china collection, surrounds an herb dip. *Above left:* On the dining room table, an old-fashioned still life of yellow and orange roses and tangerine carnations flaring up from a canton tureen. Around it—platters of seafoods and two beribboned turtles made of bread, their backs hollowed out and packed with tiny sandwiches. *Top right:* In a window bay, angels hold candles and berries.

BEADLE

PARTY DESIGNER: MILTON WILLIAMS

WEDDING PARTY ALL IN WHITE on a patio, *left,* is so simple yet looks as romantic as a bridal procession. Space around the buffet—tables scattered on the arcaded porch and lawn—is good strategy for a big reception. White cloths, white chairs, white flowers everywhere—create a wedding-day fairyland. Tables draped in snowy silk are top-frosted with fine eyelet lace. Centered on each: a Lalique basket sweetly crowded with lilies of the valley. *Above:* Tiered wedding cake, iced in an echoing design, is abloom with lilies of the valley and feathery greens. The pristine green and white are repeated in the rest of the menu: breast of capon, artichoke hearts and mushrooms; noodle soufflé, watercress and endive salad; champagne.

BIG-SCALE SPREE IN JAPANESE *left,* celebrates a birthday (could be your teen-age daughter's or your own) in a blithe way—by using oriental make-believe as an occidental icebreaker, fun-maker. Familiar, space-taking furniture is moved out of the party room and replaced by low tables, bright cushions. Each cloth is a different hue, underwriting a tiny Japanese garden of sand, sugar cubes, a Japanese maple spray holding a lantern. Place cards are attached to little favors—brass boxes filled with wild flowers. *Below:* A mood-setting start: guests shed their shoes, slip into straw slippers.

PARTY DESIGNER: MILTON WILLIAMS

SOUND STRATEGY FOR BIG PARTIES

GUEST LIST. Nothing can be duller than seeing the same people over and over again. A big party is always a great opportunity to break the mold; invite people of different ages, social groups and interests.

INVITATIONS should tell guests clearly what to expect: time, place, activities, dress. If at the same time you can pique their interest, so much the better.

SPACE. Calculate 9 square feet of dance floor for each couple (this is the nightclub allowance, adequate for everything except an old-fashioned waltz) and provide enough chairs and tables to seat half the guests at one time.

MUSIC. Your tape recorder or stereo set can be augmented with amplifiers rented from a radio store. You can rent a p.a. system with operator to program and announce or, in some areas, a packaged disc-jockey program. If you prefer music live and want to encourage local talent, a 3-piece group is all you need find room for.

COATS. Arrange a place for hanging every coat in good order. You can hire racks so that coats aren't crammed in a closet or piled higgledy-piggledy on beds.

EXTRA HELP. For a dance or larger buffet party you will need someone to serve at the buffet, one or more waiters to pick up plates and glasses, a pantry helper, coatroom attendants, possibly someone to open the door. It is also wise to have a man or men to park and return cars. Parking procedure is a local problem, and the police should be consulted and advised of the party in advance.

SAFETY. Check your insurance policy to be sure it has a comprehensive liability clause which covers your losses, property damage or injury to guests. Any services you hire should always be covered by insurance. If you are at all unsure of the stress your floors can take with no reinforcement, consult the architect or a local builder.

A TENT. For a large outdoor party, take precautions against rain. Arrange to have a tent or one of the new plastic bubbles put up adjacent to the house, so guests can move freely between the two without getting wet. Many tents have roll-up or detachable sides that are not used when the weather turns out to be fair and balmy.

DECORATIONS. Make sure you possess the right amount of table linens in the colors you need, plus whatever else you plan for decorations and table settings. You can probably rent the cloths if you don't have enough. If you are using a florist, discuss what seasonal blooms would be suitable.

PAPER DRESS-UP AT A CLUB makes a big, merry splash for very little money. Throwaways are one carefree way to turn tables in public places into a private triumph. *Below:* black and white paper runners laid over bed sheets snap up one of many tables at a country club dinner. Paper birds and flowers (printed on both sides) create a blithe centerpiece, ringed with real flower heads threaded on wire. Pink goblets are knockabout plastic.

GRIGSBY

BEADLE

WARM WELCOME IN A HOTEL starts off a charity ball with a friendly, lighthearted bang, even when the guest list is huge. To encourage camaraderie in a stately, impersonal ballroom, *above*, yellow and white polka-dot fabric curtains the arches, is festooned on the walls. Yellow flowers and plumes grace loges and tables. Hats—favors for the women—hang jauntily on chairs. Encouraging people to mingle: a fabulous buffet rather than a staid served dinner. The dessert course, *below:* a dazzling array of mouthwatering pastries and cakes are gaily lined up on a baker's rack.

ROMANTICISM IN A MUSEUM sets the dulcet mood for an anniversary party, *below*. A courtyard is brought to glorious life with miles of rosy pink fabric and candlelight. Intimate little dining tables and a towering tiered buffet table are draped with flowing floor-length cloths. On each small table: an overscale cathedral candle rising from a wreath of pink flowers. On every tier of the buffet: pastries, ices, strawberries, champagne—all in pinks.

BLAST IN A BARN— FOR TWO GENERATIONS

A freewheeling, indoor-outdoor evening of spontaneous play, supper and dancing is a fabulous formula for a big party that all your friends *and* their children will enjoy to the hilt. The one on these pages was given in a barn but the strategy that made it marvelous is easily adapted to any large splurge that jumps the generation gap.

To keep the atmosphere loose, the party was built around a barnyard theme; a natural here, it takes to simple rooms anywhere. Guests were invited to come at six o'clock— partly because many were early teen-agers, partly to make the most of the daylight outdoors. Fathers and sons played softball on the lawn until twilight, while the rest of the group sat on folding chairs and cheered. The younger crowd carried the chairs inside and put them around the table when supper was served on the barn's lower level. The upper floor was reserved for dancing. Because there would be no traffic downstairs until supper-time, all the small dining tables could be set and the cold buffet meal brought out from the house before the party began. To keep the action going, fewer places were provided than there were guests—a canny device, since people consequently ate in shifts and the party kept its pace upstairs and down.

ROLLICKING BARNYARD THEME and a red-yellow-green scheme enliven dining and dancing areas. *Above left:* On each of the dozen round dining tables, rooster-patterned paper plates, plastic glasses, edible center-pieces—radish trees sprouting string beans and green leaves, anchored in little earthen-ware pots. Country-fresh, too, the cloth's flower design. *Left:* On the barn's upper level, spectacular decorations hang near the rafters, leaving floor space free for dancing. A giant rooster peering around a post is one of many whimsical barnyard denizens home-made of papier-mâché, supersize for impact and well above eye level. *Far left:* Donkey-cart tassels from Sicily look like gaily colored pendants of a high make-believe chandelier.

BOLD COLOR AND LIGHT are big attractions inside and out. *Right:* Barn's red makes a vivid backdrop for impromptu ball game played by boys and men. Nonplayers watch or chat in the summer twilight and drift indoors, lured by party decorations, food, the sound of good music. *Far right:* In the gloaming, the wide-open barn, aglow with light, is a festive beacon. *Above:* Tablecloths of many colors, plain and patterned, transform the lower floor into a joyous dining room. Mexican peasant pottery pots and wooden serving spoons echo the simple charm of brick and beam. To save buffet table space, the centerpieces of four baskets heaped with fresh-clipped ivy and fat red candles are hung a good foot or more above the table.

FANFARE IN A GARDEN CAFE

An evening of dancing in a garden, *opposite*, is easy to stage in a matter of hours with the simplest kind of sorcery—good music, fairyland lighting, a few festive props and the terrace for a dance floor. The musical star at the party is a portable piano ready to play either on batteries or plugged into a house outlet. (Or you could just as easily hire a local combo.) On the sidelines of the terrace and across the lawns: brightly colored tables for two and garden chairs. These, plus masses of cylinders and hollowed-out balls with a votive light in each, pink plates and ashtrays, immediately create an intriguing café setting for sitters-out between the dances.

FIESTA UNDER AN AWNING

Running full speed on a Mexican theme, the terrace party on this page is kindled by a flamboyant mix of folk-art decorations, south-of-the-border food and wide-awake music. Plenty of floor space for dancing and a score of round tables ringed by chairs are geared to the size of the guest list—a big one. Hot colors and big, breezy devices establish a buoyant atmosphere: Festoons of pennant cloth caught up with paper balls and mirror crown the front door; outsize paper daisies nod from trees along the way to the terrace. Every accent is strong, every hue blatant—under an enormous awning that dominates the center of gaiety.

MARKING THE DRIVEWAY ENTRANCE, *right:* Flowing streamers hung from a hoop and a flashing red and blue mirrored medallion atop a tall pole put guests in a high jinks mood.

BEADLE

YEE

PARTY DESIGNER: JAN CURREY

GIANT BANNERS, *above*, separated by columns holding pots of paper flowers aloft, make bright excitement at one end of dance floor, define it.
ON THE TABLES, *top*, more outsize paper posies bloom in baroque Oaxaca pottery vases that are sprayed to match the solid scarlet tablecloths.

157

TURNED-ON MAGIC BY A CANDLELIT POOL

Dining and dancing under the stars is a glamorous party plot that attains peaks of perfection when it's staged on a poolside terrace and the pool itself is a candlelit centerpiece. The layout is carefully planned for the most convenience and the greatest effect. On one part of the terrace, little tables covered with flowered cloths circle the dance floor—a smooth felt-textured indoor-outdoor carpet unrolled for the evening across a generous section of concrete paving. Next to it, a live combo keeps the beat; farther along, a gaily striped tent frames the bar and screens ice-and-bottle mechanics from general view. On the opposite side of the pool, the buffet table is surrounded by plenty of uncrowded space and is a little removed to facilitate last-minute arrangement of hot food, cold plates.

After serving themselves, guests sit down to dine by shimmering candlelight—on the tables and on the clear water of the pool where a fleet of candles and flowers floats serenely around several swan decoys. The lighted boats are 6-ounce glasses centered on aluminum foil pans and secured with a bit of florist's clay. Each glass holds a votive candle that's lit with a long fireplace match before it is set adrift with a bright blossom for company. The little flames flicker throughout the evening and are reflected in the shining pans that move idly over the water.

Dancing begins at dusk when the candlelight comes into its own. Party dresses and dinner coats, snappy music, excellent food and drink, a super setting—all add up to an enchanted evening that's spent in fairyland.

BEADLE

BUFFET TABLE SETTING, *opposite,* echos overall party theme. Broadly striped cloth matches the bar tent fabric; candles in hurricane globes are like those on the dining tables; carved swans and lit votive candles bring the pool's floating charms ashore. Pink-striped plates await the meal's main attraction—a beef curry with a half-dozen many-flavored condiments, salad, lime sherbet.

THE HOSPITABLE HOUSE

H ospitality is an attitude that rings through your voice and shines through your smile; it is as instinctive as breathing. The hospitable spirit prompts myriad small touches that make your house say "welcome." Some are as concrete as the easy-to-read sign that tells guests where you live, a covered entrance path to your door, a pretty place to hang a coat or powder a nose. Some are as subtle as the way you convey to an overnight guest that he is free to rise at dawn *or* sleep until noon, the understanding with which you leave certain guests to their own devices, the cool with which you issue warm-hearted and enthusiastic spur-of-the-moment invitations—"please stay for" or "do come home with us."

In planning for guests, imagination is the greatest asset you can be blessed with. The imagination to think up delightful surprises—an offbeat place to give a party, a hammock to loll in under the sun, an unexpected spot for serving breakfast or a drink. The imagination to realize that although you may enjoy active entertainment, someone else's idea of sheer bliss is to be left alone with a book. And above all, the imagination to recall all the little things that have made, or spoiled, your fun when you were a guest. Indispensable to all hospitality is a relaxed atmosphere—the kind that comes from an intuitive understanding of comfort, thoughtful planning, frequent practice, a self-confident evaluation of what you yourself enjoy. To be truly hospitable is to share with others your own delight in living.

A GENEROUS WELCOME comes across in many ways, from a street number, *right*, high and clear for all to see (nothing spoils the fun faster than a half-hour's hunt for the house), to a living room, *opposite*, warm and attractive to put guests at ease in half a minute. Six chairs, no two alike, form a semicircle around the hearth—a cheerfully unconventional arrangement that lets everyone face the others and the fire, too. Most chairs have footstools and there's a table within reach of each. For more pleasures: bunches of flowers, a basket of apples, jars of nuts and candies on the mantel.

DECORATOR: KATHRYNE HAYS

BAILEY

ARCHITECT: ULRICH FRANZEN

LANDSCAPE ARCHITECT: LAMBERT LANDSCAPING CO.

PARKING SPACE GALORE, *above,* and room to turn in a thoughtfully planned entrance court that makes arriving so easy for all.

LIGHTED PATH, *right,* almost takes guests by the hand and leads them to the door. Soft glow plays on the landscape, too, so it's as pretty by night as by day.

LYON

SHELTERED ENTRANCE, *above,* and a path neatly defined by low gardens say come-right-in.

PORT IN A STORM is an entrance hall with a wicker kangaroo to hold umbrellas, and a place to sit while removing wet boots.

INSTANT REFRESHMENT for the spirit, *above,* comes from a tiny, perfect indoor garden that greets guests as they open the door and step inside.

GOOD OMENS, *above,* pineapples—renowned symbols of hospitality—form a lovely still life by a door.

SMALL SANCTUM, *below* and *left,* for guests: a coat closet and powder room just off the entrance hall, and all lined alike in a cool blue print.

DESIGNER: MARIAN HALL OF TATE AND HALL
BAILEY
GRIGSBY

DESIGNER: ANGELO DONGHIA OF BURGE-DONGHIA

THINGS THAT SAY WELCOME

STOLLER

ARCHITECT: DARRELL FLEEGER

ECKERT

PROFUSION OF PLANTS, *above,* flowering riotously in pots, shows the way to the front door. Just for fun, a cherubic ceramic frog serves as doorman.

MASSEY

CARVED FRONT DOOR, *above,* turns a moment of waiting into a joy. And the brick walk continues inside, beckoning guests to a cool veranda.

GAY MAILBOX, *above,* tulip-sprigged and bright as a quip, cheers anyone on the path to your house. And it's an easy sign for first-time guests to look for.

VACATIONING FIREPLACE, *left,* smiles all the while when it's brightly filled with a voluptuous basket of vivid paper zinnias and trails of ivy.

ROARING FIRE, *right,* on a cold day, invites lingering. Especially when there's a snug place to nap, a cushioned chair in which to read.

DESIGNER: STAIRCASE, INC.

MASSEY　　　KARLSON

BREAKFAST ASHORE, *above,* awaits swimmers' return. An improvised dining spot, like this one on a terrace looking seaward through an arched gate, has an easygoing air—guests love it.

LOTS OF LOLLING SPACE, *below,* makes a breezy rooftop an enticing living room for week-end visitors. Cool as water lilies: mattresses and pillows covered in fresh white sailcloth.

DELICIOUS SCENTS, *above,* from potpourri in an open container, waft toward guests as they enter the room. Fresh roses nearby add their bit to the welcome.

YEE

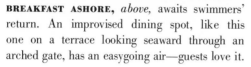

PRIMOIS-PINTO

HOARD OF WALNUTS, *above,* gathered at nutting time, sits on the living-room floor. Nutcrackers let guests know they're to help themselves any time.

FARAWAY HAMMOCK, *below,* in a meadowy garden, pleases a sunworshiper, nature lover, or just a loafer.

GRIGSBY

LANDSCAPE ARCHITECT: J. DUKE MOODY

STOY

POOLSIDE HOSPITALITY shows up in a sculptured ceramic drinking fountain, *above*, in a terrace wall; and in a comfortable cabana, *below*, for dressing in cool, tree-shaded rooms.

DESIGNER: GASTON BERTHELOT

COME-JOIN-US SEATING GROUPS, *above*, in a large living room coax party guests to mingle and talk. Banquettes make wonderful conversation wings by the fireplace; and the hassocks can be rolled anywhere they're needed.

BAILEY

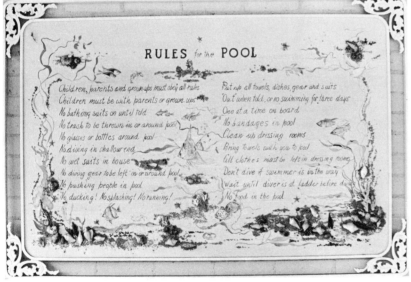

HIRSCH

CLEAR RULES FOR THE POOL, *above*, playfully illuminated, prettily framed, and mounted at the scene, are so much nicer to read than to listen to.

A COMPLETELY EQUIPPED BUT UNOBTRUSIVE BAR, *below left*, tucked into a narrow space, opens to serve with a minimum of fuss. *Below right:* Drawer fitted with metal boxes (hospital-equipment type) holds cocktail snacks.

DESIGNER: MARION HALL OF TATE AND HALL

MUSIC AND GAMES ROOM, *above*, in a basement, gives youthful guests a place to be as noisy as they please. Acoustical tiles finish the ceiling, and vinyl tile, the floor.

FLOWERS
TO GREET YOU
IN
EVERY ROOM

More than any one thing, perhaps, fresh flowers impart the essence of hospitality to a house. The smallest bunch of posies in a guest room says so clearly, "We are glad you are here." Flowers in an entrance hall issue their welcome along with the first hello. Flowers and greens and growing plants everywhere create an atmosphere of joy.

The bouquets need not be grand, nor need they be painstakingly composed. In fact, they should not be—studied arrangements are static. A marvelous armful of field flowers, casual nosegays from the garden, an unexpected combination of fruits and flowers and greens evoke an inspired grace, an uncontrived charm. In fixing flowers for your rooms, experiment in various ways—you don't need formal lessons, books of diagrams and the like. Try mixing the grand with the humble—roses from your garden with, perhaps, daisies from a meadow. Find uses for the stubby-ended buds and almost-finished blooms. Put two or three blossoms in a small bottle, or make several tiny nosegays to place on a table as you would any group of choice objects. Be inventive about containers—supplement conventional vases and bowls with jugs, mugs, empty medicine and perfume bottles. (For many inspiring possibilities, see the list at far right.) Florists' Oasis will help you put many unconventional holders to use since it can be cut to any shape. Oasis also works better than needle holders for supporting casual, natural-looking bouquets, since you can guide even the most fragile stems into the foundation material with toothpicks or skewers.

JOY AT A GLANCE, *opposite:* A golden bouquet in a yellow faience jug glows like a sunrise right in the living room. The mix includes sunflowers, green tobacco leaf—and a ceramic flower or two on the vase.

GARDEN BASKET, *above left,* of mountain laurel, cut from private woods, totes cheer to a terrace table.

GREENHOUSE GRADUATES, *left,* tuberous begonias at their peak, come forth in an Italian pot to grace a patio—and give guests a close look at perfection.

SURPRISE CARGO, *right,* of bougainvillea and fruit in a boatlike bowl from India is refreshing to come upon in an upstairs hall. Aloes serve as masts.

DESIGNER: PARISH-HADLEY

FLOWER CONTAINERS WORTH COLLECTING

Vases, pitchers, bowls of all sizes, shapes, materials—glass, pottery, silver, metal

Baskets of all sizes,

Mugs

Jugs

Crocks, pots

Jars

Buckets, tin washtubs

Tumblers

Tureens

Coolers

Urns

Boxes with sturdy linings, such as snuff boxes, tea caddies

Bottles—new or old, clear or tinted glass, originally used for perfume, medicine, wine, liqueurs, whatever

FLOCK OF CROCUSES, *above*, amid tender grass in a foil-lined wooden bowl, beams up at breakfasters.

SUMMER CENTERPIECE, *above*, of flowers and limes in an ivy-handled china basket brings delight to lunch.

OVERSIZE NOSEGAY, *above*, enlivens a living-room niche—and everyone's spirit, too. This mix was first tied in a bunch, then placed in the vase.

EMPTY COLOGNE JAR, *above*, leads a new life: With daffodils and a perfect tulip, it gladdens a guest bathroom.

TULIP FIREWORKS, *above*, and equally red hurricanes, work to spark a dining table.

TI LEAVES—three to wrap, one to tie—turn a bottle into a vase for a few sprays.

OUTDOOR ART SHOW, *above*, of blooming plants makes stretching out on a chaise even more of a pleasure.

BRIGHT SURPRISE, *above*, for a powder room: Japanese straw flowers in a Victorian pitcher, and assorted soaps in the matching ironstone basin.

THE HOSPITABLE HOUSE:
FLOWERS TO GREET YOU

FOTIADES

MINIATURE GARDEN, *above,* on a bedside table, blooms its heart out just for a guest. A Japanese umbrella-pine shades crocuses, *et al.*

YEE

SNIPPINGS OF FRESH HERBS, *above,* and, just for fun, a flower or two before a kitchen window make city visitors feel country-fresh.

TWO BRIGHT HELLOS, *below,* come from one bucket of flowers in the tiniest of foyers. A mirrored wall, floor to ceiling, reflects it all.

MASSEY

PITCHERS BRIMFUL OF REFRESHMENT, *above,* to revive travel-weary guests: on a terrace table, a crystal pitcher and its country cousin hold, respectively, iced tea and an armful of flowers.

HORST

COUNTRY STILL LIFE, *above,* of shaggy sunflowers, meadow findings, baskets and a Guatemalan scarf, plus decoupage on the guest-room mirror, express joie de vivre. Joyful too: golden walls.

DESIGNER: PARISH-HADLEY

169

THE WEEKEND'S AGENDA, served up with a welcoming while-you-dress cocktail, lists where everyone's going, and when.

BEADLE

THE PERFECT GUEST ROOM

HOLD-EVERYTHING CABINET, *above,* for a part-time guest room, rolls up to a convertible sofa, opens to reveal towels, TV, whatever.

A GENIE OF A TABLE, *above,* at bedside, fulfills every desire of sleep-over guests with its telephone, clock radio, big ashtray, cigarettes, paperbacks and magazines.

Few words of welcome or solicitude can make you feel as wanted in someone else's house as a pretty, thoughtfully appointed guest room. The perfect guest room is one that is a delight to all who stay there. If you have a room you can keep sacrosanct to that end, fine. But if you haven't (and today many of us do not), any number of other rooms—study, library, home-office, bedroom of college son or daughter —can be made, pro tem, into a guest room that anyone would love to stay in. Strip it of extraneous trappings, add the amenities you look for yourself when you go on a visit, and don't forget the ones you could cheerfully dispense with but which are necessities to some people.

Give this test to any room where you are planning to put up a guest: Try napping on the bed—the mattress should be every bit as good as your own and well-pillowed with one hard, one soft, one baby-size. Since loads of people read in bed (or they'd never go to sleep) provide a good reading light and set out a few new books and a cross section of magazines. If you live in the country, don't forget that city dwellers are apt to be cold-blooded. This means plenty of blankets on tap— maybe an electric blanket. Within easy reach try to have a clock with a luminous dial for the wakeful, a flashlight for the timid, a glass and water carafe for the thirsty, and a vacuum bottle of coffee for the guest who can't face the new day without this liquid blessing.

WISP OF A CLOSET, *left,* fitted into a family room, stores guest pillows and blankets on slim shelves. Buckling in the bedding: belts attached to shelf edges.

170

SLEEPER'S CHOICE OF PILLOWS—a firm one, a soft one, a baby pillow—and a lightweight throw for naps gives each and every guest that cared-for feeling.

DESIGNER: ALEXANDER GIRARD

Check the windows—do they have effective shades (or jalousies or pull curtains) to shut out the morning light? Inspect the closet. If it has been doing double duty, empty it. Check the hangers, keeping in mind that the wire variety from the cleaner are good for nothing except hanging Christmas wreaths. Check the chest to be sure the drawers are not overflowing with family possessions. Be sure to have a luggage rack and a wastebasket.

Now to the bathroom. If it is to be shared, clear enough space for makeup jars, bottles, shaving gear. Check the supply of extra facial and toilet tissues (and don't hide it!) and put out fresh cakes of soap. If you lack a mirror where a lady can see the back of her head, arrange one. For the forgetful (which means practically everyone) have new toothbrushes, toothpaste, shower cap, disposable slippers, razor blades, shaving cream, sun lotion. Provide aspirin, Band-Aids, cotton balls, soap flakes, cologne and shaving lotion.

Finally check the mechanics. If the plumbing gurgles, have it fixed. See that the heat turns on and off and that the windows don't put up a fight. If something (a lamp, maybe) rattles every time you cross the room, search it out and muffle it.

These are the ABC's of hospitality. There are of course any number of little extras guaranteed to make a guest purr—for instance the comforts and conveniences shown here and on the two pages that follow.

A VERSATILE STAND, *above* and *below*, that raises, lowers, tilts or not, can do so many good deeds in your guest haven. Here, a clear plastic stand is a letter-writing desk at bedside, a tea table by a sunny window.

GRIGSBY

THOUGHTFUL EXTRAS: a wall switch, *left*, by the bed to control lights in and around the room; and, *right*, for a puzzle addict, a clipboard with a new crossword.

171

PAMPERING TOUCHES

A desk, impeccably appointed with
paper, envelopes, pen, stamps, memo
pad and pencil, a lamp

Chaise longue, reclining chair or
armchair-and-ottoman, paired
with a light throw

Hat stands

Valet stand

Electric shoe-polisher

Terry bath sheet or the kind of
wraparound everyone covets
in French hotels

Full-length mirror

Small TV

Bedside radio

Sewing kit

Bath oils and salts in pretty bottles

Clothes brush

Bed board (for those with
ailing backs)

Small ironing board, electric iron

Pincushion with various size pins

Breakfast tray with legs

Baby pillow

Hangers of all kinds

Lovely sheets, blankets,
comforter, blanket covers

Tiny night-light

Electric clock with luminous dial

Bowl of fresh fruit

Flashlight

A copy of the morning paper

Books, magazines, a deck of cards

Carafe of spring water

WAKE-UP COLORS, *above,* are a bright
extra for a guest bath. So are amusing animal motifs in accessories. For instance, a
frog, *right,* holds soap in a ceramic dish.

BEADLE

AN ACCOMMODATING CABINET, *above* and
left, with a cache of towels and everything
your guests might have forgotten, is at
its best in a hall near a shared bathroom.

DESK ACCOUTREMENTS, *above,*
covered in millefleurs fabric,
may inspire your guests to
catch up on their letter writing.

CAREFREE SPREADS, *below,*
couldn't care less if a guest
stretches out for a nap—they're
made of printed sheets. You whip
up dust ruffles with bordered
sheets, use matching bottom ones
to tuck around the mattresses.

GRIGSBY

DESIGNER: VALERIAN RYBAR

ALL THE COMFORTS OF HOME, *left* and *above*, come in an armoire designed to pamper out-of-town friends who may stay a while. This built-in quickly converts a college girl's room to guest quarters when she is away.

MASSEY

WICKER TOWEL RACK, *above*, in a shared bathroom, offers each guest a colorful choice, and a bar all his own.

AN IVORY TOWER, *above*, or at least a pleasant facsimile of one, is yours to give a bookworm. Just provide privacy, unscheduled time, pillows and books galore. Sheets and cases are so gay that no spread is needed.

ANSWER TO A DRIPPING SWIMSUIT, *below*, is a drying rack for each guest (coddling can be this easy).

A CATNAP BLANKET, *below*, and especially an eye-catching one like this, subtly lets your guest know he's welcome to rest here any time he wishes.

LYON

GREAT WEEKENDS FOR GUESTS

Entertaining a weekend guest is like giving a party—the more carefully you plan in advance the more smoothly everything will go and the more relaxed everyone will be. There is one important difference. A weekend plan should be flexible enough to accommodate the unexpected—a drop-of-a-hat invitation to bring your guest to someone else's house to dinner, or an unexpected chance to spend the afternoon on a boat. But it's much easier to take surprises in your stride if your weekend program on the whole has been pretty well thought out.

Weekend invitations are almost always extended by telephone unless distance or some other consideration makes that impractical—in which case you write a note. But telephone or note, the invitation should always cover three points: when you expect your guests to arrive; how long you expect them to stay; and how—in general—they can get to your house.

Once a guest has accepted, the invitation should be followed up promptly with a bill of particulars that is both clear and complete. For guests who have never been to your house before, these should include: detailed directions for driving there, plus a simple map for the last lap after leaving the through highway; a rough idea of how much time to allow; a choice of trains—if there is a choice—in case they decide not to drive; and some indication of what kind of clothes to bring. The last is particularly important for first-timers. You can be informative, even specific, without sounding dictatorial: "We usually wear pants and shirts during the day and simple linens or cottons—street-length—for dinner." Remind them also, according to the season, of anything they may need to keep warm —sweaters for cool evenings, boots for snow. And whether they are first-timers or frequent visitors, *be sure* to tell them about any event that will call for anything dressier than sports clothes.

ARRIVING WITH YOUR GUESTS

If you live in the country or near the water the year around, your plans for weekend guests will be based on your normal household routine. But if you are taking friends with you to a house where you spend only weekends, you may have to alter your customary patterns —especially your pattern of housekeeping. Everything should be in shipshape order when you arrive. While guests are with you, you won't want to do any but the most essential daily chores, certainly no vacuuming, dusting or other cleaning. So if you can't have someone come in during the week to clean house and change the beds, do it yourself the previous weekend.

The weekend's menus, too, should be carefully planned to reduce marketing and meal preparation to a minimum. Stock up the previous weekend on liquor, staples, and anything that will keep in the freezer. You might buy the meat in town on Friday and bring it with you in an insulated bag. Plan also to bring two or three cooked dishes such as a hearty casserole or a roast and perhaps a cake or other dessert that can be counted on to travel well. Leave for weekend shopping only the special seasonal or local treats.

If there is no possibility of your arriving on Friday night until well after the normal dinner hour, you might plan to eat at a restaurant along the way. But don't consult your guests about this—it can be unnerving for them to be given options so early in the weekend. Decide in advance where you will stop, make a reservation if necessary, and simply announce that such is the program. Naturally the host will pay the check.

WEEKEND AGENDA

Working out the weekend's schedule will be the same whether you are operating on home base or at a weekend house. Your aim should be to strike a nice balance between activity and quiet relaxation, and to give your visitors periods of solitude as well as social gaiety. But when quiet time comes, suggest several places where they can be alone—to enjoy a good book or whatever. Don't make them feel they must retire to their rooms and take naps—especially if naps are not their style.

It is risky to take for granted that any weekend guest wants *only* to rest. He may be exhausted but almost certainly he is looking forward to some diversion. Remember, too, that if your community is widely known for some sport or activity, he is probably counting on seeing a bit of it, no matter how humdrum or old hat it may have grown for you.

At some point, you will probably want to offer an option between two activities. The nice point here is to make it a completely *open* option. On the other hand, if you do make a unilateral decision, keep it to yourself. Anyone is likely to feel deprived if you tell him, "There's an antique show (or a boat race or a garden tour) over at Milltown, but I decided that would be too tiring a drive."

Many a weekend has gotten off to a bad start simply because everyone sat up talking until all hours Friday night. Don't forget that just as it's the hostess' place at a dinner party to signal the rise from the table, with a house full of weekend guests it's her place to give the cue for going to bed. Make it pleasant but firm, without imputing undue weariness either to guests or yourself. Happy anticipation—"We all have a big day tomorrow" —is the best note.

Breakfast habits are so personal that it is considerate to give people a choice—a breakfast tray in their rooms, breakfast with the family at a given hour, breakfast in the kitchen whenever they feel like wandering in. If do-it-yourself breakfasts are the pattern in your household, spend a few minutes Friday night explaining how the stove works, where the toaster is. Then set out coffee, eggs, bread and anything else that might be needed plus a typed list of the whereabouts of butter, cream, and essential tools.

PARTY PROTOCOL

Laborious, long-drawn-out preparations for a dinner or cocktail party are very likely to make house guests feel ill at ease. As with any party, the more you can get done ahead of time, the better. But if there's no other way out, make firm arrangements to have a friend or some other member of the family take the visitors off on a junket for the afternoon.

House guests always appreciate time to dress as well as time to rest. So whenever a change of clothes is called for, give them due warning. If you are giving a party at home, tell them exactly when everyone else is expected. If you are taking your weekenders out, give them at least an hour to make themselves ready. It's no favor to be wakened from a deep nap fifteen minutes before party time with the cheery excuse, "You were sleeping so peacefully, I hated to disturb you."

When you take strangers to someone else's party, there's no need to stick with them every minute—they'll probably have a better time if you don't. But be sure not to leave them alone—even at a large cocktail party —until they have met the host and hostess. It takes considerable aplomb to introduce yourself without embarrassment to a hostess who has never laid eyes on you before.

HELP—WELCOME AND UNWELCOME

How much help should you expect of a weekend guest? The best assumption is: none at all. True, most people (in a house with little or no outside help) will make their beds and help clear the dinner table. But often women who are the most active housekeepers and the most thoughtful hostesses in their own houses will suddenly become drones when they are visiting —partly, perhaps, because they fear they will be more hindrance than help. And well they might be. If you operate better without company in the kitchen, the best way to fend off would-be helpers is to give them some specific small chore, preferably one to be done "later."

HAPPY ENDINGS

The Sunday evening departure should go as smoothly as any other event on the weekend schedule. And it can if everyone knows in advance when and how it will take place. If your guests are to go by train, decide ahead of time which one would be best for them to take (and refer to it in the follow-up to your invitation). That will eliminate your scurrying around at the last minute for a timetable. Let them know around mid-afternoon what time you will have to leave for the station, allow them at least a half hour for last-minute packing, and take over the clockwatching yourself— unobtrusively, of course. If they are driving home, you can't tell them what time to leave, but you can say, "On Sundays we have supper at 6:30 which should allow enough time for you to get back to town before midnight (or 10:00 or whatever)." That clearly will indicate that you expect them to leave right after supper, and if they must leave earlier they will of course say so.

DROP-OF-A-HAT INVITATIONS

With a combination of high spirits, smooth planning and proper gear, you can issue the most delightful invitations—"Right now on this heavenly day . . ." or "tonight with these same lovely people. . . ." The pleasure of spontaneity is twofold, for the joy of freedom from time's restrictions is one that hosts and guests share equally. In summer, of course, your potential is multiplied, for you can amuse and feed and pamper your friends outdoors as well as indoors and with summer's leisurely ways you are no more bound by time than you are by space. But with a lineup of good equipment and a well-stocked larder it is possible to put together delicious and inventive spur-of-the-moment meals at any time of the year. (For additions to the staples you normally have on hand for family meals, see the Gourmet Checklist at the far right and on the next page.)

Equipment that makes drop-of-a-hat invitations possible: an electric tray to keep food hot and another to keep it cold; food covers; bun and French bread warmers; espresso maker; jumbo coffee pot; waffle iron; electric skillet; broiler; hibachi; grill; extralarge ice bucket; a cooler for drinks and bottles; big wooden planks for meats; casseroles in all sizes.

To make serving and toting easy: a roving cart; folding tables; big carrying baskets; a little red wagon to transport food from indoors to outdoors.

And to whip together quick party tables without having to worry about laundry problems: a special drawer devoted to throwaway tablecloths, mats and napkins; plastic plates, coasters; candles; paper flowers on wire stems that you can stick into green Styrofoam bases —all in wonderful mix-and-match colors. Menus for Drop-of-a-hat Invitations, page 251.

LEONARD

"THE GARDEN'S ALL YOURS— PICK UP A TRAY AND EAT WHERE YOU LIKE"

Your garden is large enough for many guests to ramble in, so, to cap a country weekend, you stage a hobo supper, *left*, for neighbors and friends. Awaiting picnickers: bandanna-encased trays, each bearing a hero sandwich; two plastic dishes filled, respectively, with a cold vegetable casserole and a bean salad; a half-bottle of Chianti; fruit. At dessert time, pie will be served from its basket carrier, and coffee poured into cups with heat-saving lids.

"WE'LL HAVE A CITY PICNIC ON THE TERRACE"

Everyone's buoyant—the committee meeting went off without a hitch and, contrary to predictions, it's sunny. You're inspired to ask the group to stay for lunch, *opposite*. You set up individual tables on the terrace and link their various colors with pink accessories. You put your favorite bright idea for buffet meals into action—12-inch platters instead of dinner plates. Inside, a table near the terrace entrance becomes the buffet for a cold meat salad, French bread, cheese, fruit, and thin sandwiches of pound cake and raspberry jam.

DESIGNER: RICHARD NELSON

MAYA

**GOURMET CHECKLIST
TO HELP COPE WITH
UNEXPECTED GUESTS**

Pantry shelf:

Apricot preserves, currant
jelly, raspberry jam

Capers

Chutney

Crackers: water biscuits,
other unsalted types

Fish: anchovies, sardines,
red caviar, minced clams,
tiny Danish shrimp,
gefilte fish, tuna

Fruits: canned and
dried; applesauce

Gelatin

Meats: dried beef, tongue,
liver pâté, deviled ham,
cocktail sausages

Mustard: Dijon, English

Nuts: almonds, pecans,
pine nuts, pistachios,
walnuts

Olives: green, Greek,
ripe, stuffed

Pasta: two or three
types

Pastry canapé shells

Pickles

Rice

Soups: black bean, beef
and chicken broth
(canned and dried),
clam broth, consommé,
green turtle

Soy sauce

Tomato juice

Vegetables: artichoke
hearts and bottoms,
baked beans, beets,
cannellini beans (white),
kidney beans, dried
mushrooms, small white
onions, pimientos,
tomatoes, tomato paste,
water chestnuts

Vinegar: wine, tarragon

Continued on next page

Freezer—Prepared Items:

Casseroles, such as cannelloni, lasagne, veal with mushrooms and water chestnuts, ragoût of lamb, moussaka

Cheesecake

Rolls of cheese biscuit dough

Crepes

Duxelles

Flavored butters

Fresh bread crumbs

Leftover roast meats

Meatballs and meatloaf (made up but not cooked)

Pastry shells (rolled out and ready to cook)

Profiteroles, éclairs

Sauces such as brown (demi-glace), tomato, pesto, meat sauce for pasta

Soup bases

Stocks: beef and chicken

Freezer—Ready-made Items:

Bread, rolls, English muffins

Meat glaze

Patty shells

Phylo pastry

Freezer—Basics:

Butter (unsalted)

Cheeses: Brie, Camembert, Belle Etoile, Roquefort

Crabmeat

Egg whites

Meat: chops, chicken breasts, hamburger, shell steaks—individually wrapped

Raspberries, strawberries

Sausages: chorizo, country, frankfurters, Italian

Vegetables: corn, mushrooms, peas, snow peas, spinach

Refrigerator:

Aromatics: carrots, celery, garlic, onions, shallots

Bacon

Cheeses: cheddar, cream, feta,

Gruyère or other imported Swiss, Parmesan

Cherry tomatoes

Chocolate sauce (homemade)

Cream: heavy and sour

Dried sausages, such as cervelat, pepperoni, salami

Fruit

Gingerroot (kept in medium dry sherry to preserve)

Ham: boiled or baked, prosciutto or Westphalian

Jellied madrilene, consommé

Lemons, limes, oranges

Salad materials: cucumber, radishes, green pepper, lettuces

Bar Supplies That Aid in Cooking

Brandy

Dry French vermouth

Liqueurs in miniature bottles

Madeira

Port

Sherry

Wine: red and white jug type

And Bar Accoutrements:

Mixers: club soda, tonic, Collins mix, bitter lemon and orange

Mixes: daiquiri, Bloody Mary, sour

Olives, pearl onions

Tomato juice

"COME TO A POOLSIDE PICNIC STARTING AT DUSK"

When sundown and your guests arrive, you and the dinner are ready, for almost everything has been done ahead of time. On a plant stand you've arranged little cold vegetables to go with the drinks, which are all ready to pour. Embers glow in the hibachi, and marinated shrimps are skewered and ready to grill. Black bean soup and the main course of thinly sliced cold tongue and Westphalian ham, mustards and breads are on the patio buffet. Dessert, vanilla mousse and berries in coconut shells, waits in easy-to-tote antique stacking boxes.

ASHLEY

"WHY DON'T ALL OF YOU STAY FOR SUPPER?"

Your two weekend guests and the six friends you invited for cocktails have formed one of those magically compatible groups, and you want to keep them together longer. Fortunately, your supper menu can easily be expanded. You have more bacon, eggs, cheese, and pasta to make a generous amount of the main dish, *spaghetti alla carbonara*. And there's plenty on hand from the farmer's market for a large salad and for extra fruit flans (made with ready-baked shells). Your tea cart, which offered hors d'oeuvre with the cocktails, is handy to serve the dessert, too. Your party is on.

"WE'LL HAVE BRUNCH IN THE GARDEN WHENEVER YOU GET HERE"

Summer is racing along; you haven't seen everyone often enough. So you opt for a Sunday brunch with such elastic timing—from ten to three—that everyone can come. For flexibility's sake, you decide on a buffet meal and plan ways to keep warm fare warm and cool things cool. And you set your round patio tables with wedge-shaped mats that are easy to change as newcomers arrive. Your buffet includes a first course of melon and prosciutto; sliced cold steak; crepes filled with creamed mushrooms. Hot coffee, and champagne and orange juice for Mimosas, wait in a sheltered corner. For dessert: strawberries glacé with brioches, cream cheese, and butter chicks hatched from the freezer.

GRIGSBY

"PLEASE COME FOR A LIGHT LUNCH"

It's an uncommonly fresh summer day, you have made a lemon mousse, and suddenly you feel like asking five friends for luncheon. From the freezer, which you keep fully stocked just for times like this, you take a spinach, egg and mushroom ring, heat it, fill it with steamed carrots (pulled early in the morning from the garden), and spoon over all a spinachy cream sauce. Something crisp would be good with it—you whip up herbed melba toast. To cover the luncheon table, a checkered cloth and, over it, embroidered muslin mats. You set the places with your best things to make the impromptu meal even more delightful. Another trip to the garden adds flowers to that ever-ready basket of plastic leaves for a centerpiece. Climax to the lunch: that mousse!

"LET'S HAVE ESPRESSO AT OUR HOUSE"

You love bringing friends home for after-concert, after-play, after-almost-anything coffee and you have made a point of assembling all the gleaming professional gear the ritual calls for: an espresso machine that pressure-steams cup after foaming cup, Turkish brass mills to grind the beans at the last moment for freshness (you have both the darker beans for espresso and the lighter ones of the American type). To stage your kind of nightcap party, all you need to do on arrival is bring out sugar, lemon, demitasse cups and, from the freezer, pastries that thaw in half an hour.

"WHY NOT COME HERE TO TEA?"

It's a drizzly afternoon, the regatta has been canceled and everyone wants comforting. What better comfort is there than a fire and a good English-style tea? You bring out a card table (one with a separate top covered with stick-on vinyl—it needs no cloth) and stand it near the hearth. Next comes your silver tea service and a pair of flourishing potted plants. Crocks contain butter, plum jam, honey and marmalade, and on a good-size cutting board, you set out four fine loaves: cranberry, raisin and nut, orange, and close-grained white bread. Linen napkins reinforce the pampered feeling, and the weather is forgotten.

DROP-OF-A-HAT INVITATIONS

"DO DROP OVER FOR A DRINK"

Even though you didn't know exactly who was going to wander over to your blanket at the beach, you knew you'd want to ask a dozen or so home with you for drinks later, so you fixed everything before you left. Curried nuts you'd toasted in the cool of morning are now heaped in a bowl; glasses and cocktail napkins are set out on a tray. Martinis, vermouth cassis, and Chablis are chilling in refrigerator jugs, along with plastic containers of lovely things you made to nibble on. And out on a counter, ready to be filled on your return, wait the serving dishes you'll need for the snacks.

"THE BREAKFAST BAR
IS OPEN ALL MORNING"

With a houseful of overnight guests, you have too much to do to be running to the kitchen every time another late riser appears. Instead you spend half an hour setting out all the fixings and for the rest of the morning, it's every man for himself. Sausages and waffle batter are kept chilled until your guests are ready to cook them on plug-in appliances. If the electricity can't handle both appliances simultaneously, you post a note in big red letters on the perforated wallboard. Berries are welcome sustenance while the waffles bake. Coffee is filter style and brewed individually. Silver stands ready in a relish server.

"STAY WHERE YOU ARE
AND
I'LL FETCH THE LUNCH"

The mixed doubles playoff on your home court is so absorbing that you know you'll never get the tennis fans to trudge back to the house for lunch. But the hot dogs, hamburgers, tomatoes and onions are already packed in a big plastic container in the refrigerator since you had expected to cook them on the terrace. Borrowing the children's wagons, you load them with everything, including a snappy checkered cloth with plastic plates to match, and bread and fruit which travel to the picnic site in children's wooden pails. Borrowing youngsters to pull the wagons and electing yourself to carry the broiler with its gas cylinder, you bring lunch to a grassy place by the court. Never mind who wins the matches—the picnic may well be your guests' fondest memories.

CHAPTER 10

OPEN SKIES ENTERTAINING

Sunlight, air, water, green things—these are the magic that make for the joys of summer and of entertaining our friends out-of-doors. The sun may be a warming glow on a secluded beach picnic or a shimmering light under your patio awning. The water may be the sea in the distance or a spring-cold mountain lake that laps the supports of your cabin deck. The greenery may be an undulating meadow surrounding your house or a movable thicket of potted shrubs and flowers in your atrium. Your guests may be barefooted and blue-jeaned or wearing black tie; they may have been invited by a shout from one beach blanket to another, or by engraved invitation, but they will love an outdoor party wherever and whenever—morning brunch to midnight buffet. Whether *you* enjoy open air entertaining is another matter. You will, if you plan ahead. The whys and hows of planning are the business of this chapter.

THE WEATHER. Naturally you can't guarantee the weather, but you can keep track of forecasts and for certain parties—on boats for example—your invitations can carry a rain check proviso. Weather planning means readiness to shift the scene if the skies open. Moving a smallish group from beach picnic to covered porch or family room is something any flexible person can manage, but if you are planning a big "do," much more is at stake. For such times a wise hostess has a tent lined up just in case.

SERVICE AND EQUIPMENT. Transporting food and drink is the major effort of serving far away from the kitchen. The nearer you can locate your outdoor party to your cooking area, the easier your job will be. Special step-saving equipment is your best standby: portable cooking and serving units that plug into electric outlets located in practical places; portable coolers that keep ice icy and cold drinks and food cold; rolling carts that wheel smoothly and hold large amounts; an outside jack for the telephone.

COMFORT is always a good host's concern and arranging for it outdoors can be complicated. Everyone should be able to take his ease. You can use a mix of chairs, benches, cushions, gliders—but see to it that no one has to perch on a ledge, stand, or sit on damp grass. Provide places to set down drinks and plates and ashtrays. An accumulation of folding seats and little tables is a big help to outdoor party-givers.

TAMING NATURE. We go outdoors to enjoy ourselves and not to battle baking rays or gusty winds. These can and should be tempered. Awnings, lattice and vine-covered roofs, spreading trees, umbrellas—can keep the sun off mealtime groupings. To block the wind, there are awnings that roll up and down, strip fences, hedges and a plotted placement of furniture that takes prevailing wind currents into account. Problems vary with the place, the season, the day; so must solutions.

UNINVITED BUGS AND BITES. Mosquitos, gnats and flies should be coped with well before the party and made unwelcome throughout it. Screening an outdoor porch or terrace is a perfect solution, but many parties spill beyond the screens, so other measures are necessary. Exterminators have a big bag of tricks, but they may not be as concerned about ecology as you are, so it is a good idea to check with the county or state agricultural department for safe sprays. Some chemicals work over long periods; others help for part of a day. Your hardware store or the housewares department in most larger stores has bug-repellent torches, candles and "space" sprays.

A PRIVET-FENCED TERRACE, *opposite,* with its awning roof and slate-paved floor is an airy outdoor room. Inviting for breakfast, day 'round lounging, cocktails or dinner, the terrace is a livable mix of rugged white pieces, the greens that nature provides, potted plants and vivid cloths used on foldaway round tables. Pony-cart mobile bar is a playful and practical aid that willingly wheels drinks anywhere—within or beyond the hedge.

DESIGNER: KEITH IRVINE

ALFRESCO MEALS

When the weather is pleasant, any time is the right time for an outdoor meal. Breakfast, lunch and dinner are only the beginning: there is also the brunch after church, high tea at five, a midnight supper after summer theatre. You can think of more. And when you take pains to make the ambience gay and original, your simplest meal can seem epicurean. Decorating the surroundings can be a delightful adventure, great fun to do as well as to see, and it need not be costly. First—nature is there as a backdrop. A flowering garden gives its all. If it isn't the garden's finest hour, you can fill in with pots and tubs of greens and wild flowers, bring out your potted ferns, hang baskets of growing things, make renaissance garlands of greens studded with flowers, fruits, nuts or vegetables to loop along a fence or porch beam. If your party centers on a pool, decorate it with floating wreaths of flowers and leaves around life preservers; at night set adrift lighted oil wicks ringed with blossoms.

Have fun with your table settings. If you do a lot of outdoor entertaining you may want to build a special collection of gay pottery, wooden or ceramic-handled knives and forks, cloths and mats and napkins in strong colors that complement the brightness of nature's color scheme. On some occasions—an elegant outdoor dinner or a festive seated buffet—you may want to bring out the same fine china, crystal and silver that you use for such parties indoors. Folding chairs and tables are a good investment, and if you place a plywood round on a card table, it jumps from four to six places. Matching cloths will unite an assortment of tables whether they are identical or not. If you need to seat many guests, you can supplement your outdoor furniture with indoor chairs. Don't worry about mixing the two— you'll find that for the most part they will join forces without clashing. For serving help, bring on anything that rolls—tea cart, bar wagon, tables on wheels—plus hampers, étagères.

For centerpieces, turn to your grounds and garden—for bright vegetables, fresh flowers, grasses, fruit, green leaves. Try an edible centerpiece of beautifully arranged crudités; pile lobsters destined for the main course on an ice-filled bowl in the center of the table. Focal point of your buffet might be a pâté shaped like a pineapple, or a ham wreathed with hibiscus blossoms. For decorative night lighting you could combine tree-hung lanterns, hurricane lamps, and constellations of pin-point lights. For menus for alfresco meals, see page 249.

A HELP-YOURSELF BUFFET means the hostess does her work in advance and can be a guest herself at serving time. On an awning-shaded terrace, *opposite*, where it's easy to find either shade or sun, drinks are available at one end; sandwich makings, including toaster, at the other, with a tray for each person. Beside a pool, *right*, a big wicker hamper has carried lunch fixings, dishes and silver from the kitchen to the party.

LEONARD

GUERRERO

OPEN SKIES ENTERTAINING: ALFRESCO MEALS

A SHADY TREE, *left,* grows blossoms, then apples, and all the while is an umbrella for a terrace dining table made of sturdy planks and surrounded by a permanent bench. A low garden wall serves for extra seating, along with some chairs, when the table is set for a large buffet party.

AN EDIBLE CENTERPIECE, *below left,* of chilled boiled lobsters on an ice-filled milk-glass vase, crowned by a tempting mound of lemon halves, is ready to serve as the main course. More conventional edible centerpieces: bright arrangements of crudités, fresh fruits or colored candies.

A PARTY IN THE PINK, *opposite,* is a study in contrasts, with color used sweetly, sparingly. The pink prettiness of delicately flowered cloths and airy wreaths circling the candles emphasizes the dense green of trees and shrubs. Elegant table appointments and gilded chairs are set off by a whitewashed board fence and moss-covered bricks. Yet another proof that opposites attract: vintage champagne cooling nicely in its wood shipping crate.

GRIGSBY

PARKER

DECORATED TREES, *above*, with miniature gardens swinging in baskets from their branches shade the terrace of a 300-year-old mill whose waterfall still sings endlessly—a heavenly background for a dessert of watermelon and wine.

AN OUTDOOR FIREPLACE, *above right*, with a generous wide round hearth gives a patio a living-room coziness and ambience. Even after dining in the house, guests like to gather here for after-dinner coffee, liqueurs and conversation.

MASSEY REPORTAGE PINTO

A SUNSET SUPPER, *above*, sits smack in front of one of the greatest shows on earth. When darkness comes the hurricane lamps are lighted. This simple picnic table at the water's edge is ideal for every kind of meal at any time of day.

AN INGENIOUS SIDE TABLE, *right*, was created with a set of library steps lacquered Siamese pink to match chair seats and plates. A delightful conceit: the same steps in miniature on the table, used as stand for salt and pepper.

RUSTIC AND ELEGANT, *opposite*, the combination of an old grape- and honeysuckle-covered arbor and the fine china, crystal and silver also used indoors has a special appeal. The lacy look of the furniture belies its sturdiness.

LEONARD

PICNICS—PLAIN AND FANCY

A picnic is so much fun that the word itself has become a metaphor for lighthearted pleasure. The adventure of eating outdoors and away from a dining table appeals to everyone's love of playacting and novelty: in a city park or a pasture, beside a brook or roaring waterfall, alone on a crescent of sand or in a crowd at a football stadium parking lot. A picnic can be just about any kind of meal that's portable, from bologna sandwiches packed in bicycle baskets to a splendid fête champêtre with everyone in Manet dress.

When you plan a picnic—and planning is essential—give your prospective locale a dry run at the time of day you expect to use it. Make careful notes on how to get there to include with your invitations, then check out the terrain, the bug population, shelter from the sun and wind.

Organization is a must. You should be as careful about the details of a picnic as those of a dinner party. If the salt is forgotten, or the charcoal for the grill, there's no going into the house for it, but more likely driving ten miles. (That's been done but makes everyone nervous.) A checklist carefully made and twice checked before departure is your best forgetting insurance. Many practiced picnic arrangers have a permanent list they alter slightly for different menus.

One philosopher has divided the world into hosts and guests, and you will find that a picnic quickly separates the two. Some of the people you invite will sit back, look amiable and wait to be served; others will scurry around collecting firewood, improvising windbreaks, passing drinks. Try to include a few of these responsible souls to help you, because a picnic involves considerable exercise for more than one doer.

Providing comfort, as always, is one of the duties of the picnic-giver. Supply umbrellas and lotions against the sun, ponchos and blankets against the damp. The bare ground is not a proper seat for most people, so put such amenities as cushions, quilts and folding chairs on your list. Bring along a large anchorable cloth or tatami matting or a fold-up table to serve on. Big napkins are a wonderful help when food is drippy. They can be paper or cloth; or how about terry guest towels that don't muss, are very absorbent, and wash so easily. Plastic eating utensils are adequate and expendable, but if you use stainless steel keep a careful count.

Important to the success of any outing are properly insulated carriers for the makings of the feast, and simply designed, functional devices for on-the-spot cooking. You need wide-mouthed vacuum bottles for soup and coffee, hardy good-looking dishes and glasses and mugs. Whether your destination is fifty paces from the house or fifty miles away, the food must be easily and safely transportable. For menus for picnics, see page 249.

MID-POOL MEALS, *opposite,* are served to entranced guests on a permanent stone island furnished with firmly anchored white metal stools. Setting the table is not as hard as you might think; the depth here is 3 feet. When not a dining table, the island is . . . an island: sometimes a sunning place or stop-off point in a long swim.

The hostess' best friends: food and drink carriers

KLAPHOLZ

MARIS

WEINER

YEE GRIGSBY

BEADLE

SAILBOAT FARE, *opposite top,* has to be easy to tote (in bags and baskets and thermoses with handles) and able to wait until the race is over (in insulated and vacuum containers). This is a cooperative post-regatta picnic where the rafted-up boats share their food and drink.

TAILGATE SERVICE, *opposite, below left,* can cater to a comfortable, sit-down picnic when space permits. Light yacht tables and folding seats create an instant dining room, stow neatly into a station wagon. But whether everyone's seated or some stand, the tailgate, cloth-draped, makes a convenient, roomy buffet surface.

AT THE BEACH, *opposite, below right,* a most practical picnic can be brought, already prepared and packed into glossy paper boxes (which later carry the litter). Tatami matting is the tablecloth; napkins and wood utensils are tied to boxes. Paper plates, plastic tumblers, are pretty conveniences; the hostess' only mealtime job is to turn dessert into centerpiece.

TOTED BY CAR, *above right,* a picnic lunch packed in baskets is spread out on a peasant-print cloth, bamboo trays stand in for place mats. Napkins are linen, wine goblets the real thing. Crib quilts make gay "banquettes." Packed with the wine in the wicker hamper, hearty sandwiches, fruit, a variety of cheeses.

BICYCLE BASKETS, *right,* will carry your picnic and its setting as far as you want to pedal. In a cardboard carryall go plastic containers of salad, bread, fruit, cheese. Half-bottles of wine and their plastic goblets, kitchen-towel place mats and inflatable plastic pillows tuck in beside the carryalls.

ELEGANT FÊTE CHAMPÊTRE

BAER

"Great idea!" is what we hope this account will make you say, whether you ever find yourself hiring a trio of Renaissance musicians to play for a fête champêtre or not. But if people enjoy music indoors, why not outdoors? If you have heirloom china and silver, will fresh air hurt it? Outdoor entertaining, as we show in this chapter, can take any direction you like. Here, one way to go about it.

Inspired by French Impressionists, a man gave a kind of fairytale fête champêtre. The phrase means "rustic feast" and some people think it originated when the French nobility copied the peasant custom of giving outdoor parties, but glossed them with grace and style. To qualify as such a fête, a picnic should be beautifully served on the grass, with the very best china, silver, crystal and menu. The host had seen such picnics in nineteenth-century French paintings and asked his guests to dress in the manner of a Manet: straw hats, velvet trousers, polka-dot gowns, parasols.

Everyone met at a city house, from which they were whisked in a bus to a walnut grove where they found pale green tablecloths spread on the grass with flower-hued cushions to sit on. Wild flowers in baskets were centerpieces; place cards were thrust into apples, menus into bunches of grapes. Waiters in tail-coats served from a buffet table and a trio played ancient country gigues and sarabands while guests danced. The menu: three kinds of pâté, a *terrine berrichonne* of pork, rabbit and veal, two great roasts of lamb and veal, cold vegetables, cheese, long crusty breads, fresh fruit and wine.

PARTY DESIGNER: WILLIAM ABEEL

194

LIGHTING THE NIGHT

CLEVELAND

Darkness can be one of the many magics of nighttime outdoors, but is a lost potential if it is total and dense. We need some light—washes and pools and pinpoints—to define the darkness and create a space for us within its seemingly infinite bounds. The moon makes marvelous scenic effects when it chooses to, but we need more prosaic lighting for the times when the moon's turned off. Outdoor lighting can be handled in as many ways as indoor lighting, and it serves the same purposes: safety for moving about, illumination for party chores and amusements, and the setting of a mood.

Imitation moonlight is a good thing to start with. It is low-intensity illumination placed well above the eye: up among the tree branches, above a latticed pergola, attached high on the house or porch roof, camouflaged and diffused as much as possible. This makes fine general lighting for outdoor parties and, more than that, can be used the year round to welcome arriving guests, to play up pretty night landscape through the windows and to discourage trespassers. When you are entertaining outdoors, the exterior lighting is far more effective if you dim or extinguish the house lights that compete with it.

Pathways, steps especially, should have specific lighting both for the safety of garden strollers and for the dimensions and vistas they create. Fixtures spiked into the ground or high spotlamps with a spread lens or a series of lanterns on posts—or all three—can handle this job.

An outdoor cooking and drink-fixing center is best lighted by at least two 150-watt floodlamps aimed from two directions (to soften shadows) and placed from 12 to 20 feet above the ground in trees, on sides of buildings or on lighting poles. Permanent lighting for alfresco dining should be much softer: a kind of chandelier hung from a tree over a picnic table is festive; a reflector lamp attached to a patio table's umbrella and aimed upwards is easy to rig; a group of diffuse-light wall fixtures is effective if your table is close to the house.

Highlighting a garden statue or an especially beautiful tree whose total shape you want to see is achieved by floodlighting, usually from the ground up, from two or three directions to avoid a flat effect. You can call attention to a flowerbed or massed shrubs with high floodlighting or low mushroom-type reflectors in the beds and taller by a foot or two than the plants. Underwater lights can lend liquid enchantment to ponds and swimming pools; for clear definition, resort to overhead floodlights. There are local code regulations for installing lighting in and around water, so check with local inspectors.

There are also innumerable pro tem lighting arrangements you can make for outdoor parties. Many great effects combine the permanent with the impromptu. Use the good sampling on these pages for ideas to spark your own ingenuity.

KERTESZ

CHRISTMAS LIGHTS, *opposite,* need not shine on snow alone. Here on a warm night a string of make-believe oranges hanging from lower branches over a party punch table is appropriate, gay, and summer-lush. Flower shapes or star lights could be equally charming.
ARCHITECT: SUSANA MUELLER

DE MORGOLI

VIGIL LIGHTS, *above right,* set inside a pyramid of pink-toned cement blocks might be, like building toys, arranged in a hundred ways. **HAWAIIAN TORCHES,** *right,* are moveable kerosene-burning brass torches with 7-foot poles that can be driven into the ground.

LANDSCAPE DESIGNER: LAMBERT LANDSCAPE COMPANY

CLEVELAND

LANDSCAPE DESIGNER: WENDELL RICHARD GILBERT

ECKERT

LUMINARIAS, *above*, bordering a swimming pool, are an old Mexican invention. The festival lights are candles embedded in sand in bright paper bags. Plain brown bags look pretty this way, too. All make fine path markers.

WOOD LANTERNS, *above*, are made from redwood hanging baskets intended for plants. One basket is inverted on another, with asbestos-lined wood at top and bottom.

KEROSENE TORCHES, *below*, on tall pointed wood stakes that are dug into the ground provide not only light, they shape a round space for dinner.

LEE

LEONARD

ELECTRIC TORCHES, *below*, reminiscent of lampposts, light the way to the end of a hexagonal deck and illuminate the trees that surround it.

TINY ITALIAN LIGHTS, *above*, turn a many-tufted cryptomeria shrub into a magical forest of Christmas trees. These twinkling little lights transform any outdoor evergreen and are lovely at all times of the year.

CIRCLE OF VIGIL LIGHTS, *above*, outlines a small garden pool and plays up a reflected statue and some low planting in a corner of the lawn.

TIN LANTERNS, *above*, are hooked on wooden stakes to bring light to a completely pro tem outdoor dining space. Everything is brought here for the party: buffet, round tables, chairs and the lanterns that transform the darkness. *Below*, one lantern, decked with flowers, spreading light on the buffet table.

JAPANESE PAPER LANTERNS, *below*, with vigil lights inside, are suspended from bamboo poles for high illumination. Securely dug into the earth, the flexible poles sway safely and gently with breezes.

AN ENCLOSURE OF VOTIVE CANDLES, *above*, perched on the rails of the picket fence combines with a cooperative full moon to make a romantic late-supper setting. Nothing could be easier than creating your own effect with lots of these safe, inexpensive little candles in glasses.

COOKING IN THE OPEN AIR

Cooking out-of-doors rounds out the pleasure of alfresco dining. Guests like to drink and nibble things while they indulge in the spectator sport of cook-watching and the cook, often a male hobbyist with flourishes, finds the job both creative and ego-satisfying. More than fun, however, cooking outdoors gives us foods that cannot be prepared in the average indoor kitchen: charcoal-grilled and spit-turned meats and seafood; ember-roasted potatoes and corn, skewered oriental and mideastern dishes.

Equipment is just as necessary for this cuisine as it is inside, and a family's imagination and budget are the only limits to what they can acquire. A pit is the most primitive and inexpensive arrangement. At clambakes it is often a trench dug into the sand; for permanent backyard pits you can make excavations and line them with firebrick or stone, placing metal grills across the top. From the pit, the scale of sophistication rises up through varieties of fireplaces with or without chimneys and can include an oven, electric rotisserie and storage space as well as grill.

If you are thinking about building an outdoor barbecue you will find that a large garden center or fireplace supplier can show you prefabricated fireboxes with grill tops along with an assortment of plans for masonry structures to contain them. A fireplace should be located in the direction of the prevailing wind so that the draft is efficient and smoke is carried away.

A great many people prefer a portable grill that can be moved as the weather or party site changes. These, too, come in a variety of styles and prices, from a primitive Japanese hibachi to a complex grill that includes several motor-driven spits. Gas barbecues are also popular.

In outdoor meal planning there is one firm rule: Never experiment on your guests. This is a form of cookery that is unpredictable until you are experienced. Only a trial run with each dish will teach you such critical and important factors as how long it must cook, on how hot a fire, and how often you should baste. For menus for cookouts of all kinds, see page 250.

A PORTABLE COAL-BURNING GRILL, *left*, accommodating a quartet of river-edge picnickers, could be the hot hors d'oeuvre center at a big party or could cook an entire meal for any small group.

THE HIBACHI TABLE, *opposite*, an ingenious Japanese invention, is a teak table with a large steel plate in the center heated by propane gas from a small tank attached underneath. Diners sit on three sides, while the cook (maybe you) stands at the narrow fourth border. The Near Eastern kabobs here, assembled in advance on skewers, are to be cooked by each guest. For Japanese specialties—halved shrimp or thin slices of steak or breast of chicken—one cook might be better. Many diced or sliced vegetables are suitable, too. The hot plate will keep rice (cooked elsewhere) warm and also keep tea, sake and sauces at their best heat.

BEADLE

BEADLE LYON

OPEN SKIES ENTERTAINING: COOKING IN THE OPEN AIR

FIREBRICK-LINED BARBECUE PIT, *far left,* is dug into a prepared pebble-paved area, wouldn't work surrounded by grass or plants. The grill is extra large; here a whole lamb is cooking on it.

TABLE-CENTERED CHARCOAL GRILL, *left,* gives everyone the fun of cooking hamburgers and hot dogs to suit his own taste, while sitting comfortably around the table and enjoying everyone else.

OUTDOOR COOKING CENTER, *below,* consists of a ceramic-tiled counter over a pair of storage cabinets which flank a large grill. Grill is stored, when not in use, between the other two cabinets. The top is handy preparation center that doubles as a party buffet.

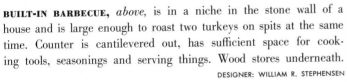

BUILT-IN BARBECUE, *above,* is in a niche in the stone wall of a house and is large enough to roast two turkeys on spits at the same time. Counter is cantilevered out, has sufficient space for cooking tools, seasonings and serving things. Wood stores underneath.

DESIGNER: WILLIAM R. STEPHENSEN

WHITEWASHED BRICK BARBECUE, *above right,* is extended on both sides by convenient work/serving counters with storage cabinets underneath. Counters are topped with bright ceramic tiles. Here the table is set for lunch with a bright flowering plant for the centerpiece. Under the plant is a well, big enough to hold a hibachi that cooks tiny sausages and other tidbits at cocktail time.

COVERED GRILL FOR ROASTING, *right,* is set in a long tile-covered table that works both for buffet and for seated dinners. Grill's cover is removable, of course. Its fire-box can be raised or lowered to control heat. Pig roasted slowly for 12 hours.

DESIGNER: LLOYD BRYAN

HOLIDAY DELIGHTS

O f all the many meanings Christmas holds for each of us, for nearly everyone it is a time for sharing: good friendship, good food and the warmth of the season. And the ways of sharing are as diverse as the themes and settings you plan for those joyful moments of family and friends together.

You can steep Christmas in a family tradition of familiar holiday sights and smells: Gingerbread and anise cookies cooling in the kitchen, tangerines, mulled wine and fresh-cut pine. Rooms garlanded with green, sparkling with candlelight. Doorways and mantels heaped with fruits—symbols of abundance and hospitality. A tree to the rafters, encrusted with a lifetime's worth of baubles—and, more important, memories.

Or you can toss tradition to the winter snows and keep your spirits blithe with ever new, joyfully unhackneyed deckings: All-out flings with color and shine. Crystally plastics and paper garlands, lit to a dazzle. A shimmering tree of wonder and light that never knew a forest. And a whole house that becomes a swirling kaleidoscope of color and music and nonstop mirth.

Or, best of all, you can choose a convivial combination of the two, adding your own imaginative flourishes to give tradition a happy twist. Even the smallest personal touches—tying perky little bows on the stems of apples in a bowl, making a centerpiece of calico and gingham fruit, decorating the *inside* of the door, or switching the menu from English turkey and plum pudding to French roast goose and *bûche de Noël*—gives the most traditional Christmas a refreshing lilt each year.

On the pages that follow, a Santa's sackful of inspiring ideas for parties, tables, mantels, doors and decorations, big and small, all through the house. All are designed to help you entwine the tradition that warms the heart with the unpredictability that delights the spirit.

TREE-TRIMMING PARTY, *opposite,* is one way to share a family ritual with cherished friends. To make a tree like this, wire candy apples (tempting fakes) to branches festooned with garlands and twinkled with lights. For the trimmers, you might serve a buffet of beef Burgundy, salad, strawberries. The table here, pattern-on-pattern, blue and white to match the room and sparklit with silver and crystal.
DESIGNER: STEPHEN MALLORY

BÛCHE DE NOËL, *left,* traditional dessert for French Christmases, is an edible sponge-cake yule log with chocolate bark and meringue mushrooms. You can turn it into a centerpiece by decking it with pinecones and holly, lighting it up with plump little candles and interspersing between them blooming pink and white crystal flower paperweights.
MASSEY

BERRY BASKETS, *left,* painted green and heaped with red and green glass currants, stack into a centerpiece for a Christmas breakfast table drawn up before the fire. The sparkly red currants, plus a smashing bouquet of red poinsettias nearby, are all you need to put any one-color-plus-white room in a holiday mood. Two touches of Christmas luxury: another berry basket, this time of silver, holding real breakfast berries and, sitting across the table, a sleek silver reindeer.

CANDLESTICKS AND TRINKETS, *below,* in delightful profusion, sprinkle across a holiday luncheon table. To create a similarly merry array, spread the table first with silver paper, then with lace, and arrange such treasures as crystal paperweights, old-fashioned ornaments and one pièce de résistance—here a Victorian Christmas tree encrusted with tiny wrapped packages, silk roses, golden horns, pearls and, on top, a rosy-cheeked wooden angel's head.

**HOLIDAY DELIGHTS:
MERRY MAKINGS
FOR PARTIES**

PARTY DESIGNER: STEPHEN BARANY

BEADLE

**HOLIDAY DELIGHTS:
MERRY MAKINGS
FOR PARTIES**

BEADLE

MINIATURE FRUIT TREE, *left,* makes a blushing centerpiece for an informal Christmas-week luncheon. You can make a tree like this by covering a Styrofoam cone first with florist's moss, then with miniature fruits—love apples, grapes, strawberries, kumquats and sugar pears, each secured with a hidden toothpick—and perching the whole on a weighted rush basket. This tree is lit up by six candles in a congenial assortment of candlesticks. Tablecloth and napkins echo fruit colors.

DESIGNER: THE GREENERY

CALICO BEANBAGS, *left below,* stitched up in fruit shapes and piled with holly in a green basket, can make a delightful country-fair centerpiece for Christmas eve supper. You might make more beanbag fruits to cluster lusciously in a garland like the one above the fireplace. For comfort, cushion the chairs with plump patchwork pillows; for a twinkle, top each bright calico napkin with a grinning gingerbread boy.

PARTY DESIGNER: STEPHEN BARANY

PEPPERMINT CONFECTIONS, *opposite page,* compose into a fantasyland centerpiece for a Christmas dinner when you use them in tempting profusion. Here a gilt and crystal epergne (or you could use a crystal compote) is ringed with candy canes shoulder-to-shoulder and crowned with a candy-cane cluster anchored in Styrofoam. For added fun, striped lollipops in the little flower holders. To make the candy clusters on each napkin, spear wrapped candies to an egg-sized Styrofoam base with florist's pins and sprig with velvet leaves.

PARTY DESIGNER: RENNY B. SALTZMAN

MASSEY

ASHLEY

MAYA

KITCHEN LUNCHEON PARTY, *far left,* sparkles like a Christmas tree with shining tin plates, bowls and baskets on the table, and copper pots trimming the walls. To make the centerpiece, heap your biggest colander with small tin utensils, pepper it with red glass Christmas bells, and ring it with merry Christmas-wrapped parcels for your guests to take home.

CHRISTMAS DINNER, *left,* is an unmistakably holiday feast even when the colors are just this side of Christmas. The centerpiece, which spills like an overflowing cornucopia onto the violet tablecloth, can be fashioned by wiring a candelabrum or tall urn with all manner of fruits, vegetables, gourds—some sprayed incredible colors, dried silvered flowers and fresh blossoms.

PRESENT-WRAPPING BEE, *bottom left,* can be a delightful afternoon for friends who might otherwise have to wrap alone. Ask guests to bring any special paper and trimmings they need; you supply extra scissors, tape, tissue paper and lots of little sandwiches and tea. To make your own beautiful presents the stars on Christmas morning, you might plan a subdued but beautiful tree like this one, using only red baubles arranged in clusters and the tiniest of white lights.

CHRISTMAS EVE SUPPER, *above,* can be set up near the Christmas tree on a table trimmed every bit as merrily. For a centerpiece, your favorite ornaments arranged under and around a clear glass dome, or pyramided on clear plastic cubes. Treats for each member of your family: a tiny red basket of after-dinner sweetmeats, a little present to open before bed.

PARTY DESIGNER: STEPHEN BARANY

SPLASHY PAPER BUFFET, *right,* that you whip up in a flash, will put everyone you invite for punch and fruitcake instantly in a holiday mood. To create your own paper fireworks, spread the table first with bright cotton cloth, then lengths of tissue-paper lace in the merriest colors you can find. The backdrop, masking-taped to the ceiling, is made of more lacework panels.

BEADLE

TRIO OF WREATHS, *below,* with ribbons—a surprise on an inside door.

PAPER FIESTA, *above,* of fringed garlands, paperfold wheels—a Mexican canopy above the door. LEE

BEAD

SHINY RED APPLES, *below,* dressed for Christmas in green velvet bows, heaped in a big crystal bowl.

CANDY-CANE BASKET, *below,* abundant with boxwood, fruit, tied with peppermint ribbons.

TISSUE-PAPER NOSEGAYS, *below,* are wired to wreathe a hall mirror.

GINGERBREAD HOUSES, *below,* on cotton snow, with ribbon-candy fence and tiny wooden "visitors."

GOLD PAPER ANGEL, *below,* with wooden head, gilt-thread hair, guards a festooned stairway.

MAGNOLIA LEAVES, *below,* splayed around lemons and sweet-gum balls.

VAN CÜYLENBURG

CANDY TREE, *right,* of candy fruits, fondants and green paper leaves, all speared with green toothpicks to a Styrofoam base.

FRAGRANT PYRAMID, *below,* of 3 dozen oranges pierced with cloves, heaped in a bowl, and chinked with cinnamon sticks.

DESIGNER: RONALDO MAIA

TREE OF SILK ROSES, *below,* wired together on a silver stand, to make a powder-room dressing table festive.

IVY TREES, *below,* standing sentry in the entrance hall; berry balls swinging gaily from the chandeliers above.

BIG GLASS JARS, *above,* lined with rows of fancy sweets around a core of tissue.

WREATH OF FRUITS, *below,* wired with paper leaves, garland a terra-cotta lady.

HOLIDAY DELIGHTS:
DECORATIONS ALL THROUGH THE HOUSE

DESIGNER: RONALDO MAIA

BOXWOOD WREATH, *above,* studded with limes and pinecone flowers, and encrusted with white berries.

SCARLET RIBBON, *below,* on a ladle handle: a pert grace note for a holiday punch-and-fruitcake buffet.

VAN CÜYLENBURG

CANDLE TREE, *above,* of candles waxed to tongue depressors in a pine-covered cone.

SWEET BASKET, *below,* woven of candy sticks and red licorice, holds other treats.

MAYA

ICICLE TREE, *below,* made of white rock candy chunks, cemented to an 18-inch cone.

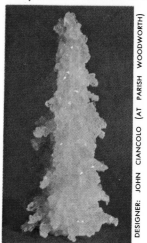

DESIGNER: JOHN CIANCOLO (AT PARISH WOODWORTH)

PAINTED SICILIAN DONKEY CART, *below,* festooned, beribboned and waiting with mugs of hot cider for frost-nipped carollers.

PAPERFOLD BALLS, *below,* and potted boxwood "trees" masquerading as holiday flowers in a plant stand, set against a backdrop of hot-hued paper lace.

PEARSON

214

BEADLE

GARLANDS OF EVERGREENS, *opposite page,* simply studded with real fruits and red velvet bows, are all you need to make a window say Christmas. To add to the spirit, you can set flowering plants—here poinsettias, cyclamen and white orchids—on sills or in clusters along the walls. On the floor, red velvet cushions to sit on and watch the festivities occurring in the tree-lit room just beyond.

HOLIDAY DELIGHTS: DECORATIONS ALL THROUGH THE HOUSE

TINY PACKAGES, *above*, each wrapped differently, then wired to a sturdy Styrofoam base just 3½ feet high.

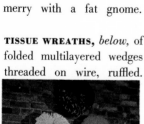

BREADSTICK TREE, *above*, in an Italian bread base, merry with a fat gnome.

TISSUE WREATHS, *below*, of folded multilayered wedges threaded on wire, ruffled.

STAIRWAY GARLAND, *above*, to climax at newel post with wreath, bow and a small grinning elf.

BERRIES AND VEGETABLES, *above*, tucked with greens into a mail basket—yours or a friend's.

ANGEL PIÑATAS, *below*, soaring on strings hooked to the ceiling and ready to release their sweet surprises to small visitors when strings are cut.

YUM-YUM TREE, *above*, with dozens of homemade holiday cookies and tiny white lights. You can ring the base with your prettiest dessert molds.

BLUE FOIL LANTERNS, *below*, to brighten the outdoors, while wine bottles chill in the snow.

ROSEMARY TREE, *below,* its fragrant branches tucked into a topiary frame and festooned with herb baskets, straw angels, shining chocolate molds tied on with raffia.

TRADITIONAL FRUITCAKE, *above,* to deck with holly sprigs, candy wreaths.

NEVER-NEVER CHRISTMAS TREE, *below,* of hundreds of chandelier prisms suspended on wires in tree formation.

TINY PRESENTS, *above,* tied with velvet ribbons, waiting on each plate to surprise the diners at a Christmas Eve supper.

DOORSIDE WREATH, *below,* of fragrant boxwood ablaze with pyracantha berries.

ASHLEY

GATHERING OF CANDLES, *below,* red tapers, green votives, and the grand-dad of them all on a silver tray.

BEADLE

POTTED POINSETTIAS, *below,* glorious on a pyramid of black boxes, forming a fascinating half-tree against a snow-white wall.

MUSIC STAND, *below,* with a red velvet ribbon to keep the place, two beribboned red candles to light up the tune.

MAYA

THE SUMPTUOUS ART OF GARNISHING

Atable can be turned into a feast for the eyes if you are a deft hand at garnishing, the sumptuous art that famous chefs have been employing for centuries to ensure that their culinary triumphs looked every whit as good as they tasted. Taste and appearance, the twin muses of the kitchen, are the inspiration behind garnishing. Basically, it consists of recognizing the decorative qualities inherent in foods, then shaping and arranging them to capitalize on these qualities. Much of the culinary sleight-of-hand that transforms a humble turnip into a flower, a fruit into a fish, or makes a lump of dough turn turtle can be mastered by anyone with the interest and patience. The tools for the job are few and inexpensive—a small, sharp paring knife, one or two cutters and possibly a couple of little gadgets like the stripper that removes the peel from a lemon or orange in one thin spiral or the fluting knife that prettily scallops the peel of vegetables. Food is one of the most malleable of materials. Think for a minute of the manifold shapes in which bread or pastry dough can be shaped and baked, the infinite ways in which the colors, form and textures of fruits and vegetables can be exploited. Or take something as humdrum as a hard-boiled egg. The white, cut into petals and given a truffle center, a chive stem and tarragon leaves becomes a flower on a salmon in aspic. The yolk, finely sieved, drifts a delicate, mimosa-like veil over a green salad. Garnishing extends your table-setting repertoire because in so many instances the garnish can double as the container for whatever you are serving—an individual portion of mayonnaise for cold lobster could be borne in a cucumber boat, lime or lemon sherbet come from the freezer to the table in a scooped-out orange basket, a seafood salad turn up in a hollowed-out acorn squash shell. In this most appetizing of arts, the possibilities are endless, limited only by your skill, imagination, materials at hand.

GREENING OF A TABLE with a mantle of lemon leaves in place of a cloth brings an ephemeral, magical freshness of springtime to an indoor luncheon party, *opposite*. The unusual and inspired table garnishment is enhanced by low finger bowls filled with clustered spring flowers, a first course of rosy shrimp couched on curried rice flecked with tomato and cucumber, edged with crisp sprays of watercress.

FOOD IS FUN when it takes new shapes. Left to right: star-shaped bread for a buffet meal breaks easily into sections. It is made by joining five braided Italian loaves at the center with a rose and leaves of bread. Croquembouche, a pyramid of caramel-glazed cream puffs, is garnished with candied violets. Fruitcake baked in candied grapefruit shell makes an intriguing tart-sweet treat for a tea party.

BEADLE

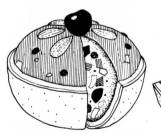

KLAPHOLZ

FUNK

DESIGNER (OPPOSITE):
RONALDO MAIA

BEADLE

SERVING ON ICE, A NEW FORM OF TABLE ART

When you serve cold food and drink at parties, remember that ice has decorative as well as refrigerating qualities. Finely crushed, carved in blocks or molded into cubes of different shapes and sizes, the frosty glamour of ice enhances everything it touches or surrounds and, as its sole constituent is water, you can even tint it in delicate pastel shades with pure vegetable dyes. To make a cold drink something special, use ice cube trays designed to form ice into fanciful shapes—spheres and sticks, hearts and flowers. If you are serving something like a Tom Collins or whiskey sour where fruit is part of the garnish, you can actually freeze the cherry or orange slice into the heart of the cube, to emerge gradually as the ice melts. The larger the piece of ice, the higher the melting point. You could arrange a whole seafood buffet of oysters, clams, shrimp, lobsters, crab legs and caviar on a huge block of ice and the ice would stay intact and the food remain chilled for hours. Crushed ice, on the other hand, dissipates quickly, but this can be retarded by chilling the container (preferably of glass or silver, both materials that hold the cold) in the freezer before packing it with crushed or shaved ice. If you don't own a battery of silver and glass bowls, trays and wine coolers, look around and you will probably find all manner of cooking equipment that can do double duty as an ice holder. For cold casseroles or soups, you can fill the water pan of a chafing dish with ice and put the food in the blazer pan on top. A copper fish-cooker packed with ice is large enough to chill four or five bottles of wine for a buffet party, while if you own an old-fashioned copper wash boiler you can ice a whole case of champagne in it. Another idea: iced tea or soup-on-the-rocks nestled in ice-filled tole mugs.

ICE IN THE HEART of a hollowed-out savoy cabbage keeps inset glass bowl of vichyssoise chilled. Leafy green of this stand-in for a tureen is a lovely contrast with summer soups.

ICEBERGS OF AQUAVIT are traditional Scandinavian way of cooling the fiery spirit and teams well with smoked fish, caviar. To make: place bottles in cardboard ice-cream container two-thirds full of water, freeze until solid, remove from carton.

ICE BOWL, *right*, for summer punch is carved from a solid block, fitted with a plastic liner so the liquid chills without diluting. The melting rate of the ice is approximately ½-inch per hour.

FROZEN GARNISHES and ice cubes shaped and colored like jewels chill and decorate summer drinks. Tangy bitters can also be captured in the ice.

FOTIADES   JEFFERY

FRUITS ON ICE nestle in the outer, ice-filled section of a heart-shaped tole tray, coeur à la crème fills the center.

ICE-PACKED RING of two half-circle *rivières*, normally used for holding flowers, turns server for a fresh cherry dessert.

FESTIVE BREADS

Festive breads are found throughout the world, wherever wheat is a staple and bakers have been inspired by tradition and fired by imagination to turn plain dough into shapes both realistic and fantastic. Given the plasticity of dough, which can be shaped, cut, pressed and formed as fancy dictates, it is possible to devise your own festive breads to suit any joyous occasion from a wedding or birthday party to a Christmas, Easter or Thanksgiving dinner. Bread can come to the table in all manner of party guises—imaginative centerpieces, serving platters, baskets, napkin rings, even casseroles for certain foods. You can roll out bread dough and shape or cut it in designs, but for greater sturdiness, when the bread is to be used as a basket handle or napkin ring, it is advisable to roll it in ropes and braid it. The following recipe for kipfel dough can be used for festive breads.

Put ¼-cup warm water in 3-quart bowl. Sprinkle 1 package dry yeast on top. Heat 1 cup milk with 6 tablespoons butter until butter melts. Add 1 teaspoon salt, 1 tablespoon sugar, let cool to lukewarm. Add the softened yeast and stir in 1½ cups sifted flour. Let rise in warm place until bubbly and light, about 1 hour. Add 2½ cups sifted flour, then turn out on floured board and knead 1 minute. Return to bowl and cover closely with plastic wrap. Let rise to double before rolling out. Bake in preheated oven.

BREAD SUNBURST, the happiest of all festive symbols, makes delightful center for tray of hors d'oeuvre, both before and after they are eaten. It can be made with yeast dough containing salt and shortening, but no sugar. Roll dough ⅛″ thick in a circle large enough to cover flat bottom of a 12″ pizza pan; trim to fit; invert a floured 8″ plate in the center; decorate as shown below. Bake in a 425° oven for 10 minutes.

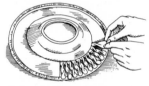

1. Lay dough on pizza pan, plate in center. Snip uncovered dough at ½″ intervals, twisting strips. 2. Remove

plate. Make eyes, dough lids from balls, strips. Make thin tapered ropes for two lips, press into place for mouth, curling up for smile.

BREAD BASKET holding a nosegay of crudités on a buffet table, *opposite,* is made from Italian bread dough. Rounded base is shaped over ovenproof glass bowl and baked. Handle of three-strand braid (see sketches *below*) is curved over similar bowl and baked, then attached to the basket with toothpicks (the handle is for appearance only, it should not be used for lifting basket). Before filling the basket, line it with plastic wrap to prevent the bread getting soggy, then fill with celery, cherry tomatoes, radish roses, button mushrooms, olives speared on long bamboo skewers.

KLAPHOLZ

1. Arrange three ropes crisscross on a cookie sheet.
2. Braid from crossover to end. 3. Tuck ends under. Braid from other end.

FOTIADES

BREAD TURTLE, *left,* is simply a round loaf of pumpernickel with small pieces of dough added to form the head, tail and feet. The surprise is inside—the shell is hollowed out and filled with tiny cocktail-size assorted sandwiches, kept moist and fresh. Circular cutout on turtle's back forms lid, topped with bright wool bow attached with toothpicks so it lifts off easily.

BREAD CASSEROLES, *above,* serve creamed seafood (fill them at last minute so they don't get soggy). To make, mold Italian bread dough over ovenproof glass bowls and bake. Cut lids from flat sheet of dough, decorate with strands and bake on cookie sheet. For napkin ring, bake braided dough around a tube of firm crushed foil, gently slide off after baking.

BREAD WEDDING CAKE, *below,* delightful and different, consists of three loaves of Italian panettone baked in 8-, 10-, and 12-inch molds, then skewered together. Braids and decorative bows, doves and flowers are pinned on with toothpicks. To control dimensions of the braids that circle each tier, shape them around the upturned greased panettone molds.

BEADLE

RING OF BREAD, *left,* the symbol of continuity, is set on the napkin beside each wedding guest's place, to be nibbled with champagne, or taken home as a keepsake. Ring is made by shaping a rope of dough into a circle, flattening it, then decorating the surface with small snippets of dough. To give a glossy brown surface, brush with beaten egg yolk before baking.

223

FANTASIES FROM FRUITS AND VEGETABLES

The art of garnishing can never resist improving on nature, even when nature's shapes are perfection, for the essence of this artifice is to decorate, adorn or embellish whatever it touches. Traditionally, all garnishes for food are made from natural materials, such as fruits and vegetables, whose color and shape lend themselves to conversion into another form. Although all the materials are completely edible, not all garnishes are made to be eaten. In some instances, such as the carved and dyed turnip flowers or the roses of curled tomato skin with which French chefs decorate platters, they are strictly for show. In other cases, notably the deftly carved fantasies of Thailand, in which fruits and vegetables counterfeit the forms of flowers and beasts, like those *opposite*, the aim is both to enchant the eye and beguile the palate, for they taste just as good as they look. The equipment for these delightful deceits is simple—nothing more than a small sharp paring knife and a big bowl of ice water to keep the carved fruits or vegetables fresh and crisp. However, since many fruits discolor rapidly when peeled (apples, pears, peaches and bananas are among the worst offenders), there is an extra step in their preparation. Put a handful of salt in the bowl of water and after the fruits are peeled, leave them in the salted water for twenty minutes, then rinse well and dry on paper towels before arranging them on the plate or platter. Prepared in this way, they will keep in perfect condition for hours and the salt, mysteriously, has no effect on the taste.

PINEAPPLE QUEEN BEE, *right,* reigns over an array of remodeled fruit. To make: take a pineapple with a good top, cut off the long center leaves. Cut out wedge at stem end, insert handful of leaves. Cut oval wings at each side, prop open with wedge of cucumber. Cut and lift out section of pineapple rind behind wings, large enough to let you remove flesh from the interior. Chop flesh in bite-size pieces, put it back in pineapple and replace section of rind. Finish off with grapes, on toothpicks, for eyes, two leaves for antennae. Surround bee with fruit flies made from halved grapes with apple or cucumber wings; piles of grapes, strawberries and tangerine sections; peeled papaya slices; peeled, halved and skinned oranges, apples cut like flowers. To make petals, cut apples in eighths, cut slice under skin three-quarters the length of each section, slice off seeds, shape tips of skin, gently lift.

HONEYDEW MELON TURNED LOTUS, *far right,* becomes a decorative dessert that separates into eight perfect sections. First slice a little off the bottom of the melon so it will stand upright, then cut in eighths lengthwise to an inch from the bottom. Gently separate sections and remove seeds from center with spoon. Cut rind away from flesh and gently pull out.

WATERMELON WHALE, *right,* aground on a meadow of fruit flowers. To make this whimsical beast, draw design on rind with grease pencil and cut out with a sharp knife, removing rind in small pieces. Undercut tail and edges to remove flesh and finish by notching edges. Cut eyes from leftover rind and pin them in place. Scoop out flesh with a melon-ball cutter, trim cavity and replace balls. Most of the flowers of the field are composed of apples sliced into petals like those above, and halved, peeled and skinned oranges. In addition: a pear fringed with green-skin petals cut vertically from blossom to stem end, the core scooped out and cavity filled with tiny carrot-strips for stamens; tangerine sections packed like buds in halved tangerine shell or clustered together to form a fat and fantastic butterfly.

SELF-SERVING MELON, *far right,* turns compote to hold a slew of melon balls. To make the base, cut off a third of the melon. Slice off the very top of this and cut a similar amount from bottom of melon. Put the scooped-out shell on the base, fill with melon balls and top with a tiny rind hat. Behold compote!

DESIGN OF FRUIT FANTASIES THIS PAGE: TURB XOOMSAI

KASPER

GRIGSBY

BEADLE

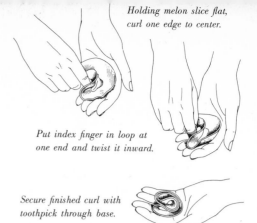

Holding melon slice flat, curl one edge to center.

Put index finger in loop at one end and twist it inward.

Secure finished curl with toothpick through base.

METAMORPHOSIS OF TWO MELONS, *left*, is simple matter of cutting, curling. To scallop edges of the cantaloupe half and honeydew slice, dig into the flesh with melon-ball cutter, cutting deeply, slightly lifting the flesh. Melon flowers are made as shown in the sketches *above*, and a melon ball of contrasting color is put in the center of each flower. The "leaves" are cut from the tender inner section of the pineapple fronds.
DESIGNER: TIND VAZQUEZ

TROMPE L'OEIL BOUQUET, *opposite*, makes a miniature centerpiece for a basket tray of crudités (raw vegetable hors d'oeuvre) presented in tiny clay flowerpots. Feigned flowers are stamped with daisy cutters or carved with a knife from turnip slices, carrots, and icicle radishes. Black olive slices supply some of the centers. Leafy celery tops provide foliage.

PERPETUAL POPPIES, *below left*, are fashioned from small white turnips, as shown in the sketches below, then dyed with beet juice and food coloring. Their "basket" consists of thin strips of orange rind woven around toothpicks set in a thick slice of pineapple. Bamboo-skewer stems of flowers are hidden by real green leaves. The ring of ice-cream roses around the basket was the result of putting ice cream in pewter molds, freezing it hard, then unmolding it onto dessert plates.

Peel turnip. Make two five-sided cuts around center. Cut out layer of turnip in between.

Round off center. Make five cuts for outer petals. Cut out area between inner, outer petals. Cut out notches to separate inner petals. Shape outside by trimming base inward. Cut out notches to separate outer petals.

Round petals off to make open flowers.

KLAPHOLZ

GARNISHING:
FRUIT AND VEGETABLE FANTASIES

OLIVES DRESSED AS CRABS, *far left,* look almost too engaging to eat. To make them, as shown in sketches at right, enlarge the holes in pitted black olives with the point of a knife, insert three-inch pieces of scallion (carrot or celery could also be used) and fringe the ends by slitting them with the point of a sharp knife.

SALAD STILL LIFE for an individual serving, *left.* For this color, taste and texture mixture, carrot tassels are combined with quartered black olives, a slice of cucumber, onion slices, a radish rose, spears of endive, romaine. To make the tassels, slice the root end of the carrot vertically and turn it 90 degrees, then slice again. See the sketch at right.

VEGETABLES IN DISGUISE, masquerading as denizens of the sea, *left center,* make an intriguing conversation piece for the cocktail hour. For the lobsters, slice one tomato, quarter another. For shrimp, slice radishes in rounds, make tails of split ovals cut from another radish. Both techniques are shown at right. Jellyfish are simply onion rings, some halved to make tentacles. Crabs are, again, olives with legs of scallion. Scampi-like creatures with scallion feelers are upper half of carrot sliced in rounds with tail made from root end cut in tassels as in salad above. For the three fantasy cucumber fish, use three cucumbers and cut as shown in sketches at right. For the first fish, cut a peeled cucumber in half lengthwise, then cut lengthwise again two-thirds of the length and fan out. For the second fish, an unpeeled cucumber is used. One quarter forms the head, with gills cut at the sides and half-round radish slices for eyes; the center section is sliced in rounds for the body; the tail consists of the final quarter with the skin cut back from the stem end and shaped into points. For the third fish, a peeled cucumber is cut in half-rounds to simulate scales, with thin rounds of carrot slipped underneath them; a sword cut from another cucumber added at the head and a fourth of cucumber peel forming the tail. Except for the tomato lobsters, all these pseudo-sea creatures should be soaked in ice water when cut to ensure crispness and curl.

SALADS ON STICKS, *far left,* with radish-rose finials radiate from a small hidden head of lettuce. Spear any combination of bite-size ingredients on a long bamboo skewer, as in sketch at right, starting with radish (cut petals toward stem end, shape with knife point). Stick skewer into lettuce. To eat, twirl salad stick in dressing, slide ingredients off.

BURNING-CANDLE TOWERS, *left,* only nonedible arrangement, dominate a vegetable centerpiece. Cucumber cups are cut like tail of the fantasy fish, but with the second layer of points and center hollowed out. To assemble, as shown in sketch, *right,* run long bamboo skewer through lettuce head and cucumber cup into hole in candle made by inserting a heated ice pick. Plant lettuce head on flower pin holder. Decorate with tomato quarters, parsley.

DESIGN OF VEGETABLE FANTASIES THIS PAGE: TURB XOOMSAI

KASPER

229

CHAPTER 13 YOUR LIQUID ASSETS

Wines and spirits are the liquid assets which make a party pay dividends in fun and pleasure. A palate-provoking aperitif or bone-dry sherry before lunch, a full-bodied red or delicate white wine with dinner can turn a simple meal into an occasion. There's nothing like a well-mixed martini or margarita to stimulate the flow of conversation at the cocktail hour, while to round off an evening with a glow of well-being and contentment a fine old Madeira or cognac, a fruit-flavored liqueur or a really good white fruit brandy can't be bettered.

The cardinal rule of successful entertaining is "be innovative." Don't always stick with the same old highballs, the stereotyped cocktail party. Instead, why not give a one-drink party and serve nothing but a selection of champagnes, or dry and medium sherries, or imported beers from all over the world? In summer, a range of white wines with a buffet of cold seafood couched on ice, or pitchers of sangria and dishes of various kinds of olives, salted almonds and cubes of sharp cheese and Virginia ham make a refreshing change from the usual mixed-drink pattern. In winter you might have an after-dinner gathering for coffee and cognacs or, if your guests are Scotch fanciers, a tasting of the different blends of light and heavy Scotches and the straight malts, the unblended whiskies now on the market that are so different in flavor and character. Then, of course, there is the wine-tasting party, which has grown in popularity over the last ten years, especially with young marrieds who find this an entertaining, economical and rewarding way of spending the evening with a group of friends while increasing their knowledge of different wines from this country and abroad.

You don't need an extensive or expensive bar or wine cellar in order to give good parties, just a willingness to experiment, without being too outlandish about it.

BASICS FOR THE BAR

The definition of a well-stocked bar differs from region to region, group to group and even season to season. For example, in some parts of the country bourbon is the popular whiskey and Scotch is seldom called for, while in others it is quite the reverse. The same is true of gin, vodka and rum. A good host will provide at least one bottle of all the basic spirits, remembering that some like their whiskies light, others heavier, and that there is no reason to waste an expensive brand of whiskey on mixed drinks like manhattans and old-fashioneds or sours when a cheaper blend will do. He'll also keep on hand a couple of bottles of good sherry, aperitifs or vermouths for those who like a lighter drink, as well as tomato juice, ginger ale and Perrier water for the occasional guest who happens to be on a diet or who doesn't drink at all.

Here is a list for a basic bar stocked for before- and after-dinner drinking; you can tailor the list to suit your requirements.

WHISKIES

2 Scotch—one light, one heavier

1 bourbon

1 blended whiskey for mixed drinks

1 Canadian or Irish whiskey

GINS

1 American gin

1 English gin (for those who prefer it in martinis)

VODKAS

1 American vodka

1 Polish or Russian vodka for drinking straight (this should be kept chilled in the freezer)

RUMS

1 light rum

1 dark (Jamaican) rum

VERMOUTHS, APERITIFS, AND BITTERS

1 dry vermouth

1 Italian sweet vermouth

1 Lillet, Dubonnet or other aperitif wine

1 Italian bitters—Campari or Punt e Mes

1 Angostura bitters for mixed drinks

FORTIFIED WINES, BRANDIES AND LIQUEURS

1 dry sherry

1 medium-dry sherry

1 vintage Madeira or port

1 fine old cognac

1 lesser brandy or armagnac

1 white fruit brandy, such as kirsch, framboise, mirabelle

2 liqueurs, one fruit flavor, 1 herb flavor

Add to or subtract from this as you see fit. You might want to add a bottle of crème de cassis or cassis syrup to make vermouth or vin blanc cassis in the summer, or a bottle of tequila or pisco if your friends have taken up margaritas and pisco sours, two delicious south-of-the-border drinks.

BUYING LIQUOR FOR COCKTAIL PARTIES

If you foresee a run of big parties, it is always a good idea to buy liquor by the case. This almost always means a saving and is a safeguard against running out of supplies over a heavily social weekend. In some states you can also buy popular liquors like bourbon, rye, gin and vodka in half-gallon, gallon or even five-gallon jugs, at a considerable advantage in price.

How do you serve liquor from such large containers? You don't. You decant it, which many people consider a far more attractive way to serve liquor than from the bottle. Decanters need not be expensive. Modestly priced decanters of contemporary design are easy to find, and secondhand shops often yield old decanters at reasonable prices. The gift bottles in which some whiskeys are packaged at Christmas are frequently pleasing enough in design to be saved and used as decanters. Be sure, though, to identify the contents, either by hanging metal, pottery or porcelain spirit labels around the necks of the decanters or making your own labels, or you may find yourself mixing up gin with vodka or bourbon with rye.

ORGANIZING A COCKTAIL PARTY

Plan your party in detail. First of all, decide on the best place to set up your bar. A temporary bar arrangement can be set up on a serving cart or table if you are having only a few guests, say six or eight. For larger groups, place a good-size table, round or oblong, at one side of the room, away from the wall so that whoever is doing the bartending, you or a professional hired for the evening, can stand behind it. If you are your own bartender, have the table close enough to the conversation centers so you can pour drinks and also enter into the general talk or you will not have much fun at your own party.

THE LIQUOR

No one is going to expect you to have all the resources of a bar, so keep the choice of drinks to a hospitable minimum. You probably have a good idea of what your guests' tastes are, and if someone should come up with an outlandish request, ask them to think again. Plan on having the usual range of spirits—a bottle or two of gin, one of vodka, one or two of Scotch, bourbon and blended whiskey and a bottle each of sweet and dry vermouth so you have the makings of manhattans or martinis. In addition, have a couple of bottles of wine drinks—chilled sherry, an aperitif and perhaps a bottle of chilled white wine, and one nonalcoholic drink such as well-seasoned tomato juice (which will come in handy for a Bloody Mary in case anyone asks for it). This, with the usual mixers—soda, water, tonic and ginger ale—should be more than adequate. If you're serving martinis, you'll save yourself time and trouble by mixing a large pitcher or bottle of them in advance (don't add ice, though) and chilling it in the refrigerator. Or, if you happen to own a large punch bowl, fill it with ice and place it on the bar; then you can stand the martini pitcher, the bottle of sherry or white wine, or any other drink that needs chilling, in it.

To estimate the amount of liquor you'll need, count on getting sixteen 2-ounce measures from a quart bottle. If you prefer to serve 1½-ounce drinks, as most leading restaurants and bars do, you'll get even more mileage from a bottle—over twenty drinks. It's a good practice to pour the first drinks with a 2-ounce measure and then cut down to 1½ ounces once the party is in full swing and the guests are happy with less strong drinks (they'll be even happier next morning). With sherry, aperitifs or wine which have a much lower alcohol content, you will, of course, serve more, say 3 to 4 ounces for sherry or aperitifs, 4 or 5 ounces of a lighter table wine. As to the number of drinks each guest will consume, that's hard to say. Four a head is a pretty good average, for while some may drink more, others will probably drink less.

With your bar set up and the drinks selected, make sure you have plenty of ice on hand. Keep a good-size bucket on the bar and have back-up supplies in a couple of inexpensive Styrofoam ice chests or barrels that can be kept behind the bar or in the kitchen.

GLASSES AND GADGETS

Always have an ample number of glasses. Rent some from a caterer if you don't think you'll have sufficient. Nothing is worse than running out of clean glasses, which is easy enough if guests put a drink down somewhere, forget it, and then come to the bar for a fresh one, because you'll have to waste time scrounging around and collecting them and dashing into the kitchen for some fast washing up.

It's not necessary, by any means, to have a different glass for every type of drink. Two basic types are really all you need: old-fashioned glasses, both single and double sizes, for highballs and drinks on the rocks; and stemmed all-purpose 10-to-12-ounce wine glasses for everything else you're likely to serve, from beer, wine or soft drinks to gin and tonic, sherry, aperitifs, even cocktails. A point in favor of the stemmed glass is that chilled but noniced drinks stay cold longer, away from the hot clasp of the hand. In any case, it is better to serve a drink in a glass that's a bit too large than in one that is definitely too small—there is less chance of spills.

Apart from liquor, ice and glasses, there are only a few things you'll need on the bar. First, a half dozen accurate jiggers, both 2-ounce and 1-ounce sizes, a sharp bar knife, a bottle opener, a corkscrew, a bar spoon, ice tongs, a board for cutting lemons and possibly a lemon stripper (a little gadget that zips the peel from the fruit in a long continuous spiral), a couple of pitchers for mixing drinks and a large pitcher of water. Unless you are going in for complicated cocktails, a metal-and-glass shaker and an electric blender are not necessary. Especially for a large party, it's best to try to simplify the bar procedure so as to keep drinks flowing smoothly.

Party food should be simple. All those little canapés that take hours to make might look pretty on the platter, but they soon become soggy and sad and someone will be stuck with the job of handing them around. Far better to arrange around the room at various points (or, if you prefer, on one big table) the kinds of food to which people can help themselves—a tray of cheeses with crackers, sliced French and pumpernickel bread; a pâté or a big hot sausage such as a kielbasa, to be sliced on a board and eaten on French bread; and possibly a mound of steak tartare or steak tartare balls rolled in parsley or finely chopped nuts, to be speared with toothpicks. (If your guests are adventurous about food, you might also make balls of kibbee, the Middle East mixture of raw ground lamb and cracked wheat.) Have a tray of the crisp raw vegetables always so popular with dieters—cherry tomatoes; red and icicle radishes; carrot, celery and green pepper strips; endive leaves; fennel; raw asparagus; snow peas; zucchini and cucumber slices or strips; green onions; cauliflower flowerets—and, for dunking and dipping, small bowls of seasoned salt and coarse salt; mustard mayonnaise or mayonnaise flavored with finely chopped garlic and anchovies; sour cream mixed with grated horseradish, chives and black pepper or with blue cheese; and wedges of lemon, which some may prefer to squeeze on the vegetables rather than saucing them.

Other good things to serve are a big bowl of marinated shrimp, Virginia ham on cornbread squares, some kind of cheese spread such as Liptauer (cream cheese, butter and heavy cream whipped, mounded and surrounded with chopped onion, anchovy, capers, chives to be mixed in as desired) or the Southwest *chile con queso,* a hot dip of melted cheese and green chiles with corn chips or bread sticks.

If you think some of your guests are likely to make an evening of it, provide more solid food in the shape of a baked ham, corned beef or roast beef to be carved as needed, and eaten on sliced French bread with a choice of mustards.

As all these qualify as finger foods, you don't need to provide plates, just an ample supply of thick paper napkins, preferably somewhat larger than the usual (and inadequate) cocktail size, to protect guests' hands and to catch any stray drips.

FOR PARTIES, GLASSES WITH MANY USES. 1. *All-purpose 18-ounce glass is fine for any wine, red or white, still or sparkling.* **2.** *Tulip-shaped champagne glass might also be used for aperitifs with soda.* **3.** *Large 22-ounce glass, originally designed for Burgundy, is equally good for beer, iced tea or highballs.* **4.** *Classic 12-ounce Bordeaux glass can serve other wines, or mixed drinks.* **5.** *Tapering 10½-ounce Burgundy glass might also be used for a Bloody Mary or a cold vichyssoise.* **6.** *Rounded 6-ounce sherry glass can double as a cocktail glass.* **7.** *Fragile 6½-ounce champagne flute might also serve fruit juice.* **8.** *Tall brandy inhaler could hold cocktails, too.* **9.** *Chimney-shaped 5-ounce brandy glass also excels for liqueurs or straight whiskies.* **10.** *Large 19-ounce tumbler is great for long drinks.* **11.** *Smaller 13-ounce tumbler takes any mixed drink.* **12.** *Slender 19-ounce tumbler is ideal for fruit punches, iced tea.* **13.** *Large 13-ounce old-fashioned glass serves any drink on the rocks.*

SELECTING GLASSES
FOR ALL PURPOSES

Nowadays, there is no hard-and-fast rule that any wine or drink must be served in only one style of glass. All that is really needed is a glass large enough for its current purpose, sensibly shaped and clear.

An average serving of wine at dinner is 4 ounces and the glass should be no more than one-third to half full. So long as you observe this custom, which allows room for the wine to breathe and the bouquet to develop, any white, red or sparkling wine may be served in an all-purpose wine glass of 10-ounce capacity or more. Don't, though, stifle wine by serving it in those dinky little so-called wine glasses some restaurants use (to their shame) for you'll be doing the wine, and your guests, a disservice. The graceful, slender-stemmed wine glasses in sketches 1, 3, 4 and 5 are the type to use. A single, all-purpose wine glass makes great sense, especially if you have limited storage space. It is always better to have plenty of glasses in one style rather than a few each of assorted ones.

Wine glasses in the classic shapes are not only beautiful but immensely versatile because you can use them for much more than the purpose they are intended for. A tulip-shaped glass like the one in sketch 4 does not have to be limited to champagne, nor does the flute in sketch 7. They can be used for parfaits and frothy whipped desserts like zabaglione. The extralarge deeply cupped Burgundy glass in sketch 3 would show off chilled summer soups like gazpacho or vichyssoise to perfection, or hold a fresh peach in champagne for dessert. The less deep, rounded wine glass in sketch 1 could double for seafood cocktails, fruit cup or a frosty sherbet or granité. Other types of glasses, such as brandy and sherry glasses, tumblers, and old-fashioned glasses, can also change their function as required. Glasses, in short, offer great opportunities for improvisation in all kinds of entertaining situations.

Beautiful glasses deserve the best of care. Never put fine glassware in an electric dishwasher. Wash it by hand. If there are greasy prints on the stems or bowls, a little household ammonia in the dishwater will remove them. Rinse the glasses first in hot and then in cold water and turn them upside down on paper towels to drain and get as dry as possible, then polish them gently with a soft lint-free cloth.

Be gentle with your wine glasses or they will get

small nicks on the rims. A nicked wine glass should be discarded, for even the smallest rough edge may cause a cut on lips or tongue. If the glasses are heirlooms or too valuable to discard, you can have the edges reground but this is an expensive procedure and only worthwhile for really fine crystal.

Always check your glassware well in advance of a party. The glasses can collect a dusty film just standing on the shelf. See that they are rinsed, polished and sparkling before you put them on the table.

CHOOSING, STORING AND SERVING WINE

A meal without wine, it has been said, is like a day without sun, and certainly there is almost no time when a glass of wine doesn't make the food taste better and the company seem livelier.

With the vast selection of wines available today, in every price range, there is no need to limit the drinking of wine to dinner parties and special occasions, or the bottle to a great (and correspondingly expensive) Bordeaux or Burgundy. Europeans drink their *vin ordinaire*, or carafe wine, as naturally as they breathe, and so can we. The reds and whites put out in half-gallon and gallon jugs by the leading American wine companies make eminently satisfactory carafe wines for everyday drinking or for informal entertaining such as buffet parties and barbecues or picnics, and they keep well if decanted into tightly corked wine bottles, or tightly capped. Once opened, whites should be refrigerated and, unless you are going to use them up quickly, it is a wise idea to do the same with reds; a little chilling won't hurt them. When you want to serve these jug wines, pour them into decanters or inexpensive liter carafes.

When the menu calls for something with more character or substance, you can go up the scale, starting with the inexpensive wines of Spain, Portugal and Chile, then going on to the medium-priced European wines from Italy, Switzerland, Austria, Alsace, the South of France, the Loire and Rhône valleys, Germany, our own American premium wines, and ending with the really first-rate, those treasured few that sell for $15 or more a bottle.

The commonsense way to buy and drink wine is to find what suits you, the food you serve, and your pocket. For everyday purposes, keep on hand a half dozen inexpensive wines, especially those like Beaujolais and the Loire whites that are best drunk young, and gradually build up a small, select collection of more noteworthy French and German wines for special dinner parties, holidays and celebrations.

When it comes to buying wine, it is literally cheaper by the dozen (or standard case); you save 10 per cent over the single bottle price. Be on the alert for new vintages and for wine sales, sample a few bottles or half bottles and make your investment when the price is right. If you have the storage space, buy slow-maturing wines such as the red Bordeaux and California Cabernet Sauvignons when they first appear on the market and cost less, and put them away until they have acquired sufficient bottle age.

Study and get to know wines. Many lesser château bottlings and little-known vineyards produce amazingly good wine in a great wine year, but the price will be well below that of the famous "names" of Bordeaux and Burgundy. You can learn a great deal about the wines of different countries by reading books written by leading authorities, such as *Wine* by Hugh Johnson (published by Simon and Schuster), Alexis Lichine's *Encyclopedia of Wines and Spirits* (published by Alfred A. Knopf), Frank Schoonmaker's *Encyclopedia of Wine* (published by Hastings. House) and several others.

Don't be a slave to vintage charts. They have their purpose, but often when a year is listed as only a fair vintage, there are exceptions. Weather varies even within a small district, and a vineyard here or there may actually turn out a very good product although the general result is not up to par. Since the price of all wines of an area is affected by the vintage reports, such exceptions are usually bargains. If you have a good wine merchant, trust his information. If he suggests a little-known wine of good vintage or a well-known wine of a generally poor vintage, he is probably offering you a good buy. Unless you have the time and money to turn yourself into a wine authority, your best guide to wine buying will always be a reputable, knowledgeable dealer, so select your wine and liquor dealer with care and talk your needs over with him.

is, after all, to his advantage to give you the kind of advice you can rely on.

STORING WINE

Today, very few of us can have a wine cellar, but anyone can find space for an adequate wine wall—an assemblage of sturdy racks in a closet, cabinet or interior hallway. One good reason, if reason be needed, for such an arrangement is that fine wine becomes agitated and unbalanced when jiggled from store to house. To be at its best when served, it needs at least a week or two to settle down, peacefully resting on its side with the wine in contact with the cork (if the cork dries out, air can seep in and spoil the wine) and then most of a day standing upright at room temperature so any possible sediment can sink slowly to the bottom of the bottle.

Ideally, your wine wall should be in a dark, draft-free spot with a constant temperature of between 55 and 65 degrees and as little vibration as possible. An inside closet, air-conditioned if you can afford it, is probably the best place available in most houses and apartments. It has proved unwise to keep bottles out in the open. Not only are they exposed to temperature changes, strong light and movement, but also to the careless hands of well-meaning friends who are apt to drag them out for a look at the label.

Stocking your wine wall is a matter of personal preference, your facilities and how much you are prepared to spend. Try to select a fairly comprehensive range of wines—reds, whites and a rosé or two—so you always have something to suit almost any kind of food or menu. It's a good idea to keep a wine log in which you record the wines you buy, with the name of the dealer, the price and a label from the bottle (removed after it is emptied, naturally) so you can check back on essential details such as the vintage and the name of the shipper and importer. This makes it easier to remember and re-order a wine you like, or try a new vintage or an old favorite.

For reds, you might start with three or four bottles from the districts of the Médoc, St-Emilion, Graves and Pomerol, château-bottled wines from excellent but medium-priced vineyards.

Pick a similar number of red Burgundies from the districts of Beaune, Pommard, Nuits-St-Georges and Gevrey-Chambertin or Chambolle-Musigny.

After this you could buy a half dozen bottles of young regional wines like Beaujolais, Côtes-du-Rhône, Châteauneuf-du-Pape, Hermitage and Chinon from France, Valpolicella from Italy, Dão from Portugal and one of the better Riojas from Spain. Add two California reds, Pinot Noir and Cabernet Sauvignon from the Napa and Sonoma valleys.

For whites, start with two or three estate-bottled Burgundies from such districts as Chablis, Meursault, Pouilly-Fuissé and Puligny-Montrachet; Muscadet, Quincy or Pouilly-Fumé from the Loire Valley; and a few of the delightfully fresh, young and flowery wines from Alsace—Sylvaner, Riesling, Traminer. If you like German wines, add two or three estate-bottled Rhines and Moselles, perhaps a Wehlener Sonnenuhr, Bernkasteler Doktor and Schloss Vollrads. From Italy, a Verdicchio or Soave, a Swiss Fendant or Neuchâtel and perhaps a Portuguese *vinho verde*. From California, a good Pinot Chardonnay.

If you like rosés, look for a Tavel or Anjou from France, a Grenache Rosé from California.

SERVING WINE

If you are serving a red wine with dinner, remove it from the rack and leave it at room temperature, upright for a few hours, then open it an hour or so before the meal to let the wine "breathe" (this merely means that as the air gets to it, the body, bouquet and flavor develop). Whites should be slightly chilled in the refrigerator (*never* the freezer) for a couple of hours, or put in a bucket of ice and water for twenty minutes to half an hour just before the dinner. Don't let them get icy, just medium cold, and open the bottle a few minutes before it is to be poured.

Make sure you have a good corkscrew, preferably one that works on the leverage principle and draws the cork out smoothly without jerking the bottle and agitating the wine, or the type that sommeliers in restaurants use. The correct method of opening table wine is shown in the accompanying illustrations.

When it comes to choosing wines to serve with food, it is impossible to be dogmatic these days. There are no hard-and-fast rules, only the guidelines of suitability

With sharp knife, cut foil below rim of neck.

Peel foil from top of bottle, wipe with cloth.

Twist corkscrew into cork, side wing out. Grip the top firmly and press wing down.

As cork rises, pull slowly, don't jerk.

Wipe inside bottle neck before pouring wine.

Fill ⅓ of the glass. To prevent drips, turn the bottle to right.

and commonsense. Wine and food should, above all, complement each other. Spicy foods like chili and curry and vinegary ones like tossed salads and vegetables vinaigrette fight wine—either they are so overpowering that they kill the flavor, or they make it taste unpleasant. Chilis and curries are best with beer. If you should want to eat salad while you are drinking wine, use lemon juice, which is less assertively acid, instead of vinegar.

As a general practice, the only wines served with soup are the fortified ones—sherry and Madeira, the traditional accompaniments for game and turtle soups, consommés and bisques. Amontillado, among sherries, and Verdelho or Rainwater, among Madeiras, have the pungency and body to hold up against a really savory broth or cream soup. The really dry sherries and Madeiras would taste a little meager and thin. Try an amontillado, at room temperature or slightly below, with a fresh mushroom soup or a Rainwater with the creamy mussel soup, Billi-Bi, to discover how perfect a combination they make.

When it comes to first-course appetizers, wine is mostly served with seafood (shellfish, seafood cocktails, smoked fish) and then it is always white. With a galantine or a pâté you would serve a white wine or a champagne, though a really coarse, strongly flavored country pâté could take a slightly chilled light red. With quiche lorraine, the savory custard tart that hails from Alsace, it would be appropriate to have a delicate Alsatian white or possibly a dry Moselle.

For main courses, the dictum about white wines with fish, red wines with red meats still holds true because it makes good sense, but it is not just the type but also the character of the dish and the manner in which it is cooked that determines the selection of the wine to accompany it.

Red wine is *de rigueur* with beef, but whereas beef Wellington should certainly be accorded the complement of a fine Burgundy or Bordeaux, it would be sheer folly to squander the same wine on a pot roast or beef stew. Better to serve an inexpensive wine that might have been used in the cooking, such as a California Mountain Red, a modest regional Bordeaux or a Mâcon Rouge. Veal, a pale and delicate meat, is a different proposition. While you might drink a light red

such as Valpolicella or a Beaujolais with a veal roast, a blanquette de veau or scalloppini cooked with white wine would definitely require a Pouilly-Fuissé, Soave or Moselle. Pork, a rich, fatty white meat, definitely needs the acidity of a white or rosé.

Red wines are usually the choice with game, although in certain cases, such as with delicate game birds like dove and quail, a white is preferable. Poultry is another matter entirely. Here the field of choice is wide. Depending on the style of preparation and your personal preference you can serve a red that isn't too heavy, a rosé or a white. A crisply roasted chicken would be equally good with a light red Bordeaux or California Cabernet Sauvignon, a Beaujolais such as a Fleurie, or a simple white Burgundy. Even duck and goose, with their darker, heavier-flavored flesh can taste just as good with a Moselle as with a more robust red wine.

Wine and cheese are classic partners and here the wine, when cheese is served as a course on its own, is invariably red. The finer the cheese, the finer the wine should be. A ripe and perfect Brie or Camembert rates a superb red Bordeaux.

Nowadays, few people serve wine with dessert—sweet dishes require sweet wines like the French Sauternes, the German *beerenauslese*, port or a California Semillon or Moscato Amabile, for which we seem to have lost the taste. If you should wish to accompany a mousse or ice cream with wine, champagne, extradry rather than the bone-dry brut, is the best choice.

Fruit is rather different. Most fresh or poached fruits marry happily with wine. A fresh pear is delicious with a light, dry red wine, or a bowl of raspberries with a rosé or light Moselle. Champagne and peaches have a divine affinity, while apples, which have a rather winey taste themselves, are enhanced by fruity white wines. Only oranges and pineapple seem really to repel wine, but they take kindly to a dash of fruit-flavored liqueur or white fruit brandy.

When you serve more than one wine at a meal, follow the customary, natural progression of white before red, dry before sweet, young before old, light before full-bodied and modest before magnificent. This is the same pattern you would follow at a wine tasting; each wine is shown to its best advantage.

STAGING A WINE TASTING

While it would take a lifetime to make the acquaintance of all the wines of the world, you can get to know more of them, and more about them, by staging a series of wine-tasting parties with a group of friends. In this way, you can sample as many as eight wines in one evening without over-indulging or over-spending, for naturally you will all share the cost.

At professional wine tastings, where there are a large number of wines to be sampled, the practice is to roll the wine around in your mouth and then spit it out. There's no need to do this with only eight wines, which is all you should attempt to taste. There is a limit to the number of wines a nonprofessional can try successfully at one session. As the average serving is 1½ to 2 ounces from each bottle, eight bottles will be sufficient for up to sixteen people, allowing for about half a bottle per person.

Don't try to taste a whole bunch of different wines; stick to those from one country or one area of a country that produces a great many wines. A wine tasting is for purposes of comparison, to judge the product of one château against another, or the white wines of the Rhine and Moselle against those of Alsace. So have an all-Bordeaux or all-Burgundy tasting, a group of representative whites and reds from Italy or Switzerland, eight wines from different vintners in the Livermore valley and Napa and Sonoma valleys of California or the vintners of New York State. Furnish your guests with pads and pencils so they can jot down their reactions and, after the tasting, offer coffee and cognac, to be sipped while everyone comments on the wines and compares notes.

ARRANGING THE TASTING TABLE

To set up your wine tasting, space out the bottles, in the order of tasting, on a large table covered with a white cloth. Put the whites first, starting with the light and brisk and going on to the richer and fuller. Follow with the reds, beginning with the lightest and least important and progressing to the greater. If you want to include champagnes, have them first or last. Then group the glasses in front of the bottles. The best glass for wine tasting is the large-bowled, all-purpose wine glass shown on page 233, which allows the taster to swirl the wine around and get the full fragrance of the bouquet. This glass will also serve for sparkling wines, but the long slim flutes that hold the bubbles are pleasanter to sip from.

You do not have to provide a separate glass for each wine, although it is nice to have two glasses per person if you are tasting both whites and reds. Instead, place several rinse bowls of water on the table so that the tasters can rinse their glasses after each wine. If this idea does not appeal to you, you can always borrow extra glasses from your wine-drinking friends, or even rent them for the evening. Provide something to clear the palate between wines—cubes of a mild cheese like Gruyère or cheddar, and pieces of French bread, breadsticks or plain unsalted crackers are best. Cheese does not help the flavor of white wines, but it makes an excellent foil for reds.

READYING THE WINES

Temperature is important if you are to get the most from a wine. Bring reds to the room where they will be served several hours ahead of time and remove the corks an hour before the tasting. When you uncork the bottles, place the corks beside them. True connoisseurs like to sniff the cork to get an idea of the condition and bouquet of the wine. White and sparkling wines should be chilled but not too icy or they will lose their flavor and taste flat. Push the bottles into wine coolers or buckets filled with ice and chill about fifteen minutes, turning occasionally to cool evenly. Or chill in the refrigerator for two hours.

TASTING THE WINES

There are three things to note about a wine: color, bouquet and taste. Pour 1½ to 2 ounces of wine into the glass (you don't have to measure, just estimate by the eye) and hold it up to the light. Is the color clear and brilliant or dull? Then roll the wine around in the glass, put your nose in the glass and sniff deeply. Does the wine have a delicate bouquet, a rich fragrance, or none at all? If the wine was made from one of the great grape varieties such as Pinot Chardonnay or Cabernet Sauvignon from which white Burgundies and red Bordeaux are made, can you detect the characteristic fragrance of the grape? Now take a sip and roll it around your mouth and over your tongue where it will come into contact with your taste buds. If you can, suck air through your lips and let it swirl through the wine, a professional's trick that points up the flavor. Finally, swallow slowly, carefully noting the body, the smoothness of the wine and the aftertaste, if any. Did the wine have a light rippling feeling in your mouth and throat, or was it round and full-bodied? Was it thin and watery? Did it have a smooth quality or was it harsh? How was the flavor—subtle or direct, delicate or rich? If the wine had an aftertaste, was it pleasing or unpleasing? When tasting white wines, consider whether the wine was flowery and a little sweet or dry, even flinty dry. Was it light, round or full? Remember, you are tasting for yourself, in order to find a wine you might like to drink regularly. So do not be unduly influenced by the opinions of the other tasters, no matter how expert. The best wine for you is the one you like best.

CHAMPAGNE, ARISTOCRAT OF WINES

"I'm only a beer teetotaller, not a champagne teetotaller," says Prossie in *Candida*, and most of us would echo that sentiment. Champagne is the supreme sparkling wine of the world. No other drink carries such a connotation of glamour and gaiety, elegance and luxury. Perhaps because of this it is usually limited to receptions, New Year's Eve and other gala occasions, which does a great disservice to a very versatile and delightful wine. Champagne is a drink for any hour, it goes with many foods and it mixes well with spirits, various fruits and flavorings and also with some pretty unexpected beverages—such as with Guinness stout, in a Black Velvet, and with fresh, cold orange juice, for California Sunshine.

If you are feeling liberal, there's really nothing better than a champagne party, and provided you serve a good American champagne or a nonvintage French champagne, it really runs you little more than the cost of a cocktail party—and you don't have all the bother of providing lots of bottles and mixing drinks all evening. Or you may prefer to serve champagne as an aperitif before a very fine dinner, as the real wine connoisseurs do, or with just one course of the meal. A bottle of champagne goes farther and fares better if it

is served with a first course of caviar, smoked salmon, oysters and other shellfish, or pâté: or as an accompaniment to a main course of roast pork or ham, cold pheasant or quail, all of which welcome its fine, dry acidity. Even little hot sausages and *choucroute garnie*, definitely bourgeois dishes, are quite at home with this aristocratic wine, so perfect with any kind of pork. And like most aristocrats, it goes on a picnic with perfect aplomb—the Edwardian fashion of feasting on a cold bird and a bottle of bubbly has yet to be bettered for outdoor eating.

Most champagne is made from a blend of black and white grapes, the former giving the wine body and the latter producing finesse and delicacy. Lately, people who like a very light, dry and delicate wine have started to drink a *blanc de blancs* champagne, which is made from white grapes only. Then there is champagne rosé or pink champagne, made either by leaving the black grapes in contact with the newly made wine long enough to allow their skins to tint the grape juice, or by carefully blending in a little red wine made from the same grape.

Vintage champagne, a blend of the wines of a single year, is more expensive than nonvintage, a mixture of wines of more than one year, but the common belief that the word "nonvintage" implies inferior quality is mistaken. While there have been some great vintage years (and a vintage is not declared unless the characteristics of that year's harvest are considered worth preserving), the quality of champagne depends on the excellence of the wines used by each house in their blends. A nonvintage wine from a top house will probably be much better than a vintage from some company you've never heard of. A number of the top French houses now produce some very deluxe—and correspondingly expensive—champagnes in addition to their vintage and nonvintage champagnes. These usually have names such as Dom Pérignon, Florens-Louis, Grand Siècle, Cristal Brut, Reserve de l'Empereur in addition to the vintage year and the name of the house. In each case, the wine is the finest cuvée, or blend, the house can offer and is therefore available only in limited quantities. These wines should be served on very special occasions that merit their superb quality—a birthday, an anniversary, perhaps, or a dinner to celebrate some very important occasion.

When it comes to serving champagne, remember that a sparkling wine is a delicate wine that should be drunk refreshingly cool but not so cold that you can neither smell nor taste it. The exception is the slightly sweet champagne that you would serve with dessert. These are better really cold, to tone down their honeyed quality, but the brut champagnes should not be over-chilled. Cool champagne just as you would white wine.

HOW TO OPEN CHAMPAGNE

First, unwind twisted end or wire cap over cork. Second, loosen wire cap and foil covering and remove. Third, tilt bottle at slight angle. Protecting hand with napkin, twist cork toward you, turning bottle clockwise with other hand.

MIEHLMANN

Continue to twist gently. As cork nears top of neck, pressure of gases inside will force it out. To pour, grasp center of bottle, with index finger on neck to give control. Pour slowly so wine does not foam up. As you stop pouring, turn the bottle to the right to prevent drips.

Opening the bottle is not difficult, but there is a knack to it, which is shown step-by-step in the pictures just above. You'll notice that the cork is not pressed up with the thumbs so that it flies out with a loud pop (a method that often causes some of the contents to fly out too, as well as exposing guests to the hazards of a flying cork), but gently twisted so the cork is gradually forced out by the pressure of gases.

Leftover champagne, in the unlikely event that you have any, presents no problem. It will keep its sparkle for twenty-four hours and not go flat if you immediately recork it, either with one of the special metal-and-rubber stoppers now on the market or by cutting a small wedge out the base of the champagne cork so you can squeeze it back into the bottle. It should, of course, be put in the refrigerator and if you don't want to drink it you can always use it in cooking, just as you would white wine. A champagne sauce for fish has a glorious delicacy.

CHAMPAGNE PUNCHES FOR WEDDINGS AND BIG PARTIES

Champagne, of course, is the preferred drink for weddings, just as it is for other joyous celebrations. When you choose a champagne for a wedding, be sure to select the brut, the dryest of all. Champagnes do vary in flavor and dryness so, unless you have a favorite of your own, shop around and try a few bottles from different companies until you find the one you think best. To estimate the amount you will need, figure on getting six drinks from each bottle. As many guests will want more than one or two glasses, it is wise to figure that you will need about half to three-quarters of a bottle per person.

If you would rather serve a champagne punch, which has the merit of stretching the supply when you have a huge guest list, there are various types from which you can choose, some rather more alcoholic than others. Here are three excellent ones.

CHAMPAGNE-SHERBET PUNCH

Combine 3 bottles well-chilled dry champagne and 1 quart lemon, raspberry, strawberry or cassis sherbet in a well-chilled silver or crystal punch bowl. Garnish with fruit: with lemon sherbet, lemon and orange slices; for raspberry, a few strawberries; for strawberry or cassis, strawberries and orange slices. The sherbet should be icy cold, but not frozen into a hard block or it will not blend. Serve in punch cups. This makes about 30-35 servings.

CHAMPAGNE-ORANGE PUNCH

Combine 2 quarts orange sherbet or 3 to 4 undiluted cans frozen orange juice concentrate, 3 bottles well-chilled champagne and 1 cup chilled Grand Marnier in an ice-cold punch bowl. Garnish with orange slices. Makes about 40 servings. If you use the frozen orange juice concentrate, you may need an extra bottle of champagne. For a brisker drink, add lemon or lime juice concentrate to taste; for a more alcoholic one, more Grand Marnier and a cup of cognac.

CHAMPAGNE-COGNAC PUNCH

Cut the peel from 2 lemons and 1 orange in long thin spirals with a sharp paring knife or the gadget called a stripper. Place in a chilled punch bowl with a large block of ice. Add ½ cup sugar, 1 bottle cognac, 2 cups water and a good dash of Angostura bitters. Blend well and, just before serving, add 4 bottles chilled champagne, either extradry or brut. This recipe makes about 35 to 40 servings.

DRINKS FOR BIG PARTIES

For parties on a grand scale other than weddings, where you may want to serve a stronger drink, choose a punch with a spirit base—cognac, rum, whiskey. Some of the best, such as Fish House Punch and Artillery Punch contain tea and, to guard against the weakening of the punch by melting ice, freeze the tea, which is nonalcoholic, into a block and use this as the chiller. (Don't try freezing anything containing wines and spirits though, or you'll end up with nothing but a liquid mess.) Select your punch and make a complete analysis of the ingredients some days before the party. Make up a batch of the essential liquors and flavorings and then try out some of this batch, adding the perishable and dilutive ingredients (tea, fruit juices, fruit) to see if they blend properly. If all seems well, mix several large pitchers of the basic spine of the punch and other pitchers containing the other ingredients and keep them all cold, ready for last-minute blending at party time. For measuring quantities, estimate 3 to 4 glasses of punch per guest. Tea, fruit juices and ginger ale can be put in round or square waxed cardboard containers and frozen, but don't use too much or they will overpower the spirits.

Martinis can be made ahead of time and dispensed like punch—perhaps from a huge glass bowl set in an ice-packed bowl. First mix the gin and vermouth in the desired proportions, pour the mixture into half-gallon bottles and chill in the refrigerator until icy.

Another good wholesale dispensable is the Bloody Mary. Prepare several jugs of a 4- or 5-to-1 mixture of tomato juice and vodka seasoned with Tabasco, lemon juice, salt, and Worcestershire sauce. Freeze more tomato juice in chunks or cubes, chill the Bloody Mary mixture and serve in a punch bowl with a tomato-ice block or in pitchers with tomato cubes. Keep a bottle of vodka, frozen in a block of ice, near at hand for pepping up the mixture. For bull shots, use frozen beef bouillon in place of the tomato juice and serve in the same manner.

Mass-produced daiquiris can also be good, provided they are properly mixed and not merely weak rum punches. Use fresh lime juice and a judicious amount of sugar syrup or Falernum for the sweetening and chill the mixture thoroughly. Serve from a bowl or jug packed in ice and pour into chilled glasses or punch cups. An excellent summer refreshment is an old Tahitian rum drink. A day ahead of the party, insert one vanilla bean in each bottle of light or medium rum and chill well. At party time, transfer the bottles to ice buckets, pour a measure of the cold, delicately vanilla-flavored rum into glasses over crushed ice and add a slice of lime.

As an alternative to cocktails and punches, it is sometimes fun for a big gathering to serve pitchers of the Spanish wine drink sangria, spritzers (chilled white wine and soda), Kir (white wine flavored with crème de cassis or cassis syrup), chilled manzanilla (a bone-dry type of Spanish sherry) or, for a very informal backyard barbecue in summer, shandygaff, that nostalgic British pub combination of beer with lemonade, ginger beer or ginger ale. Any of these drinks can be put in pitchers or bowls for easy self-service.

DRINKS FOR BREAKFAST AND BRUNCH PARTIES

Oddly enough, the choice of drinks for breakfast or brunch parties is greater than for others. First, there are the mixtures of juice and vodka—Bloody Mary, bull shot, screwdriver, salty dog and all their many off-shoots—and the sours, made with lemon juice, sweetening and different spirits such as whiskey, cognac, tequila, pisco, rum. Next, the aperitifs, like Lillet, Positano, St-Raphaël, Byrrh, Campari, Punt e Mes, Dubonnet, Chambraise, La Seine and the vermouths, light enough to go down easily, yet potent enough to give a small delicious glow. These should be served chilled, over ice, either straight or, for those who like a long drink, with chilled club soda. Twists of orange and lemon peel give them color and zest. Last, and least alcoholic, are the wine drinks, made with red or white wines or champagne: Kir, California Sunshine, sangria, spritzer or, in summer when you can get fresh peaches, the ambrosial Bellini invented at Harry's Bar in Venice. For this you puree fresh peaches in the blender with a little water, combine the puree with sugar and lemon juice to taste, before it has a chance to darken, and then serve 1 part peach puree to 3 parts champagne in a wine glass.

PUSSYFOOT DRINKS FOR TEETOTALLERS AND TEENAGERS

At every party, there will always be some guests who, for their own good reasons, are off the hard stuff. Certainly, if it is a mixed party of adults and teenagers, or a children's party, you'll want to have a repertoire of interesting, varied nonalcoholic drinks to tempt all age and taste groups. Both adults and children will bless you if you come up with something more imaginative than a glass of tomato juice poured straight from the can, or that ludicrous emulation of Daddy's cocktail, a Shirley Temple.

First, keep good bottled drinks in the refrigerator, ready to serve. Perrier, the brisk, naturally carbonated water from France, where it is often called "the poor man's champagne," is both bracing and refreshing. Serve it chilled, with a slice of lemon for extra zip. Ginger beer, the English specialty, has a pleasantly hot gingery taste on the tongue, quite different from oversweet ginger ale. If you do serve ginger ale, look around for one that is on the dry side with a good gingery tang. Another good choice is Meier's Catawba, a sparkling American grape juice with a fresh fruit flavor. Serve it plain, well-chilled, or combine it with other fruit juices. Soda water with a dash of bitters, or tonic water and bitters should also be on your list of refreshing simple-to-serve drinks.

A good brand of instant tea, soluble in both cold and hot water, is an excellent nonalcoholic bracer. For variations, add slices of fresh lime; lemon slices studded with cloves; strips of orange or lemon peel; fresh mint. You can make a delicious Tea Bowl by brewing a quart of strong tea, letting it get cold and then pouring it into tall glasses over ice cubes and adding a lemon slice, an orange slice, sugar to taste and a sprig of fresh mint to each glass. Or, for a delightfully cool and different summer drink, steep 1 bunch of fresh mint or $\frac{2}{3}$ ounce of dried mint in 2 cups of boiling water for 30 minutes, putting it in the top of a double boiler over hot water. Strain, and combine the liquid with 1 quart cold water and sugar to taste. Pour into tall glasses filled with ice cubes and garnish with lemon peel and a sprig of fresh mint dusted with powdered sugar. The French call this mint tea, although there is no tea in it. Or try serving strong coffee over crushed ice, flavored with sugar and a lemon twist, like an iced espresso.

Citrus fruits always make refreshing nonalcoholic drinks. One is that perennial favorite, lemonade. To make perfect lemonade, for each drink combine the freshly squeezed juice of 1 lemon with sugar to taste (a scant teaspoon should be sufficient) and stir until blended. Add 1 cup sparkling or plain water and stir. Serve over ice in tall glasses. To vary this, add any of the following flavorings: $\frac{1}{2}$ cup of grape juice; a jigger of cassis, cherry or raspberry syrup in place of the sugar; $\frac{1}{2}$ cup apple juice instead of water. For perfect limeade, use lime juice in place of lemon.

A popular fruit drink with the younger set is Orange Milk. For this, remove the zest from 2 oranges and place the strips in a deep bowl. Pour on 1 pint boiling milk. Cover and steep for 15 minutes. Add $1\frac{1}{2}$-to-2 tablespoons sugar and stir until blended. Chill and serve very cold. Finally, a more sophisticated drink for the young, the Pussyfoot. Pour pale ginger ale over ice in a highball or large old-fashioned glass and add a few drops of grenadine. Garnish with lemon peel, a thin half slice of orange and, if you like, a maraschino cherry.

To keep the nonalcoholic drinks flowing at a big party: a self-service setup in Victorian basins and ewers. Lemonade or Tea Bowl poured over ice in basins is replenished from fresh supplies in ewers. Glasses nest in center basin of ice.

HOW TO PLAN MEMORABLE MEALS

There's more to planning a menu than ordering half a pound of caviar and a prime rib roast or looking up recipes in a cookbook. Menu planning is a creative activity, as creative in its way as writing a play or composing a symphony, for, like other works of art, it depends for its success on a judicious balance of the various elements that mesh to form a harmonious whole.

What goes into the making of a memorable meal? Many things. A play of flavors and textures, shapes and colors that are a pleasure to the eye and the palate. A balance of courses—neither a surfeit of rich heavy foods nor a meal that is unsatisfyingly lightweight. An element of the unexpected to stimulate appetite, heighten appreciation. An awareness of what is appropriate—to the season, the occasion, or the guests. A word of caution, though. If you are doing the cooking yourself, keep the menu within your capabilities. Don't attempt an elaborate dessert or a complicated main dish unless you can really handle it, and never cook a new recipe for guests the very first time. Try it on the family beforehand, where an occasional failure won't matter.

A PLAY OF FLAVORS AND TEXTURES. Choose foods that both contrast with and complement each other. For example, team the crisp creaminess of an onion quiche with the red-meat robustness of roast beef, the colorful crunchiness of green beans and slivered almonds with a suavely sauced fillet of sole. Foods should look well together and when they do, they are apt to taste equally good. Nothing is duller than a meal where everything is one color or of a similar consistency. You wouldn't want to serve creamed chicken after a cream soup and follow that with crème brûlée; all good dishes on their own, but in sequence just too rich, bland and repetitious for words. Instead, the first course might be piquant shrimps à la Grecque or a hot consommé spiked with sherry, the dessert fresh peaches with raspberry sauce or pineapple with kirsch. A good menu should vary flavors and textures from bland to spicy, tart to sweet, soft to crisp, smooth to chewy.

A PLAY OF SHAPES AND COLORS. It goes without saying that a plate or platter should be a temptation to the eye. Never load a plate with food. It looks unattractive and one thing cancels another out. Instead devise interesting ways to serve small individual portions of accompaniments—put cranberry sauce for turkey in a scooped-out orange shell, cucumber salad for salmon in a lemon basket, pipe a vegetable puree into an artichoke bottom. Plan your vegetables so you don't serve two white types at one time, such as cauliflower and mashed potatoes. Either team the potatoes with broccoli or else make potatoes Anna, baked to a crusty brown. Give a dish a quirk of accent color—a thin slice of lemon afloat in a cup of black bean soup, a sprig of watercress in consommé or a streak of red cabbage in a coleslaw.

A BALANCE OF COURSES. Follow a hearty entrée with the merest whisper of dessert, such as an ethereal lemon soufflé, but after a light main course bring on a luscious rum-soaked gateau, a pastry confection or a mound of chocolate mousse.

AN ELEMENT OF THE UNEXPECTED. If the entrée is duck, don't stop thinking once you have arrived at orange sauce or black cherries. This time, try peaches, or figs, or even a spiced lemon compote. Be enterprising about starches. Instead of the eternal potatoes, serve kasha, chick-pea purees, even a pasta—it doesn't matter if the main dish isn't Italian. Create intriguing taste jolts by combining hot and cold foods—pass piping hot popovers with iced Senegalese soup, spoon flambéed fruits over ice cream, chilled sour cream or a hot compote.

AN AWARENESS OF WHAT IS APPROPRIATE. Let the beef at your black-tie dinner be Wellington rather than ragout. Serve an airy cheese soufflé for a summer luncheon rather than a heavy and caloric dish. If some of your guests are dieting, serve asparagus or artichokes as a first course, with a choice of a decalorized vinaigrette sauce or hollandaise for those who aren't weight-watching. Cash in on seasonal delights—shad roe or sorrel puree in spring; fresh tomato soup, corn fritters and blueberry cobbler in summer; game in fall and winter.

To start you thinking, study the menus on the following pages. All were planned for occasions illustrated in this book. These are not intended as rigid formulas, but as ideas to inspire you to create your own memorable menus. Should you want to try them, the recipes may be found in any of the good standard cookbooks.

BEAUTIFUL BREAKFAST/BRUNCH

2 SUNDAY BRUNCHES

Melon with port

Charcoal-broiled ham steaks

Zucchini frittata

Tomato salad

Warm brioches
with preserves and cream cheese

Champagne

Coffee Iced tea

Platter of Scotch salmon and sturgeon,
garnished with sliced Bermuda onion,
lemon, parsley, capers

Assorted cheeses and crackers

Chive-cheese scrambled eggs

Coffee

Wine: Gewürtztraminer

OPEN HOUSE BUFFET BRUNCH

Choice of juices (orange, grapefruit,
pineapple, apple, cranberry)
with pitcher of vodka for spiking

Omelets or scrambled eggs

Sautéed chicken livers
with onions and apples

French toast with maple syrup, fruit
preserves, cinnamon and sugar
sour cream

Coffee

Wine: Saumur

LATE MORNING BREAKFAST

Melon with ginger
or with mint and lime or lemon

Scalloped oysters

Warm crusty French bread

Lemon marmalade

Coffee

Wine: Muscadet

HUNT BREAKFAST

Toddies, hot and cold

Chicken hashed in cream

Baked Virginia ham

Baking-powder biscuits

Apples Camembert with walnuts

Coffee

Wine: Beaujolais

COLD WEATHER BRUNCH

Creamed chicken hash rolled
in giant pancakes

Poached eggs on Virginia ham

English muffins Assorted jams

Sliced grapefruit and oranges

Coffee

English tea with lemon

Wine: California Pinot Noir

MIDSUMMER BRUNCH

Chicken livers and bacon en brochette

London Broil Mushrooms in foil

Roast potatoes

Toasted bread Preserves

Breakfast cheese or Brie

Coffee

Wine: Barolo

BRUNCH COOKED
AT THE TABLE

Sautéed bananas or pineapple with
orange juice and julienne orange peel

Scrambled eggs with oysters

Hot buttered scones Crab apple jelly

Coffee

Wine: Pouilly-Fuissé

BREAKFAST AT BRENNAN'S

(a facsimile)

Eggs Tennessee Williams
(shirred eggs with chopped mushrooms,
ham, diced deep-fried potatoes)

Brioches

Café filtre

Wine: Vin rosé

French-quarter touches for "brunch at Brennan's": eggs in individual covered casseroles, individual cafés filtres, brioches in an outsize brioche mold, butter in French bistro dishes.

GARDEN BREAKFAST
FOR 20-30 PEOPLE

Prosciutto with figs or melon

Omelets with a choice of fillings

Cold sliced steak with choice of mustards

Baked tomatoes with sautéed mushrooms

French bread Small brioches

Butter Cream cheese

Strawberries glacé

Coffee

Wine: Champagne

LUNCHEON PARTIES

FESTIVE WEEKEND LUNCH

Melon cocktail with port wine

Sole poached in vermouth and Madeira

Steamed rice

Salad of lettuce and raw zucchini,
oil and vinegar dressing

Poached pears with custard sauce

Wine: Chablis

COUNTRY LUNCH

Eggs Clamart (poached eggs
in puree of green peas)

Cold roast beef

Greens salad with French dressing

Mocha soufflé

Wine: California Pinot Noir

ITALIAN LUNCH

Antipasto

Eggplant Parmesan

Rugula salad

Chocolate and almond cake

Wine: Decanters of Valpolicella
and Soave

LUNCH WITH A
MEXICAN FLAVOR

Chiles rellenos

White rice

Guacamole salad

Mango sherbet

Cold punch

ONE-DISH LUNCH

Truites à la gelée with cucumbers
and green sauce

Strawberries
with brown sugar and sour cream

Crisp cookies

Wine: California Mountain White

Truites à la gelée adorned with lily of the valley flowers cut from hard-cooked egg white, leaves of blanched tarragon. Cups cut from cucumbers could hold the sauce.

COMMITTEE MAKE-YOUR-OWN-SANDWICH LUNCH

Platters of sliced chicken, ham, cheese, hard-cooked egg, tomatoes, crisp bacon, sardines

Mayonnaise Mustard

Freshly-made toast

Crusted breads—
white, rye, whole wheat, pumpernickel

Bowl of fresh fruit

Wine: Sherry

BUSINESS LUNCH FOR 4

Cold vichyssoise

Toasted crackers

Striped bass, charcoal-broiled, mushroom and wine sauce

Parsleyed potatoes

Greens salad

Orange soufflé

Wine: Pouilly-Fumé

LUNCHEON FOR THE LADIES

Gazpacho with garnishes in sake cups: chopped onion, pepper, cucumber

Mushroom quiche

Fruit compote or melon balls

Wine: Alsatian or California Riesling

Gazpacho with garnishes in sake cups teamed with piping hot quiche.

COLD WEATHER LUNCH

Mushroom consommé Cheese Straws

Chicken Provençal

Fondant potatoes

Endive salad

Orange slices in kirsch

Wine: Château-bottled Bordeaux

LIGHT COLD WEATHER LUNCH

Lobster bisque

Cheese soufflé

Greens salad French bread

Crème brûlée

Wine: Vouvray

WARM WEATHER LUNCH

Asparagus vinaigrette

Broiled lobster tails Rice

Greens salad

Peach and blueberry brûlé

Wine: Vinho verde

LIGHT SUMMER LUNCH

Salade Niçoise with oil and vinegar

Grissini

Strawberry ice with raspberry sauce

Macaroons

Wine: Sangria

Salade Niçoise rates as a meal in itself. Arrange ingredients in an appropriately rustic bowl, pour dressing from a pottery pitcher.

KLAPHOLZ

GALA DINNERS

CELEBRATION DINNER
FOR 8

Tiny oysters Brown bread, buttered

Chateaubriand, Armagnac and truffle sauce

Belgian carrots and salsify

Salad of rugula, Boston lettuce, watercress, fresh chives

Cheese: Chèvre

Fruit with kirsch Vanilla meringues

Wines: Pouilly-Fumé
Château-bottled Bordeaux

CELEBRATION DINNER
FOR 2

Volga artichokes Rye whirls

Lemon steak Crunchy new potatoes

Tossed greens salad

Individual almond cheesecakes

Wine: Red Burgundy or California Pinot Noir

FISHERMAN'S DINNER

Avocado Bristol fashion (stuffed with crabmeat laced with dry sherry)

Poached salmon, hollandaise sauce

Fresh asparagus

Cucumber salad with chopped dill

Fresh blueberries

Wine: Chablis

BUCKS COUNTY DINNER

Oyster bisque

Roast loin of hickory-smoked pork

Horseradish-applesauce

Corn pudding

Salad of fresh spinach or dandelion greens with oil and vinegar dressing

Maple ice cream with oatmeal cookies

Wine: Champagne

ITALIAN DINNER

Melon with prosciutto

Shrimp, scampi style Fettucini

Broiled eggplant slices

Garlic olives and cherry tomatoes

Zabaglione

Wine: Soave

GOLDSMITH

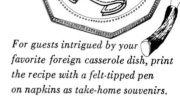

For guests intrigued by your favorite foreign casserole dish, print the recipe with a felt-tipped pen on napkins as take-home souvenirs.

DINNER IN A CASSEROLE

Swiss lentil casserole

Crusty French bread

Mixed greens salad with sliced raw mushrooms and avocado crescents

Lemon ice with crème de menthe

Sponge cake

Wine: California Zinfandel

SOUP DINNER
Served in living room

Hearty black bean soup with thin lemon slices, sliced hard-boiled egg

Hard rolls Salt sticks

Compote of fresh fruit—oranges and grapefruit with thin slices of ginger

Wine: Red Rioja

SOUTHERN-STYLE DINNER

Shrimp biscuits Sazeracs

Grilled ham steaks Hominy spoon bread

Charcoal-roasted onions

Coleslaw

Broiled pineapple slices

Wine: Vin rosé

WORKING-WIFE DINNER
FOR 4

Served in cups in living room

Clear turtle soup with Madeira

Served in dining room

Chateaubriand broiled with mushrooms

Pommes soufflés

Gateau St. Honoré

Wines: Rainwater Madeira, Burgundy

---

2 COLD WEATHER DINNERS

Bluepoints on the half-shell

Homemade thin mushroom soup

Charcoal beef tenderloin

Creamed celery and almonds

Glazed carrots, peas and artichoke bottoms

Strawberry Bavarian cream

Wines: Muscadet, Hermitage

Jellied madrilene
Pheasant baked in casserole   Wild rice
Lettuce, shredded beets,
and chopped celery-root salad
Vanilla ice cream
with mandarin oranges in Cointreau
Wine: Château-bottled Bordeaux

2 SUMMER DINNERS
Sliced honeydew melon
on thinly sliced Smithfield ham
Fish aspic with dill sauce
Beef à la Pernette   Buttered noodles
Celery with water chestnuts
and buttered almonds
Hot buttered rolls
Ice cream and raspberries
in meringue nests
Wine: Chablis, Red Burgundy

*A whole salmon in aspic to grace your
table. Decorate with flowers cut from
carrots and truffles, tarragon leaves.*

Melon and prosciutto
Veal scalloppini
with mushrooms and tomatoes
Hot French or garlic bread
Mixed greens salad
Fresh strawberries with sweet cream
Wine: Sancerre

BLACK-TIE DINNER FOR 6
Beef roulades   Homemade Melba toast
Baked red snapper with corn
bread stuffing, hot shrimp sauce
Fresh asparagus
Flan garnished with
oranges and strawberries
Wine: White Burgundy

BLACK-TIE DINNER FOR 12
Crudités: Greek olives,
raw zucchini with Lawry's seasoned salt,
pickled celery sticks
Salmon mousse de Beauzon in
cucumber shells, sauce verte
Filet Mignon, garnished with artichoke
bottoms, mushroom caps, parsley
Roasted new potatoes   Green peas
Salad of watercress, endive, cherry
tomatoes, iceberg and romaine lettuce
Cherries à la Russe
Wine: Johannisberg Riesling,
Château-bottled Bordeaux

COFFEE PARTIES

2 MIDMORNING COMMITTEE
COFFEES
Bite-size muffins
Bacon wrapped around bread
sticks, broiled
Coffee

Cheese biscuits
Orange sticks
Coffee

3 COFFEE RECEPTIONS
Watercress rolls
Ham biscuits
Water chestnuts and chicken livers
in bacon
Candied kumquats on sticks
Salted almonds
Irish coffee

Thin-sliced and buttered pumpernickel
Pigs-in-blankets (tiny sausages in pastry)
Melba toast rounds topped with peanut
butter and bacon
Cinnamon rolls
Mélange of melon balls
sprinkled with lemon juice
Coffee

Tiny baking-powder biscuits
topped with creamed chipped beef
Pint-size rolls stuffed with crisp bacon
Holes of the doughnuts, heated
Toasted and buttered pound cake
Coffee

4 AFTERNOON COFFEES
Frozen fruit salad
Toasted cheese canapés
Coffee

Cherry gelatin ring filled
with fresh fruit soaked in kirsch
Orange cake loaf
Coffee

Lemon sherbet in hollowed lemons
Almond cookies
Coffee

Peaches in champagne
Coffee

6 EVENING COFFEES
Brandied coffee mousse
Coffee   Brandy   Liqueurs

Fruit tart (black and white grapes
arranged in alternating circles
in fluted pastry shell)
Champagne   Coffee

Tray of assorted cheeses
Crisp crackers
French bread sliced thin and buttered
Salami rolls
Salted almonds
Highballs   Coffee

Choice of liqueurs:
Cherry brandy   Crème de menthe
B&B   Drambuie   Chartreuse
Nuts and raisins
Café espresso

Pêches Melba
(molded ice cream surrounded by
whole poached peaches, fresh raspberries)
Tiny cookies
Coffee   Champagne

*Diva's dessert—molded ice cream in a
silver bowl, surrounded by whole
poached peaches. In small
baskets, fresh raspberries and cookies.*

Tortoni tart   Pastries
Café diable
Champagne   Liqueurs

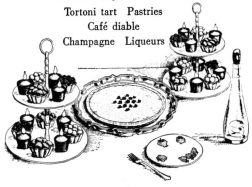

*Dessert "spectacle": Tortoni tart on a
silver dish, flanked by epergnes
bearing lighted votive candles
and berries to be sprinkled with kirsch.*

*Brandied coffee mousse, left, served in
crystal brandy snifters, coffee
bean candies sprinkled around the base.*

TEA PARTIES

HEARTY TEA IN COLD WEATHER
Cream cheese and chopped bacon sandwiches

Split and toasted English muffins
Jam   Honey

Rounds of bread topped with a seasoned slice of tomato, mayonnaise and parsley

Broiled buttered doughnut halves sprinkled with cinnamon

Hot tea   Lemon slices   Heavy cream
Decanter of sherry

ICED TEA IN WARM WEATHER
Chilled mold of cottage cheese, circled with drawn figs, mint leaves

Piping hot popovers

Iced tea with orange slice and fresh mint

2 MIDMORNING TEAS
Crisp strips of thin bacon
(to be eaten by hand)

Toast with honey

Double-strength hot tea

Thin orange slices on toast rounds, sprinkled with cinnamon-sugar, broiled

Spiced hot tea, flavored with citrus peel and spices

TEA AFTER CARDS
Curried chicken sandwiches

Cream cheese and fresh chopped tarragon sandwiches on sour rye bread

Hot cinnamon toast

Buttered toasted protein bread
Marmalade

Small fresh raspberry tarts

Hot tea

Iced tea with honey and fresh mint

TEA IN THE GARDEN
Tiny profiteroles filled with egg salad
Rolled chicken-salad sandwiches
Paper-thin ham sandwiches
Cold sliced apples on crushed ice
Slender slices of Lady Baltimore cake
Devil's food cake squares
Imported English tea

HIGH TEA IN WARM WEATHER
Rolled tuna sandwiches, asparagus tips at each end

Chopped hard-cooked egg and bacon mixture on thin sliced rye bread

Whole sugared strawberries on crushed ice

Fresh cherries in a bowl of cracked ice

Cookies   Orange cake with orange icing

Hot tea of imported loose tea leaves

Cloved lemon slices   Cream

Iced tea with orange juice, served with orange and lemon slices, fresh mint

HIGH TEA IN COLD WEATHER
Assorted tea sandwiches:
thin-sliced cucumbers on white bread, chopped watercress rolled in white bread, hot Smithfield ham on tiny baking-powder biscuits

Cinnamon toast (in bite-size triangles)

Miniature doughnuts dipped in sugar crystals, served warm

Butter cookies

Tiny gingerbread squares

Imported tea, rum for spiking

Coffee

RUSSIAN TEA
(for after-ski or late evening gatherings)
Russian Kulich (traditional fruity yeast cake cut crossways in thin slices)

Russian tea served in glasses

Choice of jam, honey, rum to flavor tea

VERSATILE COCKTAIL PARTIES

2 COCKTAIL PARTIES FOR 6-12
Cold lobster chunks on toast, dab of mustard on top

Hot stuffed mushrooms

Curried chicken spread on toast

Tiny sausages in pastry

Cherry tomatoes stuffed with pâté de foie gras, crumbled bacon on top

One-bite cream-puff shells, crabmeat salad filling

Tiny hot hamburgers, chili sauce on top

Sliced smoked turkey on buttered pumpernickel bread

COCKTAIL PARTY FOR 14 OR MORE
Stewed prunes wrapped in crisp bacon

Large brioche slices spread with pâté de foie gras
(large loaf sliced and spread with pâté, then put together as loaf)

Caviar on ice, surrounded by toast squares, lemon slices

Eggs stuffed with mushrooms

Platter of crudités:
celery, carrot and pepper sticks, cauliflowerets, cherry tomatoes, thin slices of zucchini, vinaigrette sauce in center

Platter of Swiss cheese spears, large bunch of fresh grapes in center

Served at 8:30

Onion soup   Hot buttered toast

4 MINI-COCKTAIL PARTIES FOR 4-6 PEOPLE
Crudités

Melba rounds with broiled mushroom cap on top

Melba rounds with hard-boiled egg slices topped with red caviar and dab of sour cream

Crudités

Toasted cheese rolls

Olives, water chestnuts rolled in bacon

Triscuits spread lightly with butter, sprinkled with salt, run under the broiler

Crudités

Tiny beaten biscuits, split, filled with sliced Virginia ham

Salted almonds

Crudités

Toasted peanut butter and bacon rounds (great favorite with men)

Little gherkins

Salted watermelon seeds

END-OF-SEASON COCKTAIL BUFFET
Tiny pizzas

Crudités with flavored mayonnaises

Cooled sirloin roast or stuffed double loin of pork

Mustards   Horseradish   Relishes

Thin sliced white and whole wheat breads, buttered

Small ears of hot corn with pepper, butter

Scallops seviche

Coffee

Wine: Vin rosé

Striped awning shelters tempting local foods at end-of-season party. Crudités nest in straw bowl, corn on a corn-patterned platter.

CHEESE AND SAUSAGE COCKTAIL PARTY
"Tree" of sausages and skewered vegetables

Sausages: cervelat, pepperoni, Genoa salami, braunschweiger

Vegetables: mushrooms, pickled onions, cherry tomatoes

Assorted cheese board

Cheese fondue served with squares of French bread

Basket of assorted breads

Crudités tray

Hot kielbasa, sliced on board, served on pumpernickel with hot mustard

DROP-IN COCKTAIL BUFFET
To pass
Tartar steak balls
topped with black caviar
Small fresh tomatoes
surrounding a dish of peppered salt
Tiny soufflèed cheese puffs
in pastry shells
On the buffet
Chicken in wine (coq au vin)
Seafood paella
(a Spanish rice and seafood dish)
Beef Stroganoff with noodles
Fresh peas with onions
Cheese board   Greens salad
Baked fruit compote with sour cream
Assorted cookies
Wines: California Mountain white wine,
California Mountain red wine
Coffee

LARGE COCKTAIL-SUPPER
FOR 80
Oysters, horseradish sauce
Curried bananas and bacon
Cheese rolls
Miniature bacon, tomato
and tillamook cheese sandwiches
Piroshki   Pelmeni
Hot scallops   Fried chicken legs
Crepes with fillings: shrimp and dill,
lobster, chicken
Fresh caviar with capers, onion,
lemon and sour cream
Tartar steak
Banana and apple fritters
Croquembouche   Cookies
Brie   Fruit
Wine: Champagne
Coffee

BOUNTIFUL BUFFETS

INFORMAL BUFFET DINNER
Thinly sliced corned beef
with remoulade sauce and watercress
Zucchini frittata
Salad of Chinese pea pods and shallots
Potato crisps
(potato peels soaked, salted, roasted)
Fresh cherries and Muenster cheese
Wine: Red Rioja

BLACK-TIE BUFFET DINNER
Shrimps Florentine
Cold roast beef
Hot French bread sautéed in garlic butter
Endive and watercress salad
Brie cheese   Assorted crackers
Pink grapefruit sherbet
garnished with seedless grapes
Mocha sticks
Dark roast coffee
Wine: California Cabernet Sauvignon

KITCHEN BUFFET SUPPER
Dill pickle soup
Knockwurst, bratwurst and
kielbasa sausages
Pumpernickel and rye bread
Crock of sweet butter
Mélange of fruit and berries
Coffee cake
Coffee
Cold beer

SUMMER BUFFET LUNCHEON
Jellied consommé
with caviar, sour cream and melon balls
Cucumber sandwiches
Chicken stuffed with noodles,
chicken livers, eggs, and mushrooms
Limestone lettuce salad
Rolls   Croissants
Imported cheeses   Fruit
Hot brownie pudding, vanilla sauce
Coffee   Tea   Sanka
Wine: California Pinot Chardonnay

WINTER BUFFET SUPPER
Crabmeat flambé
Roast duck, Spanish style
Saffron rice
Eggplant salad   Tossed greens salad
Chocolate roll   Compote of pears
Wine: Carafes of California Pinot Noir
and Johannisberg Riesling

LATE EVENING
"AFTER" BUFFET
(After theatre, benefit,
concert or whatever)
Spinach soup with shrimp
Boeuf en gelée
Small hollowed-out beets filled
with horseradish-flavored whipped cream
Hot corn bread
Boston lettuce salad
Assorted cheeses, crackers
Compote of plums, pears, orange, grapes
Orange cake
Wine: Beaujolais

SOUP AND SALAD
BUFFET SUPPER
Mushroom bouillon spiked with sherry
Tuna Sebastian in hollowed-out cabbage
Cheese sticks
Assorted pastries
Wine: Verdicchio

DESSERT BUFFET
Tiered epergne piled with fruit:
strawberries, pears, peaches
Muffineers of confectioners sugar,
brown sugar
Liqueurs to sprinkle on fruit:
Kirsch, Drambuie, Marsala
Coffee   Liqueurs

SALAD BUFFET
Chef's salad   Duck and orange salad
Caesar salad   Tongue and spinach salad
Salade Niçoise   Vegetable salad
Assorted dressings: mayonnaise,
green dressing, oil & vinegar
Choice of breads:
rye, pumpernickel, buttered
Chocolate roll
Coffee

KLAPHOLZ

BUFFET PARTY FOR 200
Shrimp   Crab legs   Lobster
Oysters on half-shell
Mustard sauce   Dill sauce   Red sauce
Shrimp wrapped in bacon
Sweet and sour sauce
Burritos
(kidney bean and chili casserole)
Corn chips, guacamole sauce
Smoked Nova Scotia salmon
with black bread,
capers, cream cheese, thinly sliced onion
rings, cracked black pepper
Baked ham, hot mustard
Stuffed cherry tomatoes
Boned smoked turkey
Tomatoes and
white asparagus vinaigrette
Chicken almond   Oriental rice
Charcoal-broiled fillets of beef
Belgian endive salad
Swedish rye bread with anise
Cheeses:
Le Sanglier   Pont-l'Evêque   Camembert
Imported Brie   Danish Blue
Sesame crackers   Black and rye breads
Fruit:
Fresh pineapple, strawberries,
raspberries, lady apples
Desserts:
Lemon Schumn tortes
Miniature cheesecakes   Oatmeal cookies
Chocolate torte   Sour cherries
Hazelnut torte   Lingonberry tarts
Coffee   Tea   Sanka
Wines: Champagne, Beaujolais, Vin rosé

*Pick-it-yourself
dessert: tiered
epergne piled high
with strawberries,
pears, peaches, to be
sprinkled with sugar,
spiked with
preferred eau-de-vie
in ceramic muffineers.*

*Individual servings at
an all-salad buffet:
duck and orange
salad in orange shells;
crabmeat salad in
avocado halves;
vegetable salad
in green pepper cups.*

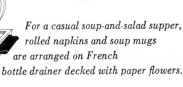

FUNK

*For a casual soup-and-salad supper,
rolled napkins and soup mugs
are arranged on French
bottle drainer decked with paper flowers.*

HOLIDAY PARTIES

CHRISTMAS EVE SHERRY PARTY
Fresh toasted almonds
Cinnamon buns with honey-bee topping
Wine: Sherry

CHRISTMAS EVE SUPPER
Herring in sour cream
Smoked sausage   Cold smoked turkey
Swedish Christmas ham
Roasted spare ribs with apple sauce
Pickled pineapple   Pickled beets
Mince pie   Ginger cookies
Christmas glögg

CHRISTMAS BREAKFAST
Milk punch or screwdrivers or
Bloody Marys
Finnan haddie with cream sauce
Swedish potato sausage
Scrambled eggs fines herbes
Stollen   Toasted English muffins
Cream cheese
Strawberry and peach preserves

CHRISTMAS LUNCH
Crudités:
celery, radishes, carrots, olives
Clear beef and sherry broth
Long Island duckling
with prune and apple stuffing
Fresh peas with creamed onions
Cranberry sauce
Sourdough bread
Mince pie with hard sauce
Molasses cookies
Wine: Red Rhône

3 CHRISTMAS DINNERS
Radishes and olives
Hot fruit compote
Roast turkey with oyster dressing
Giblet gravy
Yellow turnip soufflé
Braised brussels sprouts
Beaten biscuits
Indian pudding with vanilla ice cream
Nuts and raisins
Wines: Port   Champagne

Coquille of lobster, shrimp and scallops
Roast pheasant
Broiled apricots
filled with red currant jelly
Rice ring filled with mushrooms
Puree of green peas   Braised endive
Vanilla soufflé with peppermint sauce
Wine: Champagne

Oysters on the half-shell
Roast beef with green beans   Flageolets
Greens salad   Cheese
Snowball surprise
Christmas pudding
with rum and brandy bitters
Wine: White Burgundy
Champagne

CHRISTMAS SUPPER
Christmas casserole with chicken,
water chestnuts, mushrooms,
pistachio nuts
Baked ham
with pineapple glaze and red cherries
Cranberry-orange mold, sour cream
Herb bread
Chocolate torte   Christmas cookies
Wine: Château-bottled Bordeaux

CHRISTMAS COCKTAIL BUFFET
Cottage cheese and caviar ball
Shrimp and endive tree
Hungarian körözött
(mushroom formed from goat cheese
dotted with caviar)
Tiny round onion sandwiches
Cold sliced steak
Fruitcake

GOLDSMITH

*Fanciful shapes for holiday food: cottage
cheese ball topped with holly sprig,
ringed with caviar; "tree" of chicken
wire hung with shrimp; fat
mushroom formed from goat cheese,
butter, top sprinkled with paprika.*

HOLIDAY BRUNCH
Brandy milk punch (served in
milk-punch glasses painted with holly
and a personalized greeting
for each guest)
Chicken livers sautéed in white wine
Creamed finnan haddie on toast points
Scrambled eggs
Sliced stolen

HOLIDAY BUFFET DINNER
Rolled lamb
Egg-noodle and cheese casserole
Steamed yellow squash and zucchini
Greens salad with avocado
Whole wheat rolls
with herb and garlic butter
Poached pears on coconut
Ice cream with fruit sauce
Wine: Red Burgundy

NEW YEAR'S DAY SOUP BUFFET
Black bean soup with thin lemon slices
New England oyster stew
Tiny hot biscuits
Fruitcake

NEW YEAR'S EVE SUPPER
IN THE RUSSIAN TRADITION
Smoked sturgeon   Caviar
Smoked salmon
Cold baked ham
Coulibiac of cabbage   Coulibiac of meat
Tiny chicken bitki
(sautéed ground chicken patties
in sour cream sauce)
Beef Stroganoff
Cold striped bass in aspic
Salade Olivier   Russian vegetable salad
Plombière
(vanilla ice cream with candied fruits)
Russian torte (seven-layer hazelnut cake
with mocha filling)
Wines: Vodka   Champagne

TWELFTH NIGHT PARTY
Pollo Mestizo
(Mexican chicken casserole)
Frijoles   Rice
Greens salad   Guacamole   Tortillas
Rosca de Reyes (circular cake-bread in
which tiny china doll has been baked)
Wine: Valpolicella

DANCING PARTIES

SUPPER DANCE WITH RECORDS
IN THE LIVING ROOM
Chicken curry   Saffron rice
Lemon sherbet
Champagne

MIDNIGHT SUPPER DANCE
Double chicken consommé
Omelets with sour cream and caviar,
Roquefort butter, creamed codfish,
or curried beef fillings
Greens salad
Fresh pineapple cubes
served in pineapple shell
Champagne

DISCOTHÈQUE PARTY
Make-your-own poor-boy sandwiches.
Poor-boy rolls, caviar, sour cream,
minced onions, sliced sturgeon,
cream cheese balls rolled in truffles,
minced hard-cooked egg whites,
whipped sweet butter
Turkey mold
Celery root salad
White peaches and black grapes
in champagne
Nut crescents
Champagne punch   Black Velvet

DEBUTANTE DINNER DANCE
Hot madrilene
Straws of flaky pastry with paprika
Cold salmon, green sauce
Salad, Russian style
Roast duckling with orange sauce
Corn croquettes   Green beans
Glazed pistachio ice cream
hot chocolate sauce
Little iced cakes
Wine: Champagne

MIDSUMMER DINNER DANCE
Shrimp bisque
Squabs served with rice
Tiny French peas   Carrots in butter
Lemon ice sprinkled with
grated lemon rind
Madeleines and chocolate leaves
Wines: California Pinot Noir
Champagne

SUPPER DANCE ON A PATIO
Breast of capon,
artichoke hearts and mushrooms
Noodle soufflé
Watercress and Belgian endive salad
Croissants
Charlotte Russe
Wine: Champagne

BUFFET DINNER DANCE
Served
Creamed fresh crabmeat with sherry
White rice
Buffet
Cold roast beef and chopped aspic,
Cumberland sauce
Hot sweet and sour spareribs,
sweet and sour sauce
Ratatouille in casserole
Fresh corn on the cob
Cold artichoke halves vinaigrette
Coleslaw with carrot and green pepper
Bibb lettuce mimosa
Board of assorted cheeses
Hot crackers and French bread
Served
Fresh strawberries and sliced oranges,
brown sugar and whipped cream
Devil's food cake squares
Wine: Champagne

ALFRESCO PARTIES
CRAWFISH FEAST
Spiced crawfish
String bean salad
Homemade whole wheat bread   Butter
Coeur à la crème with strawberries
Aquavit   Beer

OPEN HOUSE
HORS D'OEUVRE LUNCHEON
Raw fava beans   Radishes
Crudités with anchovy mayonnaise
Crabmeat Orientale
Beef salad Parisienne
Leeks à la Grecque
Variety of breads   Taleggio cheese
Cold orange soufflé
Wines: California Chenin Blanc
and Zinfandel
Iced Mocha   Liqueurs

COUNTRY SUNDAY LUNCH
Cervelat salad
Cold barbecued loin of pork
with horseradish applesauce
Hot fava beans with fresh herbs
French bread   Butter
Muenster cheese, fresh cherries
Wine: Alsatian or California Traminer

LUNCH ON THE TERRACE
Iced tomato bisque
Jellied fruit and vegetable salad
Scandinavian flat bread
Wine: Vin rosé

KLAPHOLZ

*On a hot summer day serve chilled
tomato bisque in a goblet,
jellied fruit and vegetable
salad molded in shell shapes,
wafer-thin flat bread in a toast rack.*

POOLSIDE DINNER
Cold clam bisque   Water biscuits
Cooled salmon with green mayonnaise
New potatoes
Tomatoes stuffed with
smothered cucumbers
Thin brown-bread-and-butter sandwiches
Homemade peach ice cream
with fresh peaches in bourbon
Wine: Neuchâtel

BASKET GARDEN PARTY
Open-face sandwiches:
cream cheese and radish,
liver pâté with capers,
smoked salmon with dill
Fresh fruit
Brownies, date bars, small honey buns
Wine: Sangria

PICNICS—PLAIN
AND FANCY
PICNIC FROM A TAILGATE
Gazpacho
Salmon quiche
Egg and tomato salad
Peach tarts
Wine: Champagne

PICNIC ON THE GRASS
Stuffed grape leaves
Shish kebab
Cold rice salad
Rolls
Mint sherbet in lemon cups
Wine: Vin rosé

PICNICS IN BASKETS,
WRAPPED IN BANDANNAS
Hero sandwiches
Bean salad   Cold ratatouille
Peach pie   Fruit
Wine: Chianti

PICNIC AT THE BEACH
Shrimp in beer
Scallions   Cherry tomatoes
Cioppino (seafood stew served in
deep bowls)
Crisp French or Italian bread
Greens salad
Strawberries and blueberries
with maple syrup and cream
Wine: Soave

SUMMER THEATRE PICNIC
Green turtle soup
Cold roast fillet of veal   Italian sauce
Rice salad with peas and pimiento
Crème Danica   Water biscuits
Strawberries in Grand Marnier
Wine: Dry Moselle

BACKYARD PICNIC DINNER
Crudités
Country pâté   Braided bread
Baked salmon steaks with anchovy sauce
Pears à l'orange
Wine: Neuchâtel

FUNK

*Dinner is a picnic when the table is
a grassy slope, the
butler a three-tier basket
that nests everything inside.
Insulated bag keeps white wine chilly.*

PICNIC IN THE GARDEN
Antipasto
Lobster stew
Bread sticks
Frozen zabaglione
Wine: Verdicchio

SLIGHTLY FANCY PICNIC
Mushrooms à la Grecque
Cold sliced country meat loaf
Egg and chive loaf
Green bean and tomato salad
Carrot sticks
Buttered whole wheat bread
French bread
Melon with lime slices
Wine: Red Rhône

PICNIC STEAK-OUT
Charcoal-broiled or marinated steak
or cold sliced steak or sliced roast beef
Potato salad
Onion rolls, buttered
Salad greens with French dressing
Mustard pickles   Cherry tomatoes
Apple tarts, cheddar cheese
Beer

COOKOUTS

FOURTH OF JULY CELEBRATION
Tiny sausages on sticks
Spit-roasted salmon, egg sauce
Ash-roasted corn   Buttered peas
Cucumber salad   Bread sticks
Strawberry shortcake
Wine: Vin rosé
Beer

MAINE BEACH PARTY
Clam broth in vacuum jugs
Broiled live lobsters
Roast corn   Coleslaw, cooked dressing
Homemade bread-and-butter sandwiches
Banbury tarts
Beer

SOUTHERN FISH FRY
Fried pan fish   Hush puppies
Cold okra
with mayonnaise and cherry tomatoes
Individual peach or mango pies
Beer

SWISS SAUSAGE GRILL
Raclette sausage rolls
Sweet-sour red cabbage
Cherry tomatoes
Bing cherries
Chocolate ice cream sticks
Imported beer

HAMBURGER COOKOUT
Grilled hamburgers
Guacamole   Fresh tomato sauce
Shredded Monterey Jack cheese
Sliced ripe olives   Shredded lettuce
Refried beans
Colache
(corn, squash and tomato casserole)
Coffee ice cream
Beer

HAWAIIAN LUAU
Wahini cocktails in coconut shells
Macadamia nuts   Teriyaki
Roast suckling pig
Poi   Long rice
Baked sweet potatoes or yams
Baked bananas
Lomi salmon
Fruit: Pineapples, papayas, guavas,
mangoes, bananas
Wine: Champagne

CHICKEN BARBECUE
Chicken halves
(seasoned, buttered and wrapped in foil)
Small new potatoes in jackets
(individual foil packages of four
with salt, butter)
Small live lobsters
Ears of sweet corn without husks
(spread with salt-pepper-butter mixture,
wrapped individually in foil)
Wine: Sancerre

SPEAR-IT-YOURSELF
SHISH KEBABS
Platters with a selection of marinated
beef, lamb, or veal cubes, scallops,
chicken livers wrapped in bacon,
raw shrimp, cocktail franks,
raw kidneys, cooked ham cubes
Raw or parboiled vegetables:
mushroom caps, cherry or plum tomatoes,
eggplant, zucchini and green
pepper chunks, tiny white onions
Rice pilaf
French bread
Ice-cold slices of watermelon
Wine: California Zinfandel

ARIZONA STEAK FRY
Tortillas
Queso con aceitunas (cheese with olives)
Charcoal-broiled steak
Onions with oregano
Lima bean casserole
Homemade bread   Butter
Date bars
Beer

SUCKLING PIG BARBECUE
FOR 20
Grilled oysters en brochette
Grilled mushrooms filled with crabmeat
Roast suckling pig
Buttered parsnips with chopped parsley
Green peas with water chestnuts
Avocado and grapefruit salad
Hot French rolls
Lemon meringue pie
Wine: Vin rosé

NORTHWEST BEACH PARTY
Venison or tongue pasties
Planked salmon
Foil-roasted potatoes
Wilted cucumbers with dill
Toasted rye bread
Bing cherries   Tillamook cheese cubes
Wine: Pouilly-Fuissé
or California Pinot Chardonnay

OUTDOOR CHEF'S SUPPER
Crudités
Brochette of giblets
Grilled piquant chickens
Eggplant Provençal
Homemade cassis ice cream
Wine: Vin rosé

LAMB CHOP BARBECUE
Chilled chicken-avocado soup
Barbecued lamb chops
Barbecued zucchini
Tagliarini Parmesan (pasta)
Salad of tomatoes and bell peppers,
anchovy, oil and wine vinegar dressing
Cheese tray   Pears, apples, grapes
Wine: Barolo

CREOLE GARDEN PARTY
Gulf shrimp with lime and chili sauce
Sliced tomatoes   Pickled cucumbers
Creole-style barbecued game hens
Southern spoon bread   Hot biscuits
Crock of butter   Comb honey
Praline pie or watermelon
Iced coffee
Wine: Vin rosé

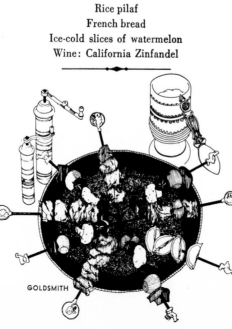

GOLDSMITH

*Great for a party cookout—shish kebab on a bed
of pilaf, alternating skewers of
meat, vegetables and lemon wedges.*

FOR DROP-OF-A-HAT INVITATIONS

These quick-to-put-together menus are based on foods in the Gourmet Checklist on pages 177 and 178. Included are dishes from the freezer, ready-to-use items on the pantry shelf, and fresh ingredients on hand in the refrigerator.

COCKTAIL GET-TOGETHER
Cheese biscuits
Mushroom cocktail strudels
(phylo pastry and duxelles from freezer)
Crudités and dip

IMPROMPTU TEA
Very thin sandwiches of Westphalian ham
with mustard butter on
whole wheat bread
Rolled watercress, tomato
and cream cheese sandwiches
Pastry canapé shells filled
with fruit preserves, heated,
sprinkled with confectioners sugar
Tiny rich chocolate cupcakes
Strawberries
to dip in sour cream and brown sugar

TOTABLE LUNCH
Jellied madrilene
with sour cream, caviar and chives
Scandinavian vegetable salad:
canned peas, carrots, beets, potatoes,
mayonnaise, dill, with
tiny Danish shrimp
Sliced cold ham, roast beef
or other cold meats
Assorted mustards   Pickles
Assorted breads
Grapes, cherries, peaches   Cookies
Ice-cold beer

SUNDAY BRUNCH
Fresh berries with cream
Brioches filled
with creamed chipped beef
and mushrooms, flavored with
Madeira and chives
(If a large brunch, perhaps serve
sautéed boiled ham and herbed
scrambled eggs in addition)
Café au lait or iced coffee
Wine: Champagne

SPUR-OF-THE-MOMENT LUNCH
Risotto made with leftover meats:
chicken, strips of prosciutto or
other ham, olives, peas, Swiss cheese,
and saffron; or lamb with currants
and pinenuts; or chicken with ginger,
chutney, and curry; or shrimp and
mussels, flavored with saffron
Salad of raw mushrooms and chives,
dressed with olive oil and lemon juice,
served on Bibb lettuce leaves
Sliced fresh fruit in kirsch
Wine: Muscadet

EXPANDABLE SUPPER
FOR 10, 20 OR MORE
Cold antipasto: tuna and white
bean salad; pepperoni and anchovies;
marinated artichoke hearts, mushrooms,
and zucchini; sardines; salamis and
prosciutto; cheese; olives,
radishes, celery or fennel
Pasta with white clam sauce
Greens salad
Pears   Gorgonzola
Espresso (could use instant in a pinch)
Wine: Frascati

LITTLE SUPPERS

LATE SUPPER
Cooked at the table
Crepes filled with smoked salmon
and sour cream or with potted shrimp
garnished with chopped parsley and dill
Greens salad
Crème Brûlée
Coffee
Wine: California
Johannisberg Riesling

SUPPER AFTER A PREVIEW
Cold rare fillet of beef
Sliced tomatoes
sprinkled with chopped basil,
oil, vinegar
Watercress and endive salad
Ice cream sundae au choix:
bowls of assorted flavors of ice cream;
whipped cream; slivered almonds,
chopped pecans; diced candied fruits,
chocolate sauce
Wine: California Mountain Red

AFTER-THEATRE SUPPER
Smoked salmon rolls
with horseradish cream
Meatballs Stroganoff
Kasha
Spinach Chinese style
Fruit magnifique   Mincemeat cookies
Wine: Beaujolais

SUPPER AFTER THE CONCERT
Assorted cheese sandwiches
Dark fruitcake   Lebkuchen
Hot chocolate   Coffee
Wine cup

---

*Main attraction at cook-it-yourself
party might be Fondue Bourguignonne—
shrimp with salmon cubes
cooked in bubbling oil, dipped in sauces.*

SUPPER AFTER
ALMOST ANYTHING
Ham and leek tarts
made in the form of pastry "skillets"
Crudités salad
Hot croissants
Champagne

*At a late supper
serve ham and
leek tarts made
in the form of
little pastry
"skillets."*

*Handles—strips of dough with hole
cut out—are baked separately, stuck
into tarts before serving.*

SUPPER FOR 2
Seafood coquilles
Hearts of palm vinaigrette
Caraway melbas
Pineapple in a pineapple shell
Wine: Muscadet

SUPPER WHEN GUESTS
COOK THEIR OWN
Seafood fondue Bourguignonne:
shrimp with salmon cubes
cooked to taste in bubbling oil
and butter
3 sauces—to dip into
Tossed greens salad
Hot fruit compote
Wine: Riesling

KLAPHOLZ

FOOD INDEX

A quick checklist to assist you in planning what goes with what for around-the-clock party meals.